THE FAITH THAT
DOES JUSTICE

THE
FAITH THAT DOES JUSTICE

Examining the Christian Sources for Social Change

Edited by
John C. Haughey, S.J.

PAULIST PRESS
New York/Ramsey/Toronto

Library of Congress
Catalog Card Number: 77-74579

ISBN: 0-8091-2026-7

Published by Paulist Press
Editorial Office: 1865 Broadway, New York, N.Y. 10023
Business Office: 545 Island Road, Ramsey, N.J. 07446

Printed and bound in the
United States of America

Contents

PART III

New Directions Envisioned

To Pedro Arrupé

General of the Society of Jesus

on the occasion

of his 50th Anniversary

as a member of

that same

Society

Foreword

The essays in this volume address a closely interconnected set of questions: To be true to its mission, what function is the Church meant to perform? What does the faith of Christians contribute to the human perception of justice? What is the theological significance of action undertaken by Christians for political or social transformation? Is justice to be looked on as one of the moral virtues that it is incumbent on Christians to practice or has it a more intrinsic link to the gift of faith which Christians have received? Does the following of Christ call Christians away from social systems into "the new creation" or is the call extended to them to concern themselves with the social systems which shape human beings?

Although the justice question addressed by this volume relates directly to the faith of Christians, it has not been a question that originated within the Church itself. It has emerged from the world, touching the Church through its members who are both citizens of this world and "the next." It is for the sake of the world first and foremost that Christians increasingly agonize over these questions. Its fragile order seems more and more imperiled, making its frequent disorder victimize both believer and unbeliever indiscriminately. Nevertheless no small reason for this volume is the attempt to bring some clarity to the relationship between Christian faith and social justice so that there can be a greater integration in the lives of those who find themselves full of concern for the world, yet wanting to be faithful at the same time.

No reader needs to be reminded of the factors which create an increasing pressure to understand what constitutes justice for individuals, groups and nations. The world grows smaller daily and the issues about which human beings come into conflict grow increasingly complex. The interdependence of nations, the proliferation of means of communication with peoples of other cultures and na-

1

tions and consequently the raising of consciousness about the human condition we all find ourselves in—these are some of the new things that must be factored into the modern experience. One can put the matter optimistically, as Vatican Council II did, and see that "the body of a new family is growing on our earth." But one can be just as certain that that body is quite unwell with one part emaciated and another stuffed. Who cannot add to the oft recited list of problems that beset this body—the disparity of ideologies, the alarming diminishment of natural resources on planet earth, the increasing recourse to violence to implement one's perception of what constitutes justice, the virtual disappearance of the family sphere of influence, the constant violation of personal conscience by the public sector, etc.?

Attempts by Christians to come to grips with the subject have not been wanting. One need only look at the deliberations of the two most recent conferences of the World Council of Churches (Uppsala in 1968 and Nairobi in 1975) to see the degree of concern Protestant and Orthodox Christianity has about the subject of social justice and Christian responsibility for the world. These provided a forum for weighing the value of a wide spectrum of opinions held by Protestant Christians about the social role of the Church in the world. The divergence within this spectrum might be seen even more clearly if one were to contrast the Hartford Statement (1975) which emphasized transcendence with the Boston Affirmation (1976) and its emphasis on immanence. One would have to conclude that the matter is still in an inconclusive stage with so many Christians.

Perhaps the drama surrounding the question is more intense in the Roman Catholic community than it is in other parts of the Church of Christ. From the last decade of the nineteenth century through the seven decades of the present century there has been a continual development of the Roman Catholic Church's understanding of social responsibility. Vatican II was an important stage in this development, but by no means a final one. If anything, since then the matter seems even further from being settled. Think, for example, of the venturesomeness expressed in the Medellín documents, fashioned by the regional conference of Latin American bishops in 1968. Then consider the pull-back from the positions adopted there by the day-to-day decisions taken by so many Latin American Church officials since then. Latin American theologians, on the other hand, have not shown the same reservations as the still-developing liberation theology attests. Finally, the 1971 International Synod of Bishops gathered in Rome to deliberate on the Church's response to the structural injustices that demean believer and unbeliever alike in so many places around the globe. Their discernment, expressed in the document "Justice in the World," is the most forthright statement to date from an official collegial body in the Church on the proper response of the Church and its members to the use and abuse of political and social power.

Soon after the dramatic deliberations of Synod '71, the Jesuit Order decided to hold its most formal kind of assembly, referred to as a General Congregation, the thirty-second such convocation held by it since the Order's beginning in the sixteenth century. In that formal consultation, held from December 1974 until March 1975, the Jesuit Order determined that the promotion of justice in the world was to become a major focus of its work in the future and a primary way of expressing the faith commitment of its membership. The deliberations of the Thirty-Second General Congregation were the immediate occasion for this volume. In a sense it had the effect of making the authors of the essays contained in this volume undertake an inquiry into the subject together which in the past they had considered only singly. In addition to being Christians, Roman Catholics, and ordained ministers in the Catholic Church, all the authors whose essays appear in this volume are Jesuits. They have addressed a question which, as we have said, is not simply Catholic nor is it peculiarly Christian. Their findings, therefore, should be of interest to all who are aware that the irresolution of the Churches on the subject of justice cannot long continue. The light which the authors have attempted to shed on the subject comes from several disciplines: history, ethics, exegesis, philosophy, biblical and systematic theology. The forum within which these essays were conceived and executed was the Woodstock Theological Center, a newly opened institute for interdisciplinary research and theological reflection located in Washington, D.C.

It remains now to give a brief introduction to the content of the essays and, to some extent, the relationship that obtains between them. The first two essays are attempts by two systematic theologians to analyze the contemporary faith situation of Christians, with particular regard to the relationship of the faith of Christians to their role in society.

In the first essay, Father Dulles analyzes the three main theologies of faith operating in contemporary Christianity, each of which has an implicit or explicit way of viewing the significance of social justice and working for a more equitable social order. Although no theology of faith could exclude such work and remain Christian, each of the three analyzed in this essay includes work for justice in quite different ways. The intellectualist conception of faith assigns it minimal importance by comparison to the performative approach, the category used by Dulles for theologies like those of the liberation theologians. At the same time he is not reluctant to point out what he sees to be the limitations of each of the theologies of faith. Common to all three is both the need to be discerning of the situation one is in and to take action upon it as part of one's faith commitment. Not only does the gift of faith enable one to perceive the ultimate meaning of human life, but it is able to affect every perception one has of concrete circumstances. When these perceptions are acted upon, the leaven of faith begins to transform society.

The second essay confronts the reason for the relative ineffectiveness of the Christian faith in transforming society. Father Dych detects a dualism running through accounts of the meaning of Christian faith, leaving believers as well as unbelievers with the idea that there are two histories, two societies, two worlds, in only one of which salvation is operative. More specifically, Father Dych analyzes the attempts of the Second Vatican Council to understand the relationship between the social role of Christian faith and society—an attempt he judges to be not altogether successful in having the Church overcome this dualism. Dych draws from some of the more promising elements in the Vatican II documents, which he foresees will be part of theological resolution of the faith/world relationship. Clearly such a resolution is needed to help Christians overcome the alienation they have allowed to develop between themselves and their world.

Among other things, these two systematic essays should have

the effect of leading one to wonder about the relationship of justice to faith and faith to justice as these have interacted as forces in the centuries of the Church's existence. The five essays which follow are the heart of this volume. They take their data from five different moments in the history of the Church and show how these moments speak to the contemporary question about faith's relationship to justice. From these five essays, one can begin to appreciate the depth of the question posed by the volume as well as the wealth of the tradition of the Church on the subject of justice. A good scribe draws from old things as well as new in order to provide the community of believers what they need to face the future. These five scribes have drawn well. For some readers the information they can cull from these essays may simply refresh the mind or reacquaint them with the tradition they have already appropriated, but for most Christians the essays will serve to introduce them to insights they did not know were part of the tradition.

The first of these essays returns to the basic source of a Christian understanding of the faith, the Scriptures, and seeks light on the questions opened up by the theme of the volume. Fr. John Donahue points out the many different ways in which justice is handled in the Hebrew Scriptures. He then shows the transformation this Old Testament vision undergoes during the intertestamental period. This makes the reconceptions found in the New Testament understanding of justice intelligible. His essay concludes with a considerable amount of insight and information on what is and is not new in the New Testament understanding of justice.

The second of the essays in this section represents the efforts of Father William Walsh, who painstakingly scoured the patristic era for the social attitudes of the Fathers. Since this would be too vast an undertaking, he focused on almsgiving as a practice and avarice as a vice as the two most concrete ways of taking a measure of how the Christians of these first centuries viewed and were taught to view material possessions, commitment to one another in community and their relationship to the world. Father Langan of the Woodstock Center reworked the material, originally compiled by Father Walsh for other purposes, into a text well suited for the purposes of this volume.

In "What Jerusalem Says to Athens," the reader will find Father Langan choosing two of the authors from the patristic era, Saints Ambrose and Augustine, as the basis for his own reflective essay on the power of Christian faith to transform the philosophical understanding of justice into one that is peculiarly Christian. Langan sees the intellectual tradition inherited by and contemporary with Augustine and Ambrose transformed specifically by their understanding of the charity Christians receive as gift of God. He shows the same power working in his own understanding of justice.

The essay by Father Richard Roach, while concentrating on the meaning of justification at the Council of Trent, uncovers much more than a sixteenth-century understanding of the importance of the works of justice which can flow from those gifted with justification. Roach's analysis lights up insights from Trent's decrees that could only have been implicit at the time they were drawn up; they awaited the major shifts in human consciousness which have taken place since then. As human beings move from an individualistic concentration on the object of their moral evaluations toward one that includes in its purview the structures of social existence, now seen not as "givens" or static and to be acquiesced in, but as susceptible of change, the decisions of Trent begin to take on new importance. Roach finishes his essay with an analysis of the two different theories about the redemption which the Tridentine Fathers entertained and shows how one reinforces the link between faith and the works of justice and how the other weakens it.

The essay by Fr. Hollenbach begins with the statement from the already mentioned International Synod of Bishops in 1971 which claims that action on behalf of justice is a constitutive element in the Church's mission. He situates that statement in the background of development of Catholic social thought which in modern times had its initial impetus from Leo XIII's encyclical, *Rerum Novarum*, in 1891. Father Hollenbach makes a number of helpful observations about the changing models of society used by the popes in this evolution, according to which they made their judgments about Christian responsibility in the world. His essay does not attempt to be exhaustive about all the features in this development though it evaluates its main features. He notes that the more recent social teachings of the Church are increasingly reserved and "humble" in both their scope and content.

The final two essays represent attempts by two theologians to sketch out future lines of development that the Church and its members could take to deepen their appreciation of the theological and religious linkage between Christian faith and action undertaken for the just transformation of society.

The first of these two prospective essays summarizes the various positions on the scope and role of the teaching Church with regard to social issues according to theologians. In the second part of his essay, Fr. Hollenbach shows why and how the religious experience of the Christian community, especially in its formal sacramental celebrations, can be a major determinant of the Church's role in the world, a point of view he sees missing in the previous analyses done by theologians. An increase in the imagination Christians bring to their communal and sacramental celebrations is called for by the author, so that the prophetic role of the Church may be more pervasive in society.

The last essay adverts to the depth and breadth of the meanings of justice as these develop in this volume and suggests that their integration could begin by the development of a justice Christology. The author sketches out some of the lines along which such a Christology might develop. Haughey thinks that until an ideal preached by the Church is seen to be lived in the person of Jesus, Christians will remain relatively passive about appropriating it.

Many deserve mention for their part in the work this volume represents. Without two Jesuit provincials, one of the New York Province, Rev. Eamon Taylor, the other of the Maryland Province, Rev. Joseph A. Panuska, this volume and presumably many subsequent ones would not be possible. Fr. Taylor has been wise and steadfastly supportive in his assisting in the creation of the Woodstock Theological Center. Fr. Panuska has been no less so, but he would also have to be thanked for giving the initial impetus that had the members of the Center decide on producing such a volume. Fr. Edward Glynn, the first director of the Center, saw the project through its first fragile months. And Mrs. Ann Bretsch painstakingly saw the work through all the stages it had to go through before it saw the light of day.

Part I
The Present Assessed

The Meaning of Faith
Considered in Relationship to Justice

Avery Dulles, S.J.

By the "meaning of faith" in the title of this chapter, I have in mind something more than the dictionary definition. I am concerned with the reality of faith itself—with faith as it concretely exists, and should exist, in today's world. The world, of course, varies from place to place, and therefore faith has a legitimate variety of forms. But there are typical features of our age, and these place certain demands on the contemporary realizations of faith. Especially in the North Atlantic community, we live in what may be called a "socio-technical" civilization. Herbert Richardson, from whom I borrow the term, defines "socio-technics" as "the new knowledge whereby man exercises technical control not only over nature but also over all the specific institutions that make up society: i.e., economics, education, science, and politics."[1]

In this socio-technical era we are, and should be, keenly conscious of man's capacity to shape the physical and social environment and consequently of man's responsibility to avoid devastating the earth and visiting misery on other people. Amid growing evidence that the benefits of technical progress are going only to a small elite, and that the world proletariat (as it might be called) is becoming frustrated and angry, even the wealthier nations of the "free world" are feeling the urgency of establishing a more equitable social system.

Christian faith has been accused both of failing to promote justice in the world and, even more seriously, of abetting injustice by inducing the wretched of the earth to accept their misery patiently, confident of abundant rewards in a future life. Faith has frequently meant little more than a confident belief in some higher or future world utterly beyond man's control and shaped by the power of God alone. If this conception were accurate, faith could rightly be accused of alienating man from his proper task in the present life and of inducing irresponsibility.

Conscious of this objection so often made by atheistic humanists and Marxists, Christians such as Teilhard de Chardin, in the first half of our century, tried to show that Christian faith could actually increase man's sense of responsibility for the earth.[2] Vatican II, in its *Pastoral Constitution on the Church in the Modern World*, favored the same thrust. It spoke of "the birth of a new humanism, one in which man is defined primarily in terms of his responsibility for his brothers and for history" (n. 55). It called upon Christians to give "the witness of a living and mature faith," a faith that proves itself "by penetrating the believer's entire life, including its worldly dimensions, and by activating him toward justice and love, especially regarding the needy" (n. 21). "The expectation of a new earth," it asserted, "must not weaken but rather stimulate our concern for cultivating this one" (n. 39). Faith, according to the Council, by casting a new light on everything, "directs the mind of man to solutions which are fully human" (n. 11).

In many post-conciliar documents, such as the Latin American Medellín documents of 1968, the statements of the International Synod of Bishops in 1971 and 1974, and the 1975 exhortation of Paul VI on "Evangelization in the Modern World," it is reiterated that evangelization—the propagation of the faith—cannot be a mere matter of words or concepts. The Gospel has to be proclaimed in an actual situation, with attention to its implications for the reordering of society. A failure to accept the social implications of the Gospel would be a lack of responsiveness to the Gospel itself, and hence a defect of faith. Faith, if it is not to be merely nominal, involves a sincere adherence to the vision of the Kingdom of God that the Gospel holds forth to us—an adherence that reveals itself concretely in the believer's manner of living and of dealing with other persons and groups.

In a great deal of the theological literature of the past decade —especially perhaps in the new German political theology and in Latin American liberation theology—an effort is being made to

show the positive bearing of Christian faith upon the transformation of human society not only in the private domain of thought
and feeling but also in the public domain of law, government, and
economics. While seeking to avoid any kind of political reductionism, Christians are increasingly conscious that faith, in the
concrete, involves certain social attitudes and commitments. The
surfacing of this consciousness entails a mutation in the concept of
faith itself—a mutation that calls for careful theological evaluation.

As contrasted with many of the medieval and early modern
theories, which attempted to define faith in terms of the spiritual
faculties of intellect and will, contemporary theologians are inclined to say with Paul Tillich that faith is a free, centered act of
the whole personality, having ramifications in all the dimensions of
our human existence, including the cognitional, the volitional, and
the emotional.[3] Drawing upon the phenomenology of religion previously developed by Rudolf Otto and others, the English philo-
sopher, Ian T. Ramsey, contended that the language of religion
rests upon disclosure experiences in which the two elements of discernment and commitment are inextricably interwoven.[4] Religious
disclosures, Ramsey held, are peculiar in that they involve a discernment of total meaning and hence a call to total commitment.
This all-encompassing and transcendent point of reference in religious experience gives rise to what is called "God-language." Although Ramsey did not, I believe, propose a new definition of
faith, one might, on the basis of his work, define it as that combination of discernment and commitment which is concomitant with
the disclosure of ultimate meaning and ultimate value.

Through a study of biblical history it would be possible to
show that revelation was given through a series of disclosure experiences, from the patriarchs, through Moses and the prophets,
down to the climactic disclosure given in the passion and exalta-
tion of Jesus.[5] These disclosures fall into a pattern in which there
are recurrent themes. The later disclosures reinforce, enrich, and
partly reinterpret the preceding disclosures. For us who live in
post-biblical times these disclosures come alive when we see them
as clues to the meaning of our own world and hence to our own
vocation. The Christian people are called, as was Israel of old, to

serve the righteousness of God in a costly way. Christian faith may accordingly be described as a combination of discernment and commitment in which we perceive and dedicate ourselves to the transcendent values disclosed by God in Jesus Christ. The discernment and the commitment are mutually interdependent aspects of the total experience of faith.

A central and recurrent theme of the biblical disclosures is that the ultimate power by which our lives are ruled is the personal reality of God, whose loving mercies surround and sustain us. Faith therefore includes not only a conviction and commitment concerning the transcendent, but a trusting obedience to God as a person who loves, who wills, who acts. So important is this element that it deserves to be made explicit in the definition of faith itself—at least if we are talking about biblical or Christian faith. Faith includes three elements: a firm conviction regarding what is supremely important, dedication or commitment to that which one believes in, and trustful reliance on the power and goodness of that to which one stands committed. The three components of faith are thus conviction, commitment, and trust.[5a]

In the classical tradition, the elements of conviction and trust have been particularly emphasized, with Catholics concentrating more on the former, Protestants more on the latter. The third component, commitment, is less prominent in the tradition, but is increasingly coming to the fore in the twentieth century under the pressure of some of the factors already mentioned. The recent developments would seem to have a solid theological grounding, inasmuch as the Kingdom of God is a reality at work within history, rather than simply a goal to which history tends. Faith, as our present mode of participation in the Kingdom, is neither the detached contemplation of a truth external to ourselves nor trust in a power totally external to the world in which we live. The truth and the power are actively at work within us. Without a sincere commitment to the healing and reconciliation of the broken world, we could not have either the discernment or the trust that is proper to children of God who share already, by grace, in the divine life opened up to us in Christ.

In the pages that follow I intend first to examine the more traditional intellectualist and fiducial theories of faith, in order to point out both the solid contributions made by these theories and the distortions to which they are subject unless viewed in the context of participation and commitment. Then I shall examine the contributions and limitations of some of the new performative theories of faith, especially as found in Latin American liberation theology.

I
INTELLECTUALIST APPROACHES

Our first group of theories center about faith as a kind of knowing. This approach has deep roots in the Patristic and Scholastic tradition, and can claim a certain foundation in the Bible, especially in the Johannine writings, in which terms such as *pistis* (faith) generally occur in close conjunction with expressions having to do with knowing and seeing, with light and truth.[6]

For Augustine and many of the Fathers, faith presented itself primarily as an illumination. Influenced by neo-Platonistic epistemology, Augustine looks on God as the changeless truth that must shine on our minds in order for us to understand. He quotes from the Septuagint version of Isaiah 7:9, "Unless you believe, you shall not understand."[7] More specifically Augustine teaches that the soul, blinded by the effects of sin, cannot go out to the spiritual and eternal unless it is healed and illuminated from above. When so healed, the soul tends by a connatural appetite to union with God. Already in this life it can enjoy fleeting anticipations of the beatific vision. Contemplative union with God is the final consummation of faith.

The Augustinian concept of faith as the beginning of wisdom and as the first step toward the beatific vision remained dominant in the Middle Ages. The monasteries were places in which, nourished by the Bible and by liturgical experience, the devout permitted their faith to flower into contemplation. The value of faith, according to this outlook, is aptly summed up in Anselm's famous formula, "Credo ut intelligam." "For I do not seek to understand that I may believe, but I believe in order to understand. For this also I believe—that unless I believed, I should not understand."[8]

The understanding of faith sought by the monastic culture is viewed as a foretaste of the heavenly vision.

Even in St. Thomas, whose general orientation is more Aristotelian, the illuminist view of faith persists. In the treatise on the theological virtues in the *Summa Theologiae*, he speaks frequently of faith as being essentially constituted by an inner light of the soul, intermediate between the light of natural reason and the light of glory, of which it is a participation and an earnest. Wherever this inner light is freely responded to, faith is present; and wherever this light does not shine or is rejected, faith is absent.

These authentically Thomist tenets, after being overlaid by a more objectivist type of Scholasticism, surfaced again in twentieth-century Thomism thanks to the probings of theologians such as Pierre Rousselot, Louis Charlier, and Marie-Dominique Chenu. The illuminist understanding of faith survives, albeit in new dress, in transcendental Thomism. In this school, attention is shifted to the pre-thematic or transcendental element in thought. For Karl Rahner, faith consists primarily in a supernatural elevation of the transcendence of the human spirit thanks to God's self-communication in grace—a communication given to every human person and thus not dependent on prior evangelization. Faith, Rahner would say, is the noetic aspect of divine grace as freely accepted by any person of good will. Although faith normally tends to seek appropriate forms of belief and expression, it is possible for faith to exist without any particular religious thematization, Christian or non-Christian.

For Lonergan, likewise, faith is identified with what the Scholastic theologians called *lumen gratiae, lumen fidei*, or infused wisdom. According to Lonergan's own preferred definition, "Faith is the knowledge born of religious love." As a result of the love of God flooding our hearts, we perceive the presence of transcendent value in our experience, and in this way the thrust of the human spirit to the transcendent is in some sort fulfilled. Faith, as the "eye of religious love," is to be sharply distinguished from beliefs. The latter are particular affirmations accepted as a result of religious faith. The love of God, according to Lonergan, reveals to us the value of accepting the word of religion.[9]

Whatever may be said of the limitations of an exclusively

illuminist interpretation of faith, this view, in my opinion, cannot rightly be dismissed. Faith is a light and it has a point of impact on the human spirit that is more basic and pervasive than assent to particular propositions. Faith arises out of the dynamic presence of God to the human spirit, and consequently gives a deep satisfaction that cannot be offered or removed by any worldly agency. Recognizing that faith transpires in an immediate encounter between the soul and God, the illumination theory contains a message of consolation for those who are not favored by worldly prosperity. The theologians of this school call attention to a dimension of transcendence or interiority that is in danger of being overlooked in other approaches.

For the contemporary believer, the most serious difficulties against the illuminist theory of faith center about the question whether it fosters responsible commitment to the building of the earthly city. From early times, proponents of the illuminist approach have tried to defend an affirmative answer. Augustine, for example, treats this question at some length in *The City of God*. Faith, he argues, lies at the basis of all authentic virtue. Where there is no love of God, there can be no true virtue, but an authentic, supernatural love of God must rest upon faith. Thus faith is at least a pre-condition for all true virtues, including that of justice.[10] Lonergan, in his *Method in Theology*, maintains that the power of God's love, apprehended in faith, brings forth "a new energy and efficacy in all goodness." Faith, he argues, is linked with human progress because it places human efforts in a friendly universe and reveals an ultimate significance in human achievement. On the other hand, faith, by overcoming human pride and covetousness, arrests the process of decay that affects the human community in a time of ideological conflict.[11]

All this being granted, we must, I think, add that the illuminist view of faith does not regularly foster an intense human concern. The primary focus of attention is the immediate relationship of the soul to God in a contemplative union that can best be achieved through relative detachment from the world. Augustine in the *Confessions* relates how powerfully he was impressed by the example of monks who fled to the desert. The highest moments of his spiritual career would appear to have been ecstatic "trips" such as that which he and his mother enjoyed at Ostia.[12]

The medieval monks, faithful to this tradition, will be able to say with Anselm: "Enter the inner chamber of thy mind; shut out all thoughts save that of God, and such as can aid thee in seeking him."[13] The most favorable environment for such a pursuit, according to the Benedictine Jean Leclerq, is "a community whose essential aim is the search for God."[14] The highest contemplation can be achieved with a modicum of material goods, as may be verified in the lives of the great mystics, such as Bernard of Clairvaux and John of the Cross. Thus the pursuit of the life of faith, seen in illuminist and contemplative perspectives, turns the mind away from social and economic problems. Preoccupation with worldly affairs is seen rather as a distraction than as the main business of the Christian life.

Increasingly, in recent years, one hears the complaint that this approach to faith, well grounded though it be in the classical theological tradition, is contaminated by Hellenistic dualism. Man is seen as essentially an intellectual being, having as his chief end an act of contemplative knowledge. The contemplative life is viewed as per se superior to the active life. As a result the believer is constantly drawn toward a certain spiritual hedonism. The long prevalence of this doctrine of faith is reckoned among the principal causes of the split between faith and the daily life of the Christian, which Vatican II, in its *Pastoral Constitution on the Church in the Modern World*, signalized as one of the more serious errors of our age (n. 43).

In my opening pages I suggested that the intellectual aspect of the act of faith is today being reconceived as a discernment within a commitment. This shift opens up new perspectives on the kind of illumination faith might bring. Where there is no commitment in loving service to one's brothers and sisters, one cannot expect to gain a genuinely Christian insight into the meaning of one's life. Where this commitment is present, it can give meaning to many aspects of life that might otherwise appear unintelligible—including the negative experiences of sacrifice, suffering, poverty, and death.

The discernment approach to faith, which I am here advocating, thus offers a certain corrective to the more Platonistic under-

standing of contemplation. Ordinarily speaking, Christian illumination is not to be found in withdrawal from worldly
preoccupations, but in situations of generous involvement and service toward others. The light of faith is given not so that we may
presently plumb the depths of the divinity in anticipation of the
beatific vision but rather that we may better interpret the meaning
of our own lives and the signs of the times in which we live. Christian contemplation, then, is not opposed to action, but is often best
achieved in the midst of active engagement. The true believer, very
often, will be a contemplative in action—*simul in actione contem-
plativus*, as Jerome Nadal was wont to say. Although there is
clearly the possibility of contemplation pursued in solitude, and
even of a life given over to solitary contemplation (in the case of
individuals who may have received this special calling), any contemplation that would result in indifference to suffering and injustice could not be anything but unchristian. It could not produce
true wisdom but only an appearance of this.

Within the intellectualist approach to faith there is, in addition to the illumination theory, a second species, which understands faith as an assent to a determinate body of revealed doctrine. According to the Catholic understanding as it developed in
early modern times, faith is a firm assent to that which the Church
authoritatively teaches in the name of God. Unlike the theory just
considered, the assent theory equates faith with belief.

On this theory, revelation is accepted not because it is seen to
fulfill any yearning for communion with God—a point stressed in
the preceding theory—but simply out of reverence for the authority of God the revealer. Faith is an act of religious submission, an
obedience of the intellect. This view comes out clearly in the teaching of Vatican I that faith is the supernatural virtue by which, with
the grace of God, "we believe the things that he has revealed to be
true, not because of their intrinsic truth perceived by the natural
light of reason, but because of the authority of the revealing God
himself, who can neither deceive nor be deceived."[15]

Although the assent theory of faith has been subjected to
severe theological criticism in the twentieth century, its positive
merits should not be ignored. Faith should in fact come to expression in articulated beliefs, and these beliefs, to the extent that they

flow from faith, are covered with the authority of the faith that inspires them. Even Karl Rahner, a proponent of the illuminist position, is willing to speak of predicamental faith as an assent to formulated truth guaranteed by a revealing God.[15a] The authenticated formulas of faith are of incalculable value in the catechetical instruction of prospective new members of the Christian community. A reverence for past formulations, moreover, does much to assure the continuity and unity of the Church in all times and places.

The weaknesses of the assent theory of faith become most apparent when we ask how it can cope with a fluid world in which man is responsible to those affected by his activity. The assent theory, tending to see the unity of faith in terms of the identity of the propositional truths assented to, is seriously threatened by rapid and radical cultural change. Where this theory flourishes in pure form, believers are taught to cling almost desperately to formulations handed down from the past, and to ignore or deny the time-conditioned character of the thought-categories and concepts used in these formulations. The faithful are not encouraged to be creative in synthesizing the data of their own experience, but are reduced to a passive submission to the approved creeds and dogmas. Faith is not seen as an interpretation of one's own life, but rather as an acceptance of mysterious information handed down long ago from on high. This kind of faith is felt to be anomalous in a world which has ceased to be dominated by the authority of the past, and which recognizes the tentative character of all systematizations. The believer experiences a severe tension within his own psyche, inasmuch as the sphere of faith has little contact with real life as actually experienced. Sometimes it is even felt that faith and the Church ought not to have any particular relevance to the world in which we presently live. This attitude, I submit, is a distortion.

Does faith, as an assent to guaranteed propositions, lead to an active participation in the quest for a just social order? The tendency in this theory is for the believer to become so concerned with right belief that he ceases to see the religious significance of working for justice on earth. Salvation is sought by preference in the ecclesiastical sphere of sacred doctrine and worship rather than in the secular sphere of economic or political life. This false orientation, so easily arising out of the assent theory of faith, is of course at the root of the charges that Christianity alienates man from his proper task and lures him into an illusory world of transcendental irresponsibility.

Up to a point, these charges can be answered from within the theory we are considering. Three important points are commonly made by defenders of the theory.

(a) Theologians who define faith as assent have never maintained that faith alone is sufficient for salvation. They have insisted upon the necessity of the additional and higher virtue of charity, which gives rise to meritorious works. Charity is held to be inseparable from the infused virtue of justice, which inclines one to give others their due. Faith without charity is incomplete, and is therefore called "dead" or "unformed."

(b) The content of faith gives motives and guidance for the building of a better social order. Faith informs the believer concerning the dignity of other persons, the divine commandment to care for the temporal needs of others, and the account that will be required from each one of us at the Last Judgment. Already in 1891, in his great encyclical on the condition of the working classes (Rerum novarum), Leo XIII wrote that the Gospel, "by inculcating self-restraint, keeps men within the bounds of moderation and tends to establish harmony among the divergent interests of the various classes which compose the state."[16] Quite recently, in 1974, the International Synod of Bishops said even more pointedly: "[The Church] can draw from the Gospel the most profound reasons and ever new incentives to promote generous dedication to the service of all men—the poor especially, the weak and the oppressed—and to eliminate the social consequences of sin which are translated into unjust social and political structures."[17]

(c) In many recent official documents, the point is made that faith cannot survive or be propagated unless the Gospel is made credible, and that credibility, at least in the circumstances of today's world, demands commitment to justice. Thus the service of faith calls for commitment to a just social order. This argument is made in the following terms by the 1971 Synod document on "Justice in the World":

The mission of preaching the Gospel dictates at the present

time that we should dedicate ourselves to the liberation of man even in his present existence in this world. For unless the Christian message of love and justice shows its effectiveness through action in the cause of justice in the world, it will only with difficulty gain credibility with the men of our times.[18]

The same argument is made in the closing section of Paul VI's Letter to Cardinal Roy, "A Call to Action" (par. 51), and seems to underlie some of the thinking behind the Synod Document of 1974. A similar thought, indeed, was at the basis of the teaching of Vatican I that the Church is a sign of credibility, in part, because of its fruitfulness on all manner of good works.[19] What is to be thought of this apologetic approach? Ideally, no doubt, the Church should so transform its members that they would devote themselves generously to the needy and the oppressed. If they did so the Gospel would win a much wider hearing than is presently the case. But it would be a mistake, in my opinion, to tie the credibility of the Gospel too closely to such works. The principal sign of credibility, it must be remembered, is not the Church but Christ. Intrinsic to Christianity is the doctrine that believers are still subject to sin. Hence the sinfulness and injustice of Christians do not necessarily deprive their message of credibility. The Church preaches not its own justice but that of Christ. The full effects of Christ's redeeming action, including the promised new age of justice, will not be experienced within history but only at the parousia. In the meantime we may expect to see some anticipations of the future Kingdom of God, in the Church as elsewhere, but these anticipations will inevitably be mingled with signs of human sinfulness.

On the basis of the three arguments just given, we may conclude that there are positive links between faith, conceived as an assent to revealed doctrine, and committed action on behalf of justice. But the propositional understanding of faith, in my opinion, causes the relationship to appear more tenuous and indirect than ought to be the case. The propositions of faith, which are generally statements of a highly speculative and abstract character, are difficult to translate into concrete programs of action. If the intellectual component of faith were to be conceived primarily as a disclosure or discernment of meaning and value, faith would have a more evident relationship to the actual world in which we live and act. Indeed it might be said, contrary to the common impression, that beliefs without any clear implications for commitment and action would be at best remotely connected with faith. If faith is a combination of commitment and discernment, the community of faith must be engaged in a constant process of discerning the signs of the times in the light of the Gospel, and thus of rediscovering the Gospel in the light of the times in which we live.

The task of discernment is a never-ending one, and one that rarely issues in universally valid and apodictic statements. Hence a Church that cultivates discernment must reconceive faith less as a set of assertions and more as a process. A Church engaged in the process of discernment will no doubt speak in more tentative and less authoritative ways than those to which it has been accustomed in previous centuries. But we cannot exclude the possibility that discernment may at times lead to clear and decisive conclusions. As the Church becomes more adept at applying the discernment process to concrete situations, it may be able to speak out more promptly, persuasively, and unanimously on current issues such as racism, militarism, ecology, and unbridled nationalism.[20] The Church's special competence, no doubt, would be restricted to the moral and religious aspects of these social questions, but that kind of input could be very important in the present moral vacuum. Believers are restlessly seeking to find a Christian meaning in the events of contemporary history and a Christian response to the challenges of our times. A theology that would confine the assent of faith to a set of sacrosanct propositions about a higher world, and would insulate faith from the contingencies of daily life, is quite evidently inadequate for our day. By bringing in the dimension of discernment, it may be possible to liberate the assent theory of faith from the sterile intellectualism and authoritarianism by which it has hitherto been plagued.

II

FIDUCIAL APPROACHES

Under my second main heading, fiducial approaches, one

might include all those theories which accent the element of personal trust. Some of these theories, as found in modern Roman Catholic personalist authors, are not far removed from the intellectualist understanding, except that they highlight the personal relationship of the believer to God or to those who speak for God. Catholic personalists, such as Jean Mouroux, frequently quote from St. Thomas:

> Anyone who believes, assents to someone's saying, and thus, in any form of belief, it seems that it is the person to whose saying assent is given, who is of principal importance and, as it were, the end; whereas the beliefs by which we wish to assent to the person are, so to speak, secondary.[21]

St. Thomas, however, in spite of the primacy he gives to the element of personal trust, remains essentially in the intellectualist tradition. For him, faith involves a trust in God as witness. The fiducial approach, as I here interpret the term, looks on God less as revealer than as Savior. As contrasted with the intellectualist notion, which stresses the recognition of what God has said and revealed in the past, the fiducial notion of faith is turned in expectation toward the future; faith therefore verges upon hope.

In general biblical usage the notion of faith *(emunah, pistis)* is much wider than in the intellectualist approach. The believer confidently relies on God, who has freely committed himself to the people of his choice, who has promised them salvation, and who has shown himself faithful to his promises in the past. The central promises in both the Old and the New Testaments are represented in the form of covenants—that is to say, collective contracts in which God, as senior treaty partner, offers to protect the people who faithfully serve him. Through the revelations given to the patriarchs, prophets, and kings, the Israelite nation was urged to rely on God's covenant promises and was blessed if they did so. Isaiah speaks for the Old Testament tradition when he asserts, "Unless you believe you shall not stand firm" (Is. 7:9).

In the Synoptic Gospels, faith is practically equivalent to trust. Praise is given to those who rely on the power of Jesus to heal, to forgive sins, and to bestow salvation and life. After the resurrection, the apostles in their kerygmatic proclamation called for confident trust in Jesus as the one in whom alone justification and remission of sins were to be sought, "for there is no other name under heaven given among men by which we must be saved" (Acts 4:12). "Let it be known to you, therefore, brethren, that through this man forgiveness of sins is proclaimed to you, and by him every one that believes is freed from everything from which you could not be freed by the law of Moses" (Acts 13:38-39). Faith, in other words, is trust in Jesus the liberator.

In Paul's letters to the Romans and Galatians, Abraham is the prototype of faith because "in hope he believed against hope that he should become the father of many nations, as he had been told" (Rom. 4:18, cf. Gal. 3:6-9). The Christians, in Pauline theology, are the spiritual heirs of Abraham. They live by the promises given by God in Jesus Christ. They are saved neither by the justice of naturally good works, nor by obedience to the Law, but by the promise of free grace stemming from Christ who is both just and obedient. If we believe in Jesus, "who has been put to death for our trespasses and raised for our justification," this will be reckoned as righteousness for us (Rom. 4:21-25).

In the sixteenth century, Martin Luther, tormented by the ecclesiastical system of justification as he understood it in his days as a monk, derived from these Pauline passages his famous doctrine of justification by faith alone. A right relationship to God, he maintained, is constituted not by the avoidance of sinful acts, nor by the performance of virtuous deeds, but solely by reliance on the merits of Christ, who will freely bestow the gifts of salvation on those who trust in his grace. "Faith," he wrote, "is a living and unshakable confidence, a belief in the grace of God so assured that a man would die a thousand deaths for its sake."[22] Luther's central concept, as John Dillenberger points out, "ruled out every attempt to justify or acquit oneself before God. One was made acceptable or justified before God in faith, that is, in the lively apprehension of God's word of love and mercy. Before God, this alone was the ground of trust."[23]

Luther's doctrine of faith is a conscious reaction against the Scholastic intellectualist understanding of faith as well as against the doctrine of justification through good works. Rejecting every suggestion of Pelagianism, Luther is anxious to stress that our salvation is due entirely to God's gracious action, rather than to anything that we do. Faith is simply the act by which we apprehend and accept God's saving action toward us in Jesus Christ.

Calvin's doctrine of faith is similar to Luther's. According to Calvin's famous definition, faith is "a firm and certain knowledge of God's beneficence toward us, founded upon the truth of the freely given promise in Christ, both revealed to our minds and sealed upon our hearts through the Holy Spirit."[24] Like Luther, Calvin stresses not simply the truth of God's word but even more the reliability of God's promises in Christ. Yet the element of intellectual assent is not missing from Calvin's definition. As compared with Luther, Calvin writes more systematically, less existentially. Characteristically he stresses not simply the external word that comes to us in Scripture but also the present and interior action of the Holy Spirit, sealing upon our heart the message of salvation.

The fiducial concept of faith, as found in the classical Protestant authors, remains very much alive today, for instance in the conservative evangelical churches and in all communities affected by the charismatic movement. There is something very imposing and attractive in a faith that brings the individual into such a lively personal relationship to Christ as Lord and God. Christians who accept this view are able to lead a deep devotional life and are sustained by a hope that is in no way shaken by adverse circumstances. Indeed the very absence of justice in the world and the very untrustworthiness of all created powers tend to concentrate the believer's hopes more intently on God, who alone can save, and who has promised salvation to all who place their trust in Jesus alone.

The theocentric or Christocentric supernaturalism of the fiducial theories can easily obscure the importance of human initiative and undermine the sense of human responsibility for the future of the world. Everything is believed to be in the hands of God, who will unconditionally fulfill his promises. This total confidence in God is logically connected with the classical Protestant positions on merit and good works.

Although he esteemed good works, Luther, followed by Cal-

vin and many others, insisted that good works do not justify and
are not essential to salvation. Perhaps with some deliberate exaggeration Luther emphasized this point in his famous 1521 letter to
Melanchthon:

> Be a sinner and sin boldly, but believe still more boldly and
> rejoice in Christ, who is victor over sin, death, and the world.
> Sin we must, as long as we live here. . . . It is enough that we
> recognize, through the riches of the glory of God, the Lamb
> who takes away the sins of the world. From him no sin will
> sever us, even though we should fornicate or commit murder a
> million times a day. Do you think that the price or ransom of
> our sins in this Lamb was so small?[25]

If we take this position without further explanation, it presents us with a radically different view of the relationship between
faith and service to the world than in the intellectualist view already examined. If Christians are concerned with salvation, as
they obviously should be, they will not be over-concerned with
doing good deeds, but will rely on the mercy of Christ, accepted in
faith, as the one effective means. Taking it for granted that the
Church is a society of sinners, one will not be led to expect that the
Church will transform the world into a place of love and justice.
Nor will the presence of injustice in the Church and in the world be
a serious impediment to the credibility of the Gospel.

In fairness to Luther, it must now be added that we have not
as yet presented his full doctrine on the relationship between faith
and good works. He consistently sees this in a positive light. In his
"Preface to the New Testament" he depicts the works of faith
primarily in confessional terms:

> If he have faith, the believer cannot be restrained. He betrays
> himself. He breaks out. He confesses and teaches the Gospel
> to the people at the risk of life itself. . . . For if works and
> love do not blossom forth, it is not genuine faith, the Gospel
> has not gained a foothold, and Christ is not yet rightly
> known.[26]

Even more explicitly does Luther bring out the relationship

between faith and service to others in his "Preface to Romans":

> Faith, however, is something that God effects in us. It changes us and we are reborn from God (Jn. 1:13). Faith puts the old Adam to death and makes us quite different men in heart, in mind, and in all our powers; and it is accompanied by the Holy Spirit. O, when it comes to faith, what a living, creative, active, powerful thing it is! It cannot do other than good at all times. . . .

> Hence, the man of faith, without being driven, willingly and gladly seeks to do good to everyone, serve everyone, suffer all kinds of hardships, for the sake of the love and glory of the God who has shown him such grace. It is impossible, indeed, to separate works from faith, just as it is impossible to separate heat and light from fire.[27]

This positive evaluation of good works, it must be added, in no way cancels out the Lutheran doctrine of justification by faith alone. As previously noted, faith justifies; good works presuppose faith. "Let him who wishes to do good works begin not with the doing of works, but with believing, which makes the person good, for nothing makes a man good except faith, or evil except unbelief."[28]

On Luther's own theory, therefore, good works are not decisive. In the life of the justified sinner, both good works and evil works will be found. Insofar as one is a believer, one will tend to do good deeds, but the deeds are not constitutive of justification. Faith, for Luther, is an interior act, real and complete in itself independently of all good works. In this respect Luther simply shares the assumption of the great majority of his predecessors and contemporaries.

Yet it is here precisely that some twentieth-century Protestants wish to qualify the views of their forebears. There is a growing tendency to insist that faith, as a sincere response to the word of God, must involve something more than an interior act of assent. This newer position is expressed, for instance, by Bonhoeffer and Barth.

Dietrich Bonhoeffer, in *The Cost of Discipleship*, polemicized against the "cheap grace" being purveyed by some of his co-religionists. Going beyond Luther, Bonhoeffer argued that faith included obedience to the word of God. "Only he who believes is obedient, and only he who is obedient believes. . . . For faith is only real when there is obedience, never without it, and faith only becomes faith in the act of obedience."[29] In the absence of a new existence created through obedience, faith will be unauthentic and will lead to "a grace which is not costly."

Bonhoeffer's idea that faith must be seen as including obedience to the word of God given in Jesus Christ agrees well with the thinking of Karl Barth. In the *Church Dogmatics*, Barth describes faith as an appropriate human response mirroring the faithfulness *(pistis)* of God revealed in Jesus Christ. As a "corresponding and appropriate answer to the faithfulness of God," faith must reproduce in itself in an analogous way the attributes and actions of Christ, especially his humility and obedience. It is thus in some sort an *imitatio Christi*.[30]

The modifications of the Reformation doctrine of faith in Bonhoeffer and Barth, in my judgment, could be interpreted as a critique of Luther and Calvin. These modern authors seem ill at ease with an exclusively fiducial understanding of faith. The intention of the Reformers was to minimize the role of the human person in justification or redemption, and thereby to magnify the role of God. In the twentieth century, when we have such an acute consciousness of the power and responsibility of man to shape the future of the world, the dualism of the Reformation is unsatisfactory. There seems to be something wrong with any theory that plays off God against all human and created agencies, so that trust in him involves a lack of trust in them.

In concluding our analysis of the fiducial approach to faith we must inquire whether it favors an ethic strongly oriented to the transformation of human society through the leaven of the Gospel. In principle, an affirmative answer to this question appears to be defensible. The exhortation to works of service and charity, so eloquently set forth in Luther's *Freedom of a Christian*, would seem to be applicable to the socio-political order, and not simply to individual acts of mercy. In some of his exhortations to princes Luther does propose an evangelical motivation for social reform, and Calvin, with his strong doctrine of union between Church and state, goes further in the same direction.

Yet on balance, this line of thought is undeveloped in Luther as in most typical advocates of fiducial faith. From his sharp antithesis between faith and works, Luther passes on to equally sharp antitheses between Gospel and law, between the heavenly and the earthly kingdoms. The evangelical precept of love, in his system, does not appear to be applicable to political society. Indeed, in his *Commentary on Galatians* Luther argues that law and Gospel are as widely separated as heaven and earth. He goes on to say: "Wherefore if the question be concerning the matter of faith and conscience let us utterly exclude the law and leave it on earth."[31]

During the Peasants' Revolt, Luther accused the rebels of having confused the two kingdoms. "It is a malicious and evil idea," he wrote, "that serfdom should be abolished because Christ has made us free. This refers only to the spiritual freedom given to us by Christ in order to enable us to withstand the devil."[32] Thus the Gospel, as understood by Luther, offers no ground for social and political liberation.

In a passage that may not be entirely fair to Luther himself, but is hardly unfair to some of Luther's successors, Ernst Troeltsch points out how the Lutheran doctrine of justification entails a lack of real interest in social reform:

> Lutheran Christian individualism has retired behind the line of battle of all external events and outward activity, into a purely personal spirituality, into the citadel of a freedom which no events of the external order can touch, a position so impregnable that neither joy nor sorrow, the world or society can capture it. This spirituality is based on nothing save the "word," which is guaranteed by the Church; it therefore regards the Church simply as the herald of the word, endowed with a purely spiritual miraculous healing power; it has no conception of the Church as an ethical organization of Christendom as a whole. . . . As soon as the Christian believer turns from this spirituality to take part in real life, he can only express his inner liberty through submission to the existing order, as a method of manifesting Christian love to the

brethren, and to society as a whole, or as something evil to be passively endured and accepted.[33]

Troeltsch in this passage paves the way for the very severe judgment on Luther's social teaching pronounced by Reinhold Niebuhr in *The Nature and Destiny of Man*. Luther's insistence on passive righteousness and on the separation of the two kingdoms, according to Niebuhr, was destined to have disastrous consequences in the history of German civilization.[34]

Is disinterest in social reform a normal consequence of the fiducial doctrine of faith? There are grounds for thinking that it is. This theory concentrates our hopes and interests not on anything that happens within history, not on anything done by human effort, not on any political or social institutions, but on God alone, whose merciful word comes to us through Jesus Christ. Salvation therefore comes to be seen in individualistic and other-worldly terms.

Among modern representatives of the fiducial position, Jürgen Moltmann is outstanding for his efforts to combine a fiducial doctrine of faith with strong commitment to social and political activism. According to Moltmann, Christian faith gives rise to an intense hope for the eschatological Kingdom, and this hope, in turn, liberates us for committed action on behalf of the human family.

The expectation of the promised future of the Kingdom of God, which is coming to man and the world to set them right and create life, makes us ready to expend ourselves unrestrainedly and unreservedly in love and in the work of reconciliation of the world with God and his future.[35]

Thus self-expenditure in this world, day-to-day love in hope, becomes possible and becomes human within that horizon of expectation which transcends this world.[36]

For Moltmann, as I read him, the object of hope is in no way dependent upon the cooperation of man. God alone by his action in raising Jesus from the dead gives us a firm hope in the future.

But that hope is inseparable from world-transformation. For Christian hope unveils the vision of an eternity of righteousness and love. Inspired by this vision, the believer thirsts for a reconciliation that still lies ahead.

> As long as "every thing" is not "very good" the difference between hope and reality remains, and faith remains irreconciled and must press toward the future in hope and suffering. . . . It is not human activity that makes the future. It is the inner necessity of the Christ event itself, the tendency of which is finally to bring out in all things the eternal life latent in him and the justice of God latent in him.[37]

We do not plan in order that God's future may come about, but because we are intent upon that future, we plan things that approximate it. Thus Christian hope brings about certain transformation of human society.

Without breaking with the basically fiducial concept of faith, Moltmann overcomes many of its characteristic weaknesses. He does away with the dualism of the two kingdoms and with the spiritualistic individualism so often found in the Lutheran tradition. For my own part, I am not sure that he entirely escapes the difficulties inherent in the fiducial approach. With his general tendency to devalue the present and the past, he seems to admit only appearances of God's action within history, and to reserve the reality of redemption exclusively to the absolute future. God, apparently, is not personally at work within history, but is present only under the mode of promise. For Moltmann, moreover, the eschatological future is the work of God alone, totally independent, it would seem, of any human cooperation. If the final reality of salvation in no way depends upon what man does within time, there seems to be no adequate motivation for human service and sacrifice.

To overcome these remaining difficulties, it will be necessary, I believe, to go beyond the fiducial concept of faith, just as the fiducial concept goes beyond the intellectualist. I turn, therefore, to the third major approach, which may be called performative.

III
PERFORMATIVE APPROACHES

At several points in these pages allusion has already been made to what may be called the performative dimension of faith. In my observations regarding Vatican II and the Roman documents issued since the Council, I mentioned the frequent insistence that the Gospel cannot be heralded by word alone, and that authentic evangelization must release energies tending to transform the world in which we live. In my discussion of the intellectualist approach, I reiterated my conviction that discernment and commitment are inseparably united aspects of the disclosure experience, so that the illumination of faith is given only within a commitment to appropriate action. Again, in my analysis of the fiducial views, I made reference to the growing opinion that the acceptance of God's word, if it is sincere, must normally include an obedient submission to what the word demands. Obedience, therefore, would seem to be a component of faith itself.

Inspired by Barth and by several contemporary theologians of the word (post-Bultmannians such as Gerhard Ebeling), the American theologian Peter C. Hodgson in several recent works has sought to reinterpret the doctrine of faith in the light of an enriched theology of the word of God.[38] The transmission of the Gospel, he maintains, is a word-event in which the word of proclamation is echoed by a word of response. Because only a total response can be appropriate to the word of God, faith is never a matter of disembodied words; it becomes incarnate in faith and praxis. Jesus made himself the faithful one by his acceptance of God's will for himself, thus passing through crucifixion to resurrection. The crucifixion—the free action by which Jesus obediently goes to his death, and through it to newness of life—is the word-event par excellence. Christian faith is the embodied word by which others respond to the word of God previously embodied in Jesus. Faith is the power of God within us, making us whole, healing the fractures of physical and social existence, and opening us to a vital participation in God's rule as it breaks into our earthly existence. "Faith is a *liberating power*," writes Hodgson, "that 'saves' life, giving it wholeness and efficacy, in the midst of bondage, estrangement and guilt."[39]

In recent Latin American liberation theology, efforts are being made to develop a new theology of faith in conscious opposition to the intellectualism and fideism of earlier European theology. Among the Catholic contributors to this new theology of faith one must reckon the Brazilian theologians Hugo Assmann and Leonardo Boff, the Chilean Segundo Galilea, the Peruvian Gustavo Gutiérrez, the Mexican José Miranda, and the Uruguayan Juan Luis Segundo. A good sampling of their views on faith may be found in a volume entitled *The Mystical and Political Dimension of the Christian Faith.*[40]

These theologians take as their point of departure the inadequacies in the traditional understanding of faith. When the traditionally minded Catholic in Latin America commits himself to the liberation of workers and peasants, writes Segundo Galilea, "the categories of his faith . . . do not inspire or illuminate sufficiently his commitments."[41] This discrepancy produces an initial crisis of faith, which must be resolved by a rethinking of the nature of faith itself.

Gustavo Gutiérrez finds fault with the traditional concept of faith as assent. Rather than being a mere assent, he writes, it must be a warm welcome of the gift of the word. Truth is not just affirmed with the mind and lips but is also brought into being as a word incarnated in life and deed. Otherwise, he remarked, faith would become dissolved in idealism.[42]

Segundo Galilea objects that the mystical or illuminationist view of faith is untrue to the Bible and is vitiated by Hellenistic dualism. Faith, he contends, ought not to be directed to an abstract, mystical contemplation in which the believer, absorbed in God, tries to imitate the angels. This Platonic form of mysticism, in his view, began to contaminate authentic Christian contemplation as Greek thought, with its antithesis between spirit and body, gained influence in the nascent Church.[43] The biblical understanding of contemplation, which involves no such dualism, is on the way to being recovered, Galilea believes, in Latin America today.

The Protestant fiducial concept of faith likewise comes in for its share of criticism. Juan Luis Segundo blames the Lutheran separation of faith from good works for having spawned an immoral neutralism with regard to political systems. The Bible, he argues, is passionately concerned with the rebuilding of the earth by persons animated by selfless love.[44]

Having rejected the intellectualist and fiducial theories of faith, liberation theology proceeds to define faith from its own perspectives. Frequently in these authors faith is described as "the historical praxis of liberation." Somewhat less succinctly, they might describe faith as commitment to revolutionary praxis in a historical situation that concretely mediates for them the word of God. Their own situation is the oppression and dependency of the third world and especially of the poorer classes.

Three terms in the definition just given seem to call for further explanation: historicity, praxis, and liberation.

(a) The historicity of faith means, in the first place, that faith does not yet exist in final, complete form. The Truth presently abides with us only insofar as it is the "Way," i.e. as a word in the midst of history. These theologians would assert, as I did in my opening paragraph, that any given act of faith must correspond to the actual historical situation in which it is made. The word of God comes to us through the historical situation, which mediates it to the believer.

In Latin America today, say these theologians, the word of God is mediated by the cry of the poor and the oppressed. "In fact encounter with Christ necessarily occurs through the mediation of the poor brother who exists as an exploited class, as a forgotten race and as a marginalized culture"—so writes Claude Geffré in a clarification of the Latin American theology.[45]

According to Gutiérrez, "History is the scene of the revelation God makes of the mystery of his person. His word reaches us in the measure of our involvement in the evolution of history." In order to hear the word of God, he contends, I have to go out of my way and, like the Good Samaritan, draw near to the "distant" person who needs my help.[46]

Assmann goes so far as to speak of the present historical situation as the primary text for the theology of liberation.[47] Other texts, such as the Bible and the documents of the magisterium, are not primary, in his view; they do not contain truth in themselves, but they have to be read in relation to our own reality and practice. The canonical texts do not become revelation until they are read in correlation with the signs of the times in which we live.

(b) The term "praxis" is a technical term in Marxism and in the critical sociology of twentieth-century neo-Marxists. A helpful introduction may be found in Charles Davis' article, "Theology and Praxis" in *Cross Currents* for Summer 1973.[48]

For Marx, praxis referred to those human activities which are capable of transforming reality and society, and thus of making the world more human. More specifically, praxis is the action that tends to overcome the alienation by which man has become separated from the fruits of his labor. Praxis is therefore revolutionary: it is directed to changing the economic and social relationships. Convinced that the existing social order is alienating, the Marxists argue that any non-revolutionary theory will inevitably reinforce the existing alienation. A theory that interprets reality without doing anything to change it is defective even as a theory, for it is distorted by its uncritical acceptance of a repressive situation.

Marx sought to lay the groundwork for a new non-alienating kind of theory, which he called "critical theory." Critical theory in his thinking is dialectically united to revolutionary praxis. It is a new consciousness growing out of efforts to overcome the contradictions in the existing society. In the dialectical unity of critical theory and revolutionary praxis, the praxis is informed by the theory, and the theory is shaped by the praxis.

Applying these principles to faith, liberation theologians say in effect that the word of God is distorted and alienating whenever it is accepted without commitment to the praxis oriented toward the Kingdom of God. But if we are authentically committed to the Kingdom, we shall be involved in the struggle to subvert the existing social order, with its institutionalized injustice, and to establish on earth a just, fraternal society. In light of that commitment we shall be in a position to discern correctly the present reality and the emerging possibilities for the future. This discernment, to be sure, will not be perfectly clear, for until the consummated Kingdom is realized, the truth cannot exist in finished form. We can, however, have a truth proportioned to our situation on the way, and we shall thereby be equipped to move forward toward greater truth.

(c) The term "liberation" in the Latin American theologians

functions somewhat as "humanization" does for the Marxists. It signifies the re-creation and total fulfillment of man, as does the biblical term "salvation." "Liberation," however, is untainted by the other-worldly connotations of the term "salvation" and calls attention to the current process by which people are extricated from their present situation of domination and dependence. In speaking of this situation, the Latin American theologians have in mind the condition of their own countries, but they point out that the concern is not merely regional, for in fact two-thirds of the human race live in a similar situation of degradation.

The term "liberation" is a substitute for "development" as used in some earlier documents.[49] After the Medellín Conference (1968), the notion of development was abandoned as being too gradualistic and optimistic; it seemed to imply that the present situation contains the seeds of the desired future. "Liberation" brings out the conflictual character of the process. On the other hand it is not tied to the rather specific political options that would be conveyed by a term such as "revolution." Unlike "development" and "revolution," "liberation" is a term that has deep roots in the Bible and in theology. It is closely connected with the biblical idea of redemption, which in some contexts signifies the manumission of a slave. Liberation connotes the "freedom with which Christ has set us free" (Gal. 5:1).

Liberation includes, but is not confined to, political and socioeconomic transformation. Gutiérrez distinguishes three levels: (i) political and social liberation of oppressed nations and social classes; (ii) liberation of humankind in the course of world history; (iii) liberation from sin and total reconciliation in communion with God through Jesus Christ.[50] In answer to the frequent charge of socio-political reductionism, liberation theologians reply that this has never been their program and is contrary to their intention. They do, however, wish to emphasize the inseparability of total redemption (or liberation) from the social, economic, and political factors, and in this way to escape the excesses of individualistic dualism.

Gutiérrez, in particular, insists that a true spiritual conversion is involved in the act of faith, as he understands it. "The encounter with Christ in the poor constitutes an authentic spiritual experience. It is to live in the Spirit, the link of the love of the Father and the Son, God and man, between men. Christians committed to an historical praxis of liberation try to live there this deep communion."[51] Elsewhere he says that commitment to liberation "gives rise to a new way of being a man and of believing, of living and thinking the faith, of being called together in an 'ecclesia.' "[52] When I make myself the neighbor of the wretched person whom I seek out in the barrios, when I take an effective option for the poor, my world changes, and I myself am transformed by my commitment to social transformation.

Liberation theology does not foster any utopian illusions about the future. We will never, of course, fully insert the Kingdom of God into historical time. But the biblical concept of the Kingdom stimulates our creative imagination so that we find ever new ways of provisionally realizing within history signs and anticipations of the promised Kingdom.[53]

In summary, then, faith as conceived by liberation theology is a transforming acceptance of the word, which comes as a free gift of God, breaking into human existence through the poor and oppressed, with whom Christ is seen to identify himself. Only in commitment to the liberation of the oppressed, and thus only in liberating praxis, can we give to the word the "warm welcome" that constitutes faith.

The dialectical interweaving of contemplation and praxis in the liberation theology of faith seems to me to be a definite advance over all the theories previously considered. The older theories, with their undialectical approach, inevitably tended to reduce man to passivity in the act of faith with the intention of giving greater glory to God. According to liberation theology the activity of God in shaping the content of faith includes, rather than excludes, the faithfulness of believers, so that their activity on behalf of justice in the world feeds back into their perception of the word of God. Faith, therefore, is not a passive waiting upon God's own decision to act, but it seizes the initiative and reshapes the world by its God-given power.

This dynamic view of faith has a more solid biblical basis than is commonly recognized. The dialectical inter-relationship between understanding and practice, between orthodoxy and orthopraxy, is suggested by certain biblical texts such as John 3:21, "Whoever does what is true comes to the light." According to this text truth is not only to be thought but also done, and the doing of truth is a condition of believing it. Further, the New Testament forbids us to look upon the Kingdom of God as exclusively future. It thus supports the contention of liberation theology that the Kingdom, in a provisional manner, is present and operative within history.[54] The Gospel, as grasped by faith, is the power of God revealing God's justice and leading to salvation (Rom. 1:16-17).[55] By keeping our eyes open to the signs of the times, we can perceive God's powerful action bringing about both judgment and salvation. Faith itself is an agent in salvation history. Paul, in Galatians 5:6, speaks of "faith working through love," thus implying that faith itself is efficaciously transforming the world according to the word of God.[56] In the struggle between faith and unfaith, the believer is assured of victory, for, as 1 John 5:4 tells us, "This is the victory that overcomes the world, our faith."[57] In view of texts such as these, it does not seem permissible to look upon faith as a merely passive virtue. Faith does not simply protect us from the world; it remakes that world.

Better than any of the theories previously considered in this chapter, the liberation theory of faith is able to cope with the problems raised by the socio-technical civilization. In the first place, the mobility of the world poses no threat to this kind of faith, for, in the view of these theologians, Christian faith is mediated by concrete historical experience. The very form of faith will bear the signature of the historical situation in which it is mediated. Actual experience of the human struggles of our own day constitutes a primary text in a sense in which not even Scripture or tradition is primary.

Second, this new theology of faith harmonizes excellently with the growing sense of the power of human initiative to shape the lives of everyone on this earth. For liberation theology, faith is not a merely passive virtue by which we accept and rely upon God's promises; it is an active engagement in the service of the Kingdom of God. Faith, according to this view, cannot exist without commitment to the implementation of the Gospel; and the experience of praxis, as we have said, helps to determine the concrete form of faith in a given time and place.

Third, the liberation theory is fully in tune with the increased sense of man's responsibility for the future of the world. Unlike the majority of intellectualist and fiducial theories, liberation theology does not place its hope of salvation solely in the action by which God will miraculously intervene in history at some future time. As I have said, liberation theology sees the Kingdom of God as presently existent and operative, and it sees faith as a force actually promoting the cause of justice and liberation.

Having sufficiently indicated my enthusiasm for the actual and potential contribution of liberation theology to a contemporary understanding of faith, I should like, before closing, to indicate certain reservations. I am not of the opinion that this theory of faith should be simply substituted for the earlier intellectualist and fiducial theories. Rather, I would say that the theories are mutually complementary and mutually corrective. Certain aspects of the complex reality of faith are better explained in other theories. The liberationist approach has limitations of its own.

Without denying the historical mediation of faith, we may continue to insist that God succeeds in making himself immediately present to the human spirit, as the transcendental theologians have so lucidly shown. If this immediacy of God were allowed to be obscured, as seems to be the case in some liberationist theologies, faith might seem to be a reaction to the historical situation rather than a response to a personal call from God.

By stressing the dialectical unity of theoria and praxis in the act of faith, the liberation theologians have recovered a very important biblical insight. But it must be kept in mind that this dialectical unity is a unity in difference. It is quite possible for a person to be a sincere believer and yet not to practice what he believes and preaches. The liberationist stress on external activity and social involvement runs the risk of minimizing the dimension of interiority in the life of faith. Luther with his advice to "sin boldly" brought out in a forceful if exaggerated way the possibility that faith may at times co-exist with actions that are inconsistent with itself. The traditional theologies of faith, in different ways, have tried to do justice to the religious significance of a personal faith that, for one reason or another, fails to achieve appropriate expression in actual conduct. In the liberation theologians I have read, there is no adequate study of the psychological complexity of

the act of faith. Liberation theology has been in dialogue with sociology and economics but not to the same extent with the disciplines that seek to penetrate to the inner depths of the human
spirit. As a result, some theologians of this school speak too glibly
about overcoming dualism and bridging the gap between theory
and action.

The effort of liberation theology to find God in the "signs of
the times" is surely a commendable one, in line with a favorite
theme of John XXIII and Vatican Council II. One may envy the
confidence of some liberation theologians that they have succeeded
in this demanding task, and have found without question where
Christ is present in the history of our time. No Christian can deny
that Jesus may come to us in the poor and the oppressed, but I
confess that I feel a certain nervousness about the insistence of
some liberation theologians that this is the way in which Christ is
necessarily to be found in our society. The correspondence between
the Gospel and Marxian class analysis is too neat to allay the suspicion that the Bible is being read through the eyes of those who
are already convinced Marxists. They quote very selectively from
the biblical passages that exalt the poor, and assert too sweepingly
that God is always on the side of the poor and the oppressed. At
times they even imply that the Christian ought to take sides with
the poor against the rich, thus engaging to the full in the existing
conflict among classes.

In this connection Richard Mouw has raised two interesting
questions. He writes:

I accept the view that a central concern of the Christian community should be to identify with the poor and oppressed. But
it seems to me that we must get clearer about what that concern comes to by dealing carefully and critically with at least
two questions. First, who are to be properly included in the
class of the "poor and oppressed" with whom we are biblical-
ly compelled to identify? Are we to include Nixon, who is
presently an outcast and despised person? What about a financially well-off used car salesman who is experiencing a painful
divorce? Or bored, pot-smoking students in an all-white su-
burban high school? Second, if we *can* clearly delineate the

class of the poor and oppressed, then how shall we go about "identifying" with them? Is Mark Hatfield doing it? Will a professor who is properly aligned with the poor and oppressed inevitably oppose the construction of a new academic library? Will he or she refuse to buy works of art for personal enjoyment?[58]

Although the rich are subject to vices that we should, on all accounts, oppose, it would be a mistake to idealize the poor. They can sin as much by envy and covetousness as the rich by pride and avarice. In the preaching of Jesus no one class is made a paragon of virtue. All are admonished to examine their motives and to repent.

The category of liberation, with its echoes of the exodus and of Easter, is theologically acceptable. It helps to bring the Gospel to life, for there is at least an analogy between God's redeeming action in Christ, liberating us from spiritual and moral servitude, and the action of military or political leaders who deliver people from poverty and oppression. The rhetoric of liberation theology, however, could engender some confusion. It sometimes seems to suggest that social or political revolution, with a corresponding redistribution of wealth and power, are an essential means of bringing the poor and oppressed the salvation promised by the Gospel. This misunderstanding would demolish the rationale for the evangelization of those who are not likely to effect social change, and would deprive many destitute persons of the consolation which the Gospel can bring them amid their sufferings. Over-influenced by the Marxist critique of religion, some look with suspicion on all direct evangelization, treating it as though it were a mere cloak for oppression. With this exaggeration in mind, Paul VI felt obliged to warn, at the close of the 1974 Synod of Bishops:

The totality of salvation is not to be confused with one or other aspect of liberation, and the Good News must preserve all of its own originality: that of a God who saves us from sin and death and brings us to divine life. Hence human advancement, social progress, etc., is not to be excessively emphasized on a temporal level to the detriment of the essential meaning which evangelization has for the Church of Christ: the announcement of the Good News.[59]

The liberation theologians are to be praised for urging all Christians to take seriously the obligation to work for a better political and social order, but in my estimation they assume too easily that some one social or economic system is endorsed by the Gospel itself. The Church does not have in its Scriptures, its traditions, and its sacramental heritage the resources it would need to make a sure choice among rival social systems. It is most difficult, or rather impossible, to deduce any specific social or political philosophy from occasional dicta of Jesus or the apostles. Christians, as individuals or in groups, will form their conscientious convictions in accordance with what seem to them to be the requirements of faith and the Gospel, but it will be most rare that the Church as such will see fit to endorse a particular system of government, political party, candidate, or platform.

Many of the conclusions of Latin American liberation theologians appear to be predicated on the assumption that capitalism is the great source of oppression in the world and Marxian socialism would bring peace, freedom, and general prosperity. On this point I personally find their statements unconvincing. Granting that laissez-faire capitalism has led to great inequities, I would think that the actual record of Marxian regimes is far from encouraging. Karl Marx may have been right when he thought that his own philosophy was entirely incompatible with Christianity.[60]

Because of the reservations I have just stated, I am ambivalent about the theory of faith proposed by the liberation theologians. My hesitations arise at just those points where it adopts the specific theses of Marxian social analysis. I am not sure whether, without these points, it would still merit the name of "liberation theology." I am confident, however, that a sound and contemporary vision of faith would accept the thesis, so brilliantly expounded by some liberation theologians, that Christian faith ineluctably involves an active concern with establishing justice on the earth.

In the letter to the Hebrews (12:2), Jesus is described as the author and finisher (or, as sometimes translated, the pioneer and perfecter) of faith. By the fidelity with which he completed the task assigned to him and carried out his own historic vocation to the end, and hence especially through the mystery of his redemptive death, he became the catalyst and paradigm of the faith that is ours. The faith of Jesus involved fidelity or faithfulness, and only in this way did it become foundational for our own faith. Our faith must be like his. As members of his body, Christians must carry out for the world of each generation the task that Jesus left unfinished. We must, so to speak, "fill up what is wanting" in Christ's faith by faithfulness in our own times (cf. Col. 1:24). By faith we accept our share in the mission of Jesus himself.

According to the Gospels, the mission of Jesus is prophetically set forth in the First Servant Song of Isaiah 42:1-4. The crucial passage reads as follows:

> Behold my servant whom I uphold,
>   my chosen, in whom my soul delights;
> I have put my Spirit upon him,
>   he will bring forth justice to the nations.
> He will not cry or lift up his voice,
>   or make it heard in the street;
> A bruised reed he will not break,
>   and a dimly burning wick he will not quench;
>   he will faithfully bring forth justice.
> He will not fail or be discouraged
>   till he has established justice in the earth;
>   and the coastlands wait for his law.

The Kingdom of peace and justice is not simply a remote ideal for which we long. In Jesus Christ the Kingdom of God has entered into history. It is already at work, albeit only germinally, transforming the world in which we live. Faith is the Christian's mode of participation in that Kingdom. Insofar as we have faith, the Kingdom takes hold of us and operates in us. This means that through faith we become instruments in the healing and reconciliation of the broken world. We become agents of justice and bearers of the power of the Kingdom. Faith, therefore, is more than intellectual assent, more than hope in what God will do without us; it is also a present participation in the work that God is doing—that is to say, in the task of bringing forth justice to nations.

NOTES

1. Herbert Richardson, *Toward an American Theology* (New York: Harper and Row, 1967), p. 16.
2. P. Teilhard de Chardin, *How I Believe* (New York: Harper and Row, 1969).
3. P. Tillich, *Dynamics of Faith* (New York: Harper, 1957), p. 4.
4. I. T. Ramsey, *Religious Language* (New York: Macmillan Paperbacks, 1963).
5. Cf. A. Richardson, *History Sacred and Profane* (Philadelphia: Westminster, 1964).
5a. I have discussed these three dimensions in my paper, "The Changing Forms of Faith," chap. 1 of *The Survival of Dogma* (Garden City: Doubleday Image, 1973), pp. 15-30.
6. See P. Benoit, "Pauline and Johannine Theology: A Contrast," *Cross Currents* 13 (1965) 339-53; also James A. Mohler, *Dimensions of Faith Yesterday and Today* (Chicago: Loyola University Press, 1969), pp. 27-41.
7. *Epist. 120*, chap. 1, no. 3 (*PL* 33:453).
8. *Proslogium*, chap. 1; in S. N. Deane (ed.), *St. Anselm: Basic Writings* (La Salle, Ill.: Open Court, 1962), p. 7.
9. B. Lonergan, *Method in Theology* (New York: Herder & Herder, 1972), pp. 115-24.
10. *The City of God*, Book 19, esp. chap. 21.
11. *Method in Theology*, pp. 116-17.
12. *Confessions*, Bk. 9, chap. 10.
13. *Proslogium*, chap. 1; Deane ed., p. 3.
14. J. Leclerq, *The Love of Learning and the Desire of God* (New York: Fordham University Press, 1961), p. 265.
15. Denzinger-Schönmetzer, *Enchiridion Symbolorum* (32nd ed., Freiburg, 1963), no. 3008.
15a. "Observations on the Concept of Revelation," in K. Rahner and J. Ratzinger, *Revelation and Tradition* (New York: Herder and Herder, 1966), p. 22.
16. Quoted from Anne Fremantle (ed.), *The Papal Encyclicals in Their Historical Context* (New York: Mentor Books, 1956), p. 191.
17. Text in J. Gremillion (ed.), *The Gospel of Peace and Justice* (Maryknoll: Orbis, 1976), p. 597.
18. Text *ibid.*, p. 521.

19. Denzinger-Schönmetzer, *op. cit.*, no. 3013.

20. E. Schillebeeckx, in *God the Future of Man* (New York: Sheed and Ward, 1970), gives an enlightening treatment of the process by which moral imperatives are perceived in concrete social situations.

21. *Sum. Theol.* 2-2.11.1; cf. J. Mouroux, *I Believe: The Personal Structure of Faith* (New York: Sheed & Ward, 1959), p. 59.

22. "Preface to Romans," in J. Dillenberger (ed.), *Martin Luther: Selections* (Garden City: Doubleday Anchor, 1961), p. 24.

23. *Ibid.*, p. xxvi.

24. *Institutes of the Christian Religion*, Bk. III, chap. 2, par. 7.

25. Quoted in J. A. Moehler, *Symbolism* (New York: E. Dunigan, 1844), pp. 212-13.

26. "Preface to the New Testament," in Dillenberger, *op. cit.*, p. 18.

27. "Preface to Romans," *ibid.*, pp. 23-24.

28. "The Freedom of a Christian Man," *ibid.*, p. 71.

29. *The Cost of Discipleship* (New York: Macmillan Paperbacks ed., 1963), p. 69. Elsewhere Bonhoeffer declares: "Faith is a participation in this being of Jesus (incarnation, cross, and resurrection)"—*Letters and Papers from Prison* (enlarged ed., New York: Macmillan Paperbacks, 1972), p. 381.

30. *Church Dogmatics* IV/1 (New York: Scribner's, 1956), p. 634.

31. Quoted by Reinhold Niebuhr, *The Nature and Destiny of Man*, vol. 2 (New York: Scribner's, 1964), p. 192.

32. Quoted *ibid.*, p. 194.

33. E. Troeltsch, *The Social Teaching of the Christian Churches* (New York: Harper Torchbook ed., 1960), vol. 2, p. 540.

34. *Op. cit.*, vol. 2, p. 195.

35. J. Moltmann, *Theology of Hope* (London: SCM Press, 1967), p. 337.

36. *Ibid.*, p. 338.

37. *Ibid.*, pp. 215-16.

38. See especially his *Jesus—Word and Presence* (Philadelphia: Fortress, 1971), pp. 136-217, 270-81.

39. *New Birth of Freedom* (Philadelphia: Fortress, 1976), p. 333.

40. *Concilium*, vol. 96 (New York: Herder and Herder, 1974).

41. S. Galilea, "Liberation as an Encounter with Politics and Contemplation," *ibid.*, p. 21.

42. G. Gutiérrez, "Liberation, Theology, and Proclamation," *ibid.*, pp. 67-70.

43. S. Galilea, *art. cit.*, p. 21.

44. J. L. Segundo, "Capitalism—Socialism: A Theological Crux," *ibid.*, p. 122.

45. C. Geffré, "Editorial: A Prophetic Theology," *ibid.*, p. 16.

46. "Faith as Freedom: Solidarity with the Alienated and Confidence in the Future," *Horizons* 2/1 (Spring 1975) 32.

47. H. Assmann, *Theology for a Nomad Church* (Maryknoll: Orbis, 1976), p. 104.

48. *Cross Currents* 23/2 (Summer 1973) 154-68.
49. G. Gutiérrez, *A Theology of Liberation* (Maryknoll: Orbis, 1973), pp. 25-37.
50. *Ibid.*, pp. 36-37, 176-78; cf. Assmann, *op. cit.*, p. 55.
51. "Faith as Freedom . . . ," p. 40.
52. "Liberation, Theology, and Proclamation," p. 58.
53. L. Boff, "Salvation in Jesus Christ and the Process of Liberation," *Concilium* 96, pp. 90-91.
54. J. Miranda, *Marx and the Bible* (Maryknoll: Orbis, 1974), pp. 201-229.
55. *Ibid.*, pp. 163, 172, 244-45.
56. *Ibid.*, p. 256.
57. *Ibid.*, p. 249.
58. Richard J. Mouw, "New Alignments and the Future of the Evangelicism," in P. L. Berger and R. J. Neuhaus (eds.), *Against the World for the World* (New York: Seabury, 1976), pp. 123-24.
59. Paul VI, "Closing Address" (Oct. 26, 1974), *Synod of Bishops— 1974* (Washington, D. C.: USCC, 1975), p. 12.
60. In his rather acerbic review of Miranda's *Marx and the Bible*, J. L. McKenzie comments: "The Bible was there for him (Marx) to study, had he wished to do so; he could have found for himself that ineffable harmony which Miranda hears echoing among the spheres. I think Marx was altogether right in finding religion alien to his theories. It takes more than a perception of the basic ugliness and viciousness of poverty to share a common vision of the redemption of humanity"—*Journal of Biblical Literature* 94 (1975) 280-281.

The Dualism in the Faith of the Church

William Dych, S.J.

Ten years after the publication of the Second Vatican Council's study of the relationship between the Church and the modern world it is still worth noting the novelty of both the question and the Council's answer in the history of the Church. It is true that all of the councils of the Church addressed "modern" or "contemporary" questions, but they were intramural questions of Church doctrine and Church discipline. It is also true that a hundred years earlier the First Vatican Council addressed this question in its study of the relationship between faith and reason, but with results very different from those of Vatican II's study. Looking back after ten years it is worth asking to what extent the significance of either the question or the answer has penetrated into the theology, the preaching and the life of the Church.

We shall look first at the question and try to clarify the terms. How is the Council using the terms "Church" and "world" in studying their inter-relationship? No precise definition of Church is given, but putting together the various elements mentioned in the early paragraphs we can say that by Church the Council means "a community of men united in Christ and led by the Holy Spirit on their journey toward the kingdom of their Father."[1] What does the Council mean by world? World means "mankind and its history," "the whole human family along with the sum of those realities in the midst of which that family lives," "the world as the theater of man's history, carrying the marks of his energies, tragedies and triumphs."[2]

What are to be related, then, are not two static entities, nor two abstract concepts, but two histories, that of the community journeying toward the Kingdom and human history in the broadest sense of the word. The Council says that these two histories are "truly and intimately linked,"[3] and so it wants to explain how it understands "the presence and activity" of this community within this larger history.[4] In asking how the Church is to be present and how it is to act in the modern world the Council in effect is asking what it means to be Church in our contemporary situation. The answer cannot be deduced from a timeless essence of the Church, nor learned exclusively from the Church's past history and tradition, but includes an understanding of the contemporary situation in which the Church finds itself. In this sense the Council is making non-theological knowledge or "secular" experience an intrinsic part of its ecclesiology.

Before examining more closely how the Council elaborates this "intimate link" between the life of the Church and the life of the contemporary world it is important to realize how and why this became a question in the first place. Just as the Council of Trent makes sense only in the context of the Protestant Reformation, and just as the First Vatican Council's constitution on faith makes sense only in the context of the post-Enlightenment emergence of reason and science as autonomous sources of truth, so too the question raised by Vatican II and the answer it gives makes sense only within a particular historical and cultural context. We shall mention just two elements in this cultural context, and these among the more obvious.

There is, first of all, the famous critique of religion by Karl Marx, a critique which has had massive influence in shaping the world in which the Church presently exists, and to which it is trying to relate itself. Parts of that critique are well-known, but it perhaps is worthwhile quoting one passage as an example:

> Religious suffering is at the same time an expression of real suffering and a protest against real suffering. Religion is the sigh of the oppressed creature, the heart of a heartless world, and the soul of soulless conditions. It is the opium of the people.[5]

Just as the effect of opium is not to remove the real causes of pain, but to deaden one's sensitivity to it, so too can religion function for

Marx as a false and pseudo-remedy. If the roots of what he calls real suffering and oppression lie in an unjust social and economic order, in circumstances, situations and structures that lie within man's power to change and improve, then the real remedy for that suffering and oppression is changing that order, not in promising a justice hereafter that, like opium, can alleviate the pain of the present. Such a promise can be alienating in the sense that by focusing our attention elsewhere it can deaden our sensitivity to the actual situation and our capacity to change it.

The real issue for the believer and for the Council, then, is not Marx's materialism or his atheism, but to what extent religion can function in this alienating way. The real issue for the Council is not the existence or non-existence of God, but the social function of theism as we know it. When Marx calls for "changing" rather than "interpreting" reality, the real question for Christian philosophy and theology is not the "objective" truth of their theories, but whether their theories have functioned as an ideology alienating man from reality.

Before looking at the Council's response to this we want to consider another critique of religion not unrelated to the former and likewise having a massive influence on the formation of the modern secular mentality to which the Council is speaking. The critique of Freud comes not from an analysis of human society, but from an analysis of the human psyche. In his analysis faith is an "illusion," which does not mean necessarily that it is false. In Freud's terminology that would be a "delusion." The illusory for Freud is a functional, not an ontological category. His method is not capable of judging the truth claims of faith, but only what function the choice to believe performs in the life of the believer.[6]

Measured, then, not against the existence or non-existence of some objective referent, but against their function in one's perception of and response to an empirical situation, we can say that faith images and religion are illusory whenever God is used to fill in gaps, whenever religious answers are given to non-religious questions, or religious solutions to non-religious problems. To the extent that this happens, faith can function as a defense against or an escape from the demands of the real world.

I shall give but one example which, I think, illustrates very well the capacity of faith and religion to function both as an opiate and as an illusion in our contemporary cultural situation. When Camillo Torres[7] left the priesthood of the Roman Catholic Church in South America, he did so, he says, with regret. He had found it a joy and an honor to be a minister of the Church's sacraments. But these sacraments had become empty gestures, because in the actual situation in which the Church was existing they were not touching the real needs and the real suffering of the people. An exclusively ritualistic and cultic understanding of the Church's ministry can render the Church and its ministers blind to and incapable of performing the real ministry that is needed.

His question, then, was not whether the Church in South America was "objectively" the true Church, but, in the words of Vatican II, what kinds of "presence and activity" were required in order to be Church in that concrete situation. His question was not whether sacraments "really" caused grace, but what concrete realities constituted the grace of Jesus Christ here and now, and whether the grace being "really" caused by the sacraments was "cheap grace." To ask these questions is to try to see the "link," once again in the words of Vatican II, between the Church and the modern world. Torres is saying in the terminology of Marx and Freud that religion was functioning as an opium for the people, that the theology of Church and sacraments was an ideology, and that his own role as priest in those structures was an illusion.

We have been looking at two of the most famous critiques of religion formulated during the past century, and two which have had great influence in shaping the contemporary, secular mentality in which we live. Looked at in broader perspective, it is clear that both critiques are products of the Enlightenment and continuations of its spirit in the contemporary world. The Enlightenment can be seen as first and foremost an assertion of freedom and autonomy: the autonomy of reason and science over against revelation, the autonomy of the secular state and the secular university over against the Church, the autonomy of the moral conscience over against clerical control. In all these instances religion is experienced as bondage, as a shackle upon the development of all that is genuinely human in the secular world. In this spirit the Freudian and Marxist critiques of religion call for liberation from the bondage of the illusions and ideologies that alienate man from the real world in which he is living.

Such in part is the highly secular mentality, both inside and outside the Church, which forms the context in which the text of Vatican II was written, and in which it must be read and understood. J.B. Metz has pointed out the Church's initial reaction to the Enlightenment and the emergence of modern secular culture.[8] With the break-up of Christendom as a cultural phenomenon and the Church retreating from, or, rather, being pushed out of the public forum, that is, the political, social, cultural and intellectual life of the secular world, the tendency was to interiorize and individualize religion. Religion became an affair between the individual and God, and the journey toward the Kingdom became the interior journey of the soul toward God in both Catholic and Protestant forms of pietism and quietism. In the light of the New Testament such a view can only be seen as a truncated version of Christianity which does not do justice to the social and political implications of the Gospel message.

We can see, therefore, that the Second Vatican Council's attempt to relate the Christian community in its journey to the Kingdom to the modern world in its social, economic and political history is an attempt to bring Christianity back into the public forum and to show the responsibilities of that community in the social and political order. We shall now look more closely at that attempt, and then ask whether or not it succeeded, and this in two senses. Did it succeed in the practical sense as a pastoral constitution exhorting Christians to certain kinds of actions? Did it succeed in the theoretical sense of presenting Christian faith in such a way that it escapes the charges of ideology and illusion made so powerfully against it during the past century?

The Council says, as we have already seen, that the Church, that is, the Christian community journeying to the Kingdom of its Father, "is truly and intimately linked to mankind and its history." What is the nature of this link? They are themselves "a community composed of men,"[9] says the Council, so that it could be thought that as men they are part of human history with its duties and responsibilities, and as Christians they are part of another history or journey, with its duties and responsibilities. The link, then, would simply be in the one individual taking part in two different histories, but not in the two histories themselves. Such an understanding of the relationship would be open to the charge of in-

teriorization and privatization as elaborated by Metz, and would
fail to integrate religion into the social and political dimensions of
human existence.

The Council does not stop with such an interpretation, but
proposes a closer link when it returns to the question later:

> This Council exhorts Christians, as citizens of two cities, to
> strive to discharge their earthly duties conscientiously and in
> response to the Gospel spirit. They are mistaken who, know-
> ing that we have here no abiding city but seek one which is to
> come, think that they may therefore shirk their earthly re-
> sponsibilities. For they are forgetting that by the faith itself
> they are more than ever obliged to measure up to these duties,
> each according to his proper vocation.[10]

The faith itself obliges them more than ever to measure up to
earthly responsibilities, so that their journey in faith to the Kingdom of their Father is itself somehow linked to the history of
mankind and its responsibilities. Before seeing how the Council
elaborates this "somehow," let us see how it echoes the same
thought with regard to hope and charity that is said about faith in
the passage just quoted:

> Therefore, while we are warned that it profits a man nothing
> if he gain the whole world and lose himself, the expectation of
> a new earth must not weaken but rather stimulate our concern
> for cultivating this one. For here grows the body of a new
> human family, a body which even now is able to give some
> kind of foreshadowing of the new age. Earthly progress must
> be carefully distinguished from the growth of Christ's King-
> dom. Nevertheless, to the extent that the former can contrib-
> ute to the better ordering of human society, it is of vital con-
> cern to the Kingdom of God.[11]

Eschatological expectations must not weaken but stimulate concern for this earth, so that Christian hope precisely as Christian
has something to do with human hopes in the sense of inner-worldly hopes, the latter being of "vital concern" to the former.

Finally, the Council repeats the same thought with regard to charity:

> For this reason, love for God and neighbor is the first and greatest commandment. Sacred Scripture, however, teaches us that love of God cannot be separated from love of neighbor: "If there is any other commandment, it is summed up in this saying, thou shalt love thy neighbor as thyself. . . . Love therefore is the fulfillment of the Law" (Rom. 13:9-10; cf. 1 Jn. 4:20). To men growing daily more dependent on one another, and to a world becoming more unified every day, this truth proves to be of paramount importance.[12]

Does the Council give any reason why the love of God cannot be separated from love of neighbor, or why eschatological faith and hope in a new earth must not weaken but stimulate our responsibility for this one?

It offers two images of this relationship, and also makes two statements connecting the soteriological work both of Jesus and the Spirit to temporal hopes. One image we have already mentioned, when the Council says that the body of the new human family now growing "even now is able to give some kind of a foreshadowing of the new age."[13] A little earlier the document had said that those who dedicate themselves to the earthly service of men "make ready the material of the heavenly kingdom by their ministry."[14] This work is directly connected with the soteriological role of the Holy Spirit when the Council says of developments and improvements in the social order that "God's Spirit, who with a marvelous providence directs the unfolding of time and renews the face of the earth, is not absent from this development."[15] Finally, it is said that Jesus "was crucified and rose to break the stranglehold of the evil one, so that this world might be fashioned anew according to God's design and reach its fulfillment."[16]

To sum up, the Council has been trying to establish a "true and intimate link" between the Christian community and secular history. To assert that Jesus died and rose "so that the world might be fashioned anew" and that the Holy Spirit is directing the unfolding of time and renewing the face of the earth, and that this process is a preparation for and a foreshadowing of the eschatological Kingdom, is indeed to assert a very true and intimate link. Hence the Christian's faith and hope in Jesus, the Spirit and the Kingdom is directly related to this world and should stimulate his concern and responsibility. It is also clear from the *Sitz im Leben* of this document why the Council placed such emphasis on this intimate relationship. In the context of the Marxist and Freudian critiques it had to present Christian faith, hope and love in such a way that they would lead not to alienation from the world but involvement in and responsibility for it.

In evaluating the success of Vatican II's attempt to relate Christian faith and hope to the secular world, let us say, first of all, that it represents real development beyond the analogous position taken by Vatican I. I say "analogous" because the problematic of the relationship between the Church and the secular was different in the two Councils. For Vatican II, as we have seen, the problem was relating the Christian community with its otherworldly beliefs and hopes to secular history in all of its dimensions. For Vatican I the secular was "natural knowledge" or reason, the first fruits of the Enlightenment; faith was a body of revealed, supernatural truths, and the problem was their relationship. What kind of a relationship did Vatican I see between faith and the secular?

The Council begins by asserting that there are two "orders" of knowledge "distinct not only in their principle, but also in their object."[17] Between these two orders of knowledge there exists what we might call a negative and extrinsic relationship. It is negative because the Council says that the two orders cannot contradict one another, and extrinsic because the ground of this non-contradiction lies not in either body of knowledge, but in the fact that the same God who revealed the mysteries also endowed the human soul with the light of reason, and God cannot contradict himself.[18] Given this distinction in source and object, there is the possibility of subsequent cooperation: right reason can show the foundations of faith and cultivate a "science of divine things"; faith, on the other hand, can liberate reason from errors.[19]

This is a much less "intimate link" between faith and the secular than the one worked out in the Second Vatican Council. If

Jesus did indeed die so that this world, that is, the secular, might be fashioned anew, and if the Holy Spirit is directing the unfolding of time and renewing the face of the earth, and if developments in secular history are preparing the material for and giving some foreshadowing of the Kingdom to come, then there exists more than a relationship of non-contradiction between them. We can say that the negative and extrinsic relationship between faith and the secular of Vatican I is replaced by a positive and intrinsic relationship.

Vatican II was in a position to make that change because of the entire rethinking of the relationship between the "natural" and the "supernatural" that took place between the Councils. If one accepts the Augustinian starting point about the human nature of Christ, namely that it is simultaneously created and assumed,[20] and makes that the prime analogate for understanding the entire relationship between the "natural" and the "supernatural," as Rahner does in his theory of the supernatural existential, then the distinction between the purely "natural" and the "supernatural" becomes a logical and not a real distinction. Likewise and analogously, if one applies the same Christological principle in soteriology, then the distinction between salvation history and secular history becomes not a material distinction, but a formal distinction. There are not two histories running side by side and concurrently, but salvation, if and when it is taking place, must be taking place in secular history. Such systematic principles make it obvious why Christian faith precisely as Christian faith, and not just because Christians are also men, increases earthly responsibilities, why eschatological hope should stimulate inner-worldly hopes, and why love of God cannot be separated from love of neighbor.

It seems clear, then, that there is real doctrinal change with regard to the theology of the secular between the First and the Second Vatican Councils, and, if one admits some measure of legitimacy to the Marxist and Freudian critiques, and it seems that Vatican II does, then that change is real doctrinal development in Newman's sense. But was the Council consistent and consequent in the application of these principles? Looking back after ten years, is further development possible, given the theological principles available to the Church, and necessary, given the present situation of the Church in the world? I say "necessary" in the practical, not the theoretical sense, for, as Newman observed, "the chain of logic hangs loose at both ends."[21] The final judgment in systematic theology, as in moral theology, is not a theoretical, but a practical and prudential judgment, based on one's perception of the present situation of the Church and of the world. Otherwise, theology becomes an idealist history of ideas, not the history of a reflecting historical community whose identity, following the insights of the First and Second Vatican Councils in their attempt to come to terms with the post-Enlightenment secular world, is "intimately linked" with the identity of that secular world.

I shall try to illustrate what I mean by "consistent and consequent" by two examples from the conciliar document. The first has to do with the mission of the Church:

> Christ, to be sure, gave his Church no proper mission in the political, economic, or social order. The purpose which he set before it is a religious one.[22]

The text includes a reference to an address of Pius XII which reads as follows:

> Its divine founder, Jesus Christ, has not given it any mandate or fixed any end of the cultural order. The goal which Christ assigns to it is strictly religious. The Church must lead men to God, in order that they may be given over to him without reserve. . . . The Church can never lose sight of the strictly religious, supernatural goal. The meaning of all its activities, down to the last canon of its code, can only cooperate directly or indirectly in this goal.[23]

That the Church has a religious purpose or goal, and that all of its activity must cooperate toward this end, is without question. But that this assertion should or can include the denial that the Church has a proper mission in the political, social or economic order, that its mission is "strictly religious" in this exclusive sense, seems hardly consistent with the principles enunciated by the Council.

Perhaps some quibble is possible with regard to the word "proper," but if the Holy Spirit is at work in developments in the social order,[24] the same Holy Spirit who is guiding the Church, how can Christians have no proper mission in the social order? Perhaps the text does not mean Church in the sense of the Christian community as it was defined in the first paragraph, but Church as the institution or the hierarchy. But on what grounds is the institutional weight of the Church or its leaders excused from obligations that are said to be incumbent on all the members?

Does the problem not lie with the Council's category of the "strictly religious," or, more precisely, with the word "strictly"? Does not isolating the strictly religious in this way open the door once again to the critiques of religion, the very door which the whole thrust of the document tries so hard and so successfully to close? Let us grant for the moment that there is such a thing as a "strictly religious" vocation in the Church. How, nevertheless, can it be said of the entire Church that it has no proper mission in the political, economic or social order? Does this not once again turn the distinction between political, economic and social hopes and eschatological hope into a separation between the two?

Let us move now to the second example, which also involves turning a necessary distinction into a separation. On the one hand, the Council stresses repeatedly the intimate link between the Church and the contemporary world. The Church is a community composed of men,[25] men who are citizens of two cities with corresponding responsibilities,[26] and who, therefore, cannot but share the joys and the hopes, the griefs and the anxieties of the men of this age.[27] On the other hand, the Church keeps getting separated from human history and placed over against it. Thus, "the people of God and the human race in whose midst it lives render service to each other,"[28] and at another point enter into "dialogue" with each other. Prescinding from the theological problem of identifying the Church with the people of God, especially after saying that "Christ died for all men,"[29] that the Holy Spirit "offers to every man the possibility of being associated with this paschal mystery,"[30] and that God "has a fatherly concern for every man,"[31] and prescinding from the difficulty of imagining the people of God as not part of the human race, but only "living in its midst," the formulation here and the thinking behind it reveal something more important. They betray the deep-seated and still unresolved elitism and particularism of the Church. Despite the repeated insistence on being at one with the problems, the griefs, and the anxieties of the men of this age, the Church really still feels itself to be not only outside of, but above secular problems and concerns. This probably accounts too for the fact that the tone of so many of the texts is patronizing rather than genuinely compassionate.

When one adds to this the first inconsistency we discussed, that its elitism is in the name of and is based on religion, that its strictly religious mission absolves it from having any "proper mission in the political, economic or social order," we have perhaps a classic expression of ideology. Moreover, if having a strictly religious mission means that the Church need be less involved in or less compassionate for social, economic and political problems or injustices, we can also see how tenaciously illusions function, an illusion at least as old as Jesus' story of the Good Samaritan, where the priest and the Levite hurried past their fallen neighbor on strictly religious missions.

What is the real importance of the inconsistencies we have been discussing in Vatican II's *Pastoral Constitution on the Church in the Modern World*? They are important not because of the theoretical problems they reveal, but because of their practical consequences in the life and mission of the Church. Ideas do have consequences, a *Wirkungsgeschichte* in Gadamer's phrase. I shall mention here a few examples of where I see the inconsistencies in the text mirrored in the life of the Church.

A Catholic prison chaplain said to me not long ago that it was true that living conditions in his prison were inhuman, that the inmates left the prison less human than when they entered. This he could and did sympathize with, but his main responsibility as priest and chaplain was the *spiritual* well-being of the men. This meant to him regular opportunity for Mass, confession and other religious duties. This is a not uncommon attitude at many levels of Church life, echoed also in parish priests, who see their main responsibility to be the religious needs of the people, however much they are aware of and sympathetic toward social problems like hunger or housing. This practical, pastoral attitude mirrors, I think, the "strictly religious" and "no proper social mission" statement in Vatican II.

In contrast to this there was a meeting of prison chaplains in New Orleans recently to discuss the problem of prison reform. They saw their mission as priests and as chaplains to do something about the social problem of prison reform, and had no difficulty in seeing this as properly priestly work and as work proper to the mission of the Church. For their ecclesiology sees the Church there in that situation as called upon to serve others, not to serve itself. Nor need this be watered down to a process of "pre-evangelization" or preparation for the real work of the Gospel. Serving others is the real work of the Gospel. This second group seems to me to be using the best insights of Vatican II, and in its practice to have moved beyond the inconsistencies of its theory. If one agrees with Schillebeeckx's definition of theology as "the reflective and critical self-consciousness of Christian praxis,"[32] it is theological reflection upon such pastoral practices as this that will bring about genuine development beyond the theology of Vatican II.

Another example comes to mind in the difficulties that Dorothy Day had with Cardinal Spellman in New York in the late 1940's. There were those in the Church who saw Cardinal Spellman's Mass as doing something more religious and spiritual and more properly the mission of the Church than Dorothy Day feeding the poor and the hungry. (Today Dorothy would probably also fall under the criticism of the neo-orthodox on the left for not having changed structures, and for believing that hunger is satisfied bite by bite.) Is the notion of the religious and the spiritual behind the opinion adequate to the present situation of the Church and its mission? It brings up James Baldwin's criticism of religion and the spiritual as he found it growing up in Harlem. The trouble with the salvation being offered to people in the ghetto was that "it stopped at the church door."[33] How can what is going on on both sides of the church door be brought together, so that the outside will be genuinely religious and spiritual, and the inside genuinely real, and not ideology and illusion?

To begin with, is there not something wrong in the way that the problem tends to be posed? There seem always to be two things

to be put together, whether as in earlier discussions it be the natural and the supernatural, or as in more recent discussions, religious hope and secular hopes, material needs and spiritual needs,
God's activity and man's activity in furthering the Kingdom. This
way of posing the problem always places the two poles in inverse
proportion, so that emphasizing one means not putting enough emphasis on the other. Do we not get into this position because of a
basic dualism in Catholic thought, both in its philosophy, as for
example body-soul anthropology, and in its theology, as for example the two natures model in Christology? I shall simply allude
here to Schoonenberg's study of the principles that should govern
our understanding of the relationship between God and the world
and his conclusion that whenever we are faced with the alternative
of God or man, God's activity or man's activity, it is a false alternative.[34] Their relationship stands in direct, not inverse proportion.
His concern was the false alternative in Christology of emphasizing either the humanity or the divinity of Jesus, but would not the
same principles obtain in all of the polarities we discussed earlier?
Have we not turned logical distinctions into real distinctions (natural and supernatural), and formal distinctions into material distinctions (body and soul) and *thereby* come up with "objects" or
"things" to be put together? In the language of William Lynch,[35] it
is only because we have allowed analogous images and notions to
become univocal that we are in a position to "add" the natures of
Christ and come up with a "two," or to allow eschatological hopes
to be not only distinguished from, but separated from secular
hopes.

I would suggest as a way out of these false alternatives and as
a way of avoiding turning polarities into dichotomies the reflections of Dietrich Bonhoeffer on the nature of transcendence, the
religious and the spiritual. Bonhoeffer's reflections are especially
valuable because they are based on his own non-religious, secular
activity. His notion of transcendence and the spiritual grows out of
the secular, and does not have to be added to or imposed upon it.
Bonhoeffer is famous, of course, for his proposal of a "non-
religious Christianity," a proposal based on the performance of
religion in Pius XII's sense in the social and political situation of
Nazi Germany. That proposal is ironic coming from a man whose

writings are so religious, also in Pius XII's sense, right up to the final entries in his prison diary. What actually emerges from that diary, however, is not a religionless Christianity, but a new notion of religion, transcendence and the spiritual.

A few months before his death, in the diary entry for August 3, 1944, Bonhoeffer presents the outline for a book on Christian faith that he never lived to write. "Who is God?" he asks in chapter two,[36] and for his development it is important to note that his question is not "What is God?"—the question of classical theism and Christology. Summarizing his sketchy reply, no answer is to be found in metaphysics, which extends concepts from the finite to conceive of an infinite, absolute, all-powerful, all-knowing being. Therein lies nothing qualitatively different, but only "a piece of prolonged world." True experience of God comes in encountering Jesus Christ, and, more precisely, in encountering the transformation of human existence into something qualitatively different in his "existence for others." This existence for others, this freedom from self and transcendence of self, is the genuine experience of transcendence. Faith is participating in this new existence of Jesus.

Bonhoeffer never lived to develop these thoughts, so we can only try to interpret what he means. Our relationship to God is not mediated primarily by concepts that are analogous to his being, but by a new kind of life that is analogous to his life. This qualitatively new kind of life is revealed in Jesus' existence for others, his self-transcendence. One can know Jesus, and thereby know God, by participating in this life of existence for others. The kind of knowledge Bonhoeffer means here is what Aquinas would call knowledge by connaturality, knowing God by participating in God's life, so that grace and truth are ultimately one, and knowledge and love are ultimately one. But the point that Bonhoeffer is stressing is that it is self-transcendence for the sake of one's neighbor ("the here and now, the finite, the tangible and attainable, not the infinite and the unattainable") that is genuine self-transcendence. In his own terminology, the measure of one's self-transcendence for the *Vorletzte* (the penultimate, that is, finite, innerworldly realities) is the measure of one's self-transcendence to the *Letzte* (the Ultimate, that is, eschatological realities). Hence God must be found and experienced in human form.

Unlike some other spiritualities, which would have one love one's neighbor for God's sake, or have one find Christ in one's neighbor, and where the movement is from God to man, Bonhoeffer's movement is from man to God. When the neighbor is actually loved for his own sake, that is, when there is genuine love and compassion, then God is being known and loved, not as another "object," but in the quality of the relationship and by connaturality. Hence Rahner could say in another context that wherever in the world real love is present, there God and Jesus Christ are present.[37] God can, of course, be objectified into another object, the commandment to love God and neighbor can be separated into two commandments, the religious and the spiritual can be hypostatized into a separate realm, and then we have the pseudo-problem of getting them back together.

That raises questions in what we might call the epistemology of faith: How do we know God, and what is the nature of the knowledge involved? Let us say, first of all, with Bonhoeffer and with many others today, that in religious knowledge or knowledge of God experience is primary, and, secondly, that one can experience the infinite and the absolute not by going around or above the finite and the relative, but by going through them. It is the attempt to go around or above that deprives religion of its roots in real experience. This is simply to say that all knowledge of God is mediated, something which Catholic theology has always said in asserting that all of our knowledge of God is analogous. The only difference is that Catholic theology has tended to stress that the concepts we apply to God are analogous, whereas what is being stressed here is that it is primarily the experience itself upon which the concepts are based that is analogous. Furthermore, this is not meant in the sense that the finite is the starting point, simply the springboard from which one can then leap into an unmediated knowledge of the infinite, as for example in speculation about the nature of the Trinity in itself. It is not simply the starting point but the permanent basis, so that it is by growth in human experience as such that one can grow in the knowledge of God. This is the reason why Rahner wants to identify our knowledge of the Trinity in its relationship to us in time with knowledge of the Trinity in itself.

There is one further aspect that should be mentioned, and this I think is well expressed in an image that St. Paul uses in expressing his epistemology of faith.[38] Someday, he says, we shall see or know God face to face, and that is a future and therefore hoped-for event. Here and now we know God "through a mirror dimly," or "through a glass darkly" in other translations. The mirror is the medium through which we can know God dimly or imperfectly, another way of expressing the mediated or analogous nature of this knowledge. There is no reason why that cannot be expanded to include other aspects of that experience besides the knowledge aspect—our hope in God, our love or reverence for God—and this includes not only the positive moments in that experience *(theologiae gloriae)*, but also the negative moments *(theologia crucis)*. If there must always be a mirror, then love for God cannot be separated from love for neighbor, and eschatological hope must be mediated and become concretized in secular hopes.

Paul situates our direct or unmediated knowledge of God in the future: someday we shall see him face to face. This is a point greatly stressed by both Moltmann and Metz in their theologies of hope: all theological statements are eschatological statements,[39] that is, statements about the future, and therefore expressions of hope. To leave out the hope dimension in our knowledge of God leads either to presumption, that is to say, a Church already in possession of divine truth and therefore untouched by time and the secular, the root of triumphalism and elitism; or it leads to despair: the finite has no ultimate meaning and cannot lead to God.

To situate all of this more directly in the context of our study of Vatican II's analysis of the relationship between faith and the secular, let us ask one final question. If one experiences God in and through experiencing the finite, and this for the Christian is preeminently through the humanity of Jesus, how does the contemporary Church experience Jesus, since he is just as invisible to it as the invisible God? At least the beginnings of an answer to that can be found in the words placed on the lips of Jesus in Matthew's Gospel.[40] The scene is the inauguration of the final Kingdom, and the Son of Man is admitting some to the Kingdom and dismissing others, separating the sheep from the goats. The line is drawn between those who fed and clothed and welcomed and visited the king when he was in need, and those who did not. Both groups deny this, the former that they had fed him when he was in need, and the latter that they had not fed him when he was in need. The king's answer is that when they did it for the least of his brethren they were doing it for him, and when they did not do it for the least of his brethren they did not do it for him.

This text can be watered down to mean that the Son of Man will consider what is done to the least of his brethren as having been done to himself. Then it can lead to a "loving Christ in others" spirituality where the most important thing is serving him in some explicitly religious sense. But the surprise of the first group belies this interpretation, for they had no intention of serving the Son of Man when they did what they did. The norm is simply what they did or did not do to the least of his brethren. If we identify Jesus with the Son of Man, is there any realistic sense in which we can say that what was done for the least of his brethren was actually and really done for him?

If we consider that all faith statements are also statements of hope, including our belief in the resurrection of Jesus, then we do not have to consider the resurrection of Jesus as a "past event," already finished and complete. If, moreover, Jesus really loves the least of his brethren, then their suffering is really his suffering too. If we think in less individualistic categories, then the destiny of Jesus is bound up with the destiny of all his brothers and sisters. God saves and redeems his people, and the individual in and through the people, including the man Jesus. If the suffering of Jesus is still going on, not in the sense of his historical suffering, but in the sense of his compassion for the least of his brethren, if we develop a soteriology of compassion rather than expiation, of "dying with" rather than "dying for," then doing something for the least of his brethren is in the most realistic sense doing it for him. The contemporary Church, therefore, not only can, but must experience Jesus in and through the least of his brethren.

This is not to deny that the Church must also "remember" Jesus in its liturgical celebration as he commanded, nor that it must pray and contemplate. The question is how these religious activities can be intrinsic within, and not added to the Church's mission of service in the contemporary world. The question is how a religious mission can be understood in such a way that it does not exclude, but intrinsically includes a mission in the secular order without ceasing to be properly religious. The Son of Man in Matthew's story seemed to have no trouble whatsoever with this problem. Perhaps it is the dualism in our theology of faith, and of hope and charity as well, that creates the necessity of putting things together that never should have been separated in the first place. Resolving that dualism would lead, I think, to something that the Roman Catholic Church began to do, although not with complete consistency, by its statements on the role of the present-day Church found in the Second Vatican Council's *Pastoral Constitution on the Church in the Modern World*.

NOTES

1. *Gaudium et Spes*, 1. Hereafter G.S.
2. G.S., 2.
3. G.S., 1.
4. G.S., 2.
5. K. Marx, *Early Writings* (New York: McGraw-Hill, 1964), pp. 43-44.
6. L. Dewart, *The Future of Belief* (New York: Herder and Herder, 1966), p. 20.
7. Cf. Camilo Torres, *Revolutionary Priest*, ed. J. Gerassi (Vintage Books, 1971).
8. J. B. Metz, *Zur Theologie der Welt* (Mainz, 1968).
9. G.S., 1.
10. G.S., 43.
11. G.S., 39.
12. G.S., 24.
13. G.S., 39.
14. G.S., 38.
15. G.S., 26.
16. G.S., 2.
17. Denzinger-Schönmetzer, *Enchiridion Symbolorum*, 3015. Hereafter D.S.
18. D.S., 3017.
19. D.S., 3019.
20. Felix Malmberg, *Über den Gottmenschen* (Freiburg: Herder, 1960), pp. 38ff.

21. John Henry Newman, *An Essay in Aid of a Grammar of Assent* (London: Longmans, Green, 1961).

22. G.S., 42.

23. Pius XII, "Address to the International Union of Institutes of Archeology, History, and History of Art," March 9, 1956: AAS 38 (1965), p. 212.

24. G.S., 26.

25. G.S., 1.

26. G.S., 43.

27. G.S., 1.

28. G.S., 11.

29. G.S., 22.

30. *Ibid.*

31. G.S., 24.

32. E. Schillebeeckx, *The Understanding of Faith* (New York: Seabury, 1974), p. 154.

33. James Baldwin, *Go Tell It on the Mountain* (New York: Dial Press, 1955).

34. P. Schoonenberg, *The Christ* (New York: Herder and Herder, 1971), pp. 13ff.

35. William Lynch, *Christ and Apollo* (New York: Sheed and Ward, 1960).

36. D. Bonhoeffer, *Widerstand and Ergebung* (München: Siebenstern, 1951), p. 191. English translation: Diary entry for August 3, 1944.

37. K. Rahner, "Über die Einhert von Nächsten-und Gottesliebe," in *Schriften Zur Theologie VI*, p. 283.

38. 1 Cor. 13:12.

39. Cf. J. Moltmann, *Theologie der Hoffnung* (München, 1966), p. 12, and J. B. Metz, *Zur Theologie der Welt* (Mainz, 1968), p. 83.

40. Mt. 25:31-46.

Part II
The Tradition Plumbed

Biblical Perspectives on Justice

John R. Donahue, S.J.

I

THE OLD TESTAMENT

Introduction

Contemporary Catholic theology as well as official Church teaching is engaged in reflection on problems of the relation of Christian faith to the quest for justice in the modern world. While such reflection has a precedent in the social encyclicals of Leo XIII and his immediate successors, contemporary thought is characterized by rooting the reflection in the biblical heritage rather than in a natural law philosophy. This emphasis in Catholic theology resonates well with statements of scholars of other denominations. G. von Rad writes: "There is absolutely no concept in the Old Testament with so central a significance for all relationships of human life as that of $s^e d\bar{a}q\bar{a}h$ [justice/righteousness]."[1] H. H. Schrey, in a study prepared for the World Council of Churches, states: "It can be said without exaggeration that the Bible, taken as a whole, has one theme: The history of the revelation of God's righteousness."[2]

The centrality as well as the richness of the biblical statements on justice is the very reason why it is difficult to give a "biblical definition" of justice which, in the Bible, is a protean and many-faceted term.[3] Justice is used in the legal codes to describe ordinances which regulate communal life (e.g., Ex. 21:1—23:10) and which prescribe restitution for injury done to person and property, as well as for cultic regulations. The Hebrew terms for justice are

68

applied to a wide variety of things. Scales or weights are called just when they give a fair measure and paths are called just when they do what a path or way should do—lead to a goal.[4] Laws are just not because they conform to an external norm or constitution, but because they create harmony within the community. Acting justly consists in avoiding violence and fraud and other actions which destroy communal life and in pursuing that which sustains the life of the community.[5] Yahweh is just not only as lawgiver and Lord of the covenant; his saving deeds are called "just deeds" because they restore the community when it has been threatened. The justice of Yahweh is not in contrast to other covenant qualities such as steadfast love *(hesed)*, mercy *(rah^{a}min)* or faithfulness *('^{e}munāh)* but, in many texts, is virtually equated with them.[6]

In general terms the biblical idea of justice can be described as *fidelity to the demands of a relationship.* In contrast to modern individualism the Israelite is in a world where "to live" is to be united with others in a social context either by bonds of family or by covenant relationships. This web of relationships—king with people, judge with complainants, family with tribe and kinfolk, the community with the resident alien and suffering in their midst and all with the covenant God—constitutes the world in which life is played out.[7] The demands of the differing relationships cannot be specified *a priori* but must be seen in the different settings of Israel's history.

The present essay will attempt to describe some of these relationships and to indicate how this general notion of justice as fidelity to the demands of a relationship is concretely manifest. We will mention certain ways in which both the individual and Yahweh can be called just and then turn to a characteristic element of Hebrew thought: justice as concern for the marginal people in society, the widow, the alien, the poor. In the second section of the essay we will describe certain transformations of the Old Testament ideas of justice which took place in the intertestamental period, and in the final section we will address certain aspects of a New Testament theology of justice. In doing this we hope to show how the contemporary realization that faith must be involved in the quest for and expression of justice, far from being foreign to biblical thought, recovers a core of the biblical heritage which, when neglected, brings the danger of reducing this heritage to a manual of personal piety.

The Just Individual

In the Book of Job and in Proverbs the just person preserves the peace and wholeness of the community.[8] Such a one "upholds the weak hands and him who was stumbling" (Jb. 4:3-4), cares for the poor, the fatherless and the widow (Jb. 29:12-15; 31:16-19; Prov. 29:7) and defends their cause in court (Jb. 29:16; Prov. 31:9). The just are good stewards of their land and of work animals, and their relations with their workers create peace and harmony (Jb. 31:13). They live at peace with their neighbors and are a joy to their families (Jb. 31:1-12; Prov. 23:24). From justice flows peace and prosperity to the land and to all in the community. In the Psalms the just person is the one who calls upon Yahweh as a source of strength with a confidence which is based on faith in the justice of Yahweh, that is, Yahweh's fidelity to his promises. Yahweh rewards according to justice (Ps. 18:20) and "leads me in the paths of righteousness, for his name's sake" (Ps. 23:3). The justice of Yahweh is saving help. The psalmist cries "In thy righteousness deliver me" (Ps. 31:1) and vindication comes from the justice of God (Ps. 35:24). The response to this experience of and hope for the saving justice of Yahweh is to praise him, which, in the Psalms, is equivalent to praise of the justice of God (Pss. 35:28; 71:16, 18-19; 89:16).

The justice of the individual is summed up in Psalm 112, a wisdom Psalm. The Psalm begins with a command to praise the Lord (Ps. 112:1), and then calls blessed the one who fears the Lord. Such a one will be rich in land and descendants, "wealth and riches are in his house and his justice endures forever" (Ps. 112:3). Such a one "conducts his affairs with justice" and his heart is "firm, trusting in the Lord." The just one gives freely to the poor and "his justice endures forever" (Ps. 112:9). The double statement of justice enduring forever in the context of both possessing wealth and distributing it captures the biblical notion that the goods of this earth are the sign of the right relationship with Yahweh as well as the means to create harmony within the community.

The statements on justice in Job, Proverbs and the Psalms reveal that justice is a harmony which comes from a right relationship to the covenant Lord and to the neighbor to whom a person is related by covenant bond. The realism of biblical thought is expressed by the fact that the sign of justice is peace, prosperity and fertility on the land. At the same time biblical thought has a dialectical counter to the naive view of Proverbs 11 that the unjust suffer and the just prosper. Such a view provides the arena for the problem of theodicy in Job. Job has lived a just life and yet he suffers. He is so convinced of his justice that he is ready to call Yahweh unjust (Jb. 39:8). The answer to Job is that Yahweh is Lord even of the destructive powers of nature (Jb. 38:1—40:5; 40:6—41:26). Job is called on to have faith—"Do you have faith in him that he will return?" (Jb. 40:12). He is restored (Jb. 42:10-17) when he discards his last support, his integrity as a claim on God's justice and accepts it as gift.[9] What Job expresses in mythological and dramatic form the Psalms express in confessional form—the justice of God is both gift and mystery and the attempt to crystallize it by human standards can result in destroying the proper relation with Yahweh. To live justly is to rejoice in the good things of life and at the same time to be able to recognize that life is a gift even in the face of loss and destructiveness. To be just is to be open to the world as gift and God as mystery.

The Justice of Yahweh

Throughout the Old Testament Yahweh is proclaimed as just (2 Chr. 12:6; Neh. 9:8; Pss. 7:9; 103:17; 116:5; Jer. 9:24; Dan. 9:14; Zeph. 3:5; Zech. 8:8). The justice of Yahweh is not deduced from reflection on his nature, but is intrinsic to the covenant relationship (Hos. 2:19; Jer. 9:24). Breaking of the covenant or turning away from Yahweh is a failure of justice. At the conclusion of the song of the vineyard (Is. 5:1-17), Yahweh indicts the people he "planted" and watched over which Isaiah captures by means of a poetic word play:

And he looked for justice *(mispat)*, but behold bloodshed *(mišpāh)* for righteousness *(sedāqāh)*, but behold a cry *(se'āqāh)* (Is. 5:7).

The justice of God embraces an element of forensic judgment on the sins of the people. Justice is often equated thus with punishment. In Isaiah 10, there is an indictment against the infidelity of Israel which begins:

> Woe to those who decree iniquitous decrees
> and the writers who keep writing oppression
> to turn aside the needy from justice
> and to rob the poor of my people from their right (Is. 10:2).

The chapter then threatens Israel with the same punishments which were visited upon Assyria when "the Lord will destroy both soul and body" (Is. 10:18). However, from this destruction a remnant will be saved "for destruction is decreed overflowing with righteousness" (Is. 10:22). In like vein when the rulers have made a covenant with death (Is. 28:14) their faithlessness will be overcome by Yahweh's restoring love:

> And I will make justice the line
> and righteousness the plummet.
> Then your covenant with death will be annulled
> and your agreement with Sheol will not stand (Is. 28:17-18).

The anger of Yahweh leads to a justice which can overcome even the power of death. While Yahweh's justice restores the afflicted and condemns the wicked, caution should be exercised in describing the Lord of the Old Testament as vindictive. Though Yahweh punishes sinners there is no text in the Old Testament where his justice is equated with vengeance on the sinner. Yahweh's justice is saving justice where punishment of the sinner is an integral part of restoration.[10]

The justice of Yahweh receives special emphasis in the enthronement Psalms (Pss. 47, 93, 95—100). These Psalms are cultic in origin and may have been used either at the enthronement of the king as Yahweh's vice-regent or in an annual festival celebrating the reign of Yahweh.[11] Here, as in some other places in the Psalms, justice is virtually personified. $S^e d\bar{a}q\bar{a}h$ is a messenger who goes before Yahweh (Ps. 85:14); justice and righteousness are the foundation of his throne (Ps. 97:2). In these Psalms Yahweh is hailed as king because he is victor over hostile powers (Pss. 47:2; 98:2), the world is established or made firm (Pss. 93:1; 96:10) and all creation returns praise (Pss. 96:11-12; 98:4-8). As victorious king Yahweh will rule in justice. He is called mighty king "lover of justice" (Ps. 99:4); "he will judge the world with righteousness and the peoples with equity" (Ps. 98:9) and his reign will be a dawning of light for the just (Ps. 97:17).

The justice of Yahweh is, therefore, his saving power, his fidelity to his role of Lord of the covenant. It is also his indictment of sin and his call to return or conversion. Justice represents a victory over evil powers which threaten the destruction of the world. It is manifest both in the historical lives of the people and as an object of their eschatological hope.

Justice and the Widow, the Orphan and the Poor

Characteristic of all strands of Israel's traditions is concern for the widow, the orphan, the poor and the sojourner in the land. In the legal traditions as represented by the covenant code and the Deuteronomic legislation we find the following texts:

> You shall not wrong a stranger or oppress him. You shall not afflict any widow or orphan (Ex. 22:21-22)

> . . . and the sojourner, the fatherless and the widow who are within your house shall come and be filled; that the Lord your God may bless you and all the work of your hands that you do (Dt. 14:29, cf. Dt. 15:7).

This concern for the defenseless in society is not a command designed simply to promote social harmony, but is rooted in the nature of Yahweh himself who is defender of the oppressed.[12] There are a series of texts, again from different traditions, which portray Yahweh in this role:

For the Lord God executes justice for the fatherless and the widow and loves the sojourner giving him food and clothing (Dt. 10:18).

Give justice to the weak and the fatherless,
maintain the right of the afflicted and the destitute,
rescue the weak and the needy (Ps. 82:3-4).

The Lord works vindication and justice
for all who are oppressed (Ps. 103:6 cf. Pss. 140:12; 146:7).

In one of the earliest texts immediately following the revelation of "I am" at the burning bush, Yahweh reveals himself as a compassionate Lord who enters Israel's history to free them from oppression:

Then the Lord said, "I have seen the affliction of my people who are in Egypt, and have heard their cry because of their taskmasters; I know their sufferings and I have come down to deliver them out of the hand of the Egyptians" (Ex. 3:7-8).

Therefore, Yahweh reveals himself as a God who is compassionate to the oppressed and their vindicator. When Israel is the oppressed one he leads them out of slavery; when they inherit the land he again emerges as the protector of the landless.

When Israel forgets the covenant it is the prophets, most explicitly Amos, Isaiah and Jeremiah, who proclaim to Israel that their fidelity to the covenant Lord must be manifest in concern for the poor and the oppressed. The prophet in Israel is not one who foretells, but one who *forthtells*. He speaks not with foresight into the future but with insight into the ways in which people have broken the covenant. The prophet is one who is called not only to speak on behalf of Yahweh, but one who speaks on behalf of those who have no voice.[13]

Amos, one of the earliest prophets (c. 760-750 B.C.), is one of the strongest to call Israel to return to justice. One of the transgressions of Israel is that:

They sell the righteous for silver
and the needy for a pair of shoes,
they trample the head of the poor into the dust of the earth
(Am. 2:7).

And the people will be punished because:

You trample upon the poor
and take from him exactions of wheat (Am. 5:11).

Amos culminates his judgment against the rich and exploiters of
his day by proclaiming that their injustice negates their worship of
Yahweh:

I hate, I despise your feasts,
I take no delight in your solemn assemblies . . .
but let justice roll down like waters
and righteousness like an ever-flowing stream (Am. 5:21, 24).

The imagery here is striking. One function of the cult (feasts and
solemn assemblies) was to pray for the water and flowing streams
which would assure fertility and hence life to the land. By compar-
ing justice and righteousness with water and a stream, Amos,
speaking in the name of Yahweh, shows that without justice the totality of life is barren.

Two of the most striking texts which affirm Yahweh's concern
for the poor and show that faith in him involves the doing of justice are from Jeremiah and Isaiah. In these texts the core of
Israel's faith, knowing God and praising him in the cult, is equated
with the doing of justice. In chapter 22 Jeremiah is commanded to
deliver a word of the Lord to the king:

Thus says the Lord: Do justice and righteousness, and deliver
from the hand of the oppressor him who has been robbed.
And do no wrong or violence to the alien, the fatherless and
the widow (Jer. 22:3-4).

Later in the same chapter the king, Jehoiakim, is censured for not following the way of his father Josiah:

> Woe to him who builds his house by unrighteousness,
> and his upper rooms by injustice.
> Did not your father eat and drink
> and do justice and righteousness?
> Then it was well with him.
> He judged the cause of the poor and the needy;
> then it was well.
> Is this not to know me? says the Lord (Jer. 22:13, 15-16).

The conclusion of this passage is one of the strongest in the Old Testament for equating true religion with the doing of justice. Josiah, the one king who is praised by Jeremiah and the Deuteronomic school, is remembered not simply for his reform of the cult or promulgation of the Torah (2 Kgs. 22:1—23:25). He is the one who "knew" Yahweh, and the knowing of Yahweh is taking the cause of the poor and the needy. Here there is no division between *theoria* and *praxis*, between faith and the doing of justice.[14] Justice is concrete. It combines non-exploitation of the poor and taking their cause. The doing of justice is not the application of religious faith, but its substance; without it, God remains unknown.

Isaiah 58 begins with a cry to declare to the people their transgression. The people assemble for worship and ask of Yahweh righteous judgments (Is. 58:2). They come in fasting and prayer, but hear no answer (Is. 58:3). The answer of Yahweh appears in verses 4-7. The cultic fast which the people choose is a charade because "in the day of your fast you seek your own pleasure and oppress your workers." Then the true fast demanded by Yahweh is described:

> Is this not the fast I choose:
> to loose the bonds of wickedness,
> to undo the thongs of the yoke,
> to let the oppressed go free and to break every yoke?
> Is it not to share your bread with the hungry,

and bring the homeless poor into your house;
when you see the naked, to cover him,
and not to hide yourself from your own flesh? (Is. 58:6-7).

In verse 8 the request of the people for "righteous judgments" is
then answered. If they observe the fast as called for by Yahweh:

Then shall your light break forth like the dawn,
and your healing shall spring up speedily;
and your righteousness shall go before you
and the glory of the Lord shall be your rear guard (Is. 58:8).

In these texts justice as fidelity to the demands of a relationship is
described most concretely. A people cannot be just before the covenant God, they cannot know or worship him, when they do not
heed his call to take the cause and defend the rights of the poor
and oppressed in the community.

Concluding Remarks on the Old Testament

1. To live in Old Testament terms is to be open to relationships. For the Israelite death is not simply the cessation of life
but the end of a relation to Yahweh, to fellow Israelites and to the
land. In most general terms justice is fidelity to this threefold relationship by which life is maintained. What these relationships concretely involve assumes different forms in different literary traditions as the social and religious world of the Old Testament
evolves. For example, in the early period the command to take the
cause of the widow, etc., is given to the whole community; with the
rise of the monarchy it becomes a royal task, and when the monarchy fails ethically and historically, Yahweh becomes the defender.[15]
2. While justice is central to the Old Testament, it is impossible to view texts on justice in isolation from a host of other concepts such as loving mercy, truth, covenant fidelity, vindication,
and saving deed, as well as law and statute. A reading of the Old

Testament which seeks the path of justice leads one into many other paths of Israel's faith.

3. *Realism* characterizes Israel's view of justice. Injustice is not simply a bad moral attitude but a social cancer which destroys society and a physical force which can bring chaos to the goods of the earth. So, too, the fruits of justice are portrayed most realistically—harmony and peace in personal relations (Job, Proverbs); fertility and rain in due season (Joel); freedom from slavery and oppression (Deutero-Isaiah); hope in the face of sinfulness (Psalms).

4. Although human justice may fail, Yahweh's endures. The Lord's justice has a forensic quality in that he calls people to account when they forget or break the covenant relationship. It is also salvific in that Yahweh restores harmony to the world, intervenes on behalf of his people, forgives their sin and saves them from bondage.

5. The marginal groups in society—the poor, the widows, the orphans, the aliens—become the scale on which the justice of the whole society is weighed. When they are exploited or forgotten neither worship of God nor knowledge of him can result in true religion.

6. The religious world of the Old Testament is not our world. We have difficulties with both the anthropomorphism of the picture of Yahweh and the interventionist or salvation history perspective of the Old Testament. Nor is our world the social world of the tribal confederacy, the centralized monarchy or the community of exile and restoration. Old Testament statements on justice need not only application, but interpretation. Despite the gulf between the Old Testament and our world certain constants remain. The expression of religious faith by confrontation with the evils which destroy the social fabric of society is no new phenomenon but as old as the eighth-century prophets. The God who spoke long ago as one compassionate to the oppressed and vindicator of the poor remains the Lord of the Jewish and Christian heritage. The call to see the quest for justice as integral to faith in the God of Abraham, Moses and the prophets must be heard by all who claim this book as either Bible or Testament.

II
THE INTERTESTAMENTAL PERIOD

A general description of the meanings of justice in the period from the exile to the time of Jesus is helpful not only in noting the transformations of the notions of justice within Judaism itself, but also in providing a context for New Testament statements on justice. During this period the Hebrew terms for justice and Greek translations retain the same wide connotations which we find in the early period.[16] Justice is associated with mercy (2 Esd. 8:36; Tb. 3:2; Sir. 44:10), goodness of heart (Tb. 14:11; Wis. 1:1), love of neighbor (Jub. 7:20; 20:2), compassion for the poor and weak (Asmp. Mos. 11:17), truth (Tb. 1:3; 3:2; 4:6; Wis. 5:6; 1 Mc. 7:18; 4 Ezr. 7:114), harmony in family and social relations (Jub. 7:20; 31:12; 7:26). Along with these, justice is closely identified with a number of individual qualities—integrity, courage, constancy, self-control, steadfastness amid poverty and illness, intelligence and knowledge.

While maintaining continuity with the meanings of justice in the Old Testament, justice in this period undergoes three major transformations: (1) emphasis on the justice of the individual and a sectarian stress between the just and the unjust, (2) the establishing of justice as a characteristic of the end time, or the influence of eschatology on justice (3) the shift in language whereby *sedāqāh* means almsgiving or care for the poor.

1. The Just Individual

The stress on the justice of the individual arises when Psalms which were originally cultic laments become codified in a book and become the prayers of individuals. In certain of these Psalms (e.g., Pss. 18, 25, 26, 31, 35, 51) justice is keeping the statutes of the Lord, and freedom from guilt. The Lord is at one and the same time the only just one and the one who rewards a person "according to my righteousness" (Ps. 18:24). During the intertestamental period reflection on the call to be just before the Lord, coupled with a growing awareness of the transcendence of God, leads to a theology where God alone is just (Sir. 18:2; 1QH. 1:4) and that man alone is devoid of justice (Dan. 9:18; Sir. 5:8). The justice of the individual is a striving for innocence and purity in the face of Hellenization and religious syncretism. This individualization of justice is vividly portrayed in the departure address of Tobit to his son, Tobias (Tb. 4:1-21). Tobit tells his son:

> Remember the Lord our God all your days, and refuse to sin or transgress his commandments. Live uprightly all the days of your life, and do not walk in the ways of wrongdoing (Tb. 4:5).

Tobit goes on to counsel his son to give alms and share his goods with the poor, but the social motive is absent. Instead:

> For charity delivers from death and keeps you from entering the darkness (Tb. 4:10).

The son is also urged to avoid immorality, to marry a woman from the Jewish people, to avoid pride, to honor the dead and to persevere in prayer. What in the earlier period were manifestations of justice incumbent on the whole community become, for Tobias, a rule of life.

In this context the rise of Pharisaic notions of justice can be understood.[17] The Pharisees originated in the movement of the pious or "separated ones" who were conscious of the evils of Hellenization and sought to preserve the sanctity of God by careful observance of his revelation, the Torah. The *Psalms of Solomon* give examples of early Pharisaic piety. God is a "righteous judge" who is no respecter of persons (2:19), and at the same time he is "merciful and good" (10:7). The Lord is vindicator of the just since he will punish sinners, and those who fear the Lord will rise to life eternal (3:4). The just person remembers the Lord at all times (3:3), and "his will is always before the Lord." True justice will be established with the advent of the Davidic Messiah who will be "a just king" (17:32) and who "will direct every man in the works of righteousness by fear of God" (18:8). Care should be exercised in describing Pharisaic piety as a "righteousness by works" piety. In observing the Law the Pharisee did not hope to merit or gain salvation, but attempted to recognize that the sovereignity of God applied to every area of human life and that the Torah made present to daily life the distant God. Nonetheless Pharisaic piety fosters the individualization of justice.

Allied to the individualization of justice is the rise of the motif of suffering as a sign of justice. In the Old Testament the command was to remain faithful to the covenant God amid suffering and see God's saving power as the vindication of his justice. In the intertestamental period suffering itself becomes a sign of a just person. This emphasis culminates in the *Wisdom of Solomon*.[18] Here the unjust "lie in wait for the just man" who is inconvenient to them and reproaches them for sins against the law. The just one is a reproof to their thoughts because "his manner of life is unlike others" (2:12). The unjust plan to test the just one with tortures and plan to put him to death (2:18-20). However, the death of the just one will be a vindication of God's justice since:

The righteous man who has died
will condemn the ungodly who are living (4:16).

At the Final Judgment the vindication of this suffering just one will take place (5:1) and those who persecuted him will say:

We thought that his life was madness
and that his end was without honor.
Why has he been numbered among the sons of God?
And why is his lot among the saints?
So it was we who strayed from the way of truth,
and the light of righteousness did not shine on us (5:4-5).

In this diptych (chs. 2 and 5) from the *Wisdom of Solomon*, suffering itself becomes a stage in the manifestation of God's judgment on sinners and a prelude to the hope of vindication. This conjunction of justice and suffering provides the background for the Pauline idea of the cross as a stumbling block (1 Cor. 1:23) as well as a manifestation of the saving justice of God (Rom. 4:25).

2. *Eschatological Justice*

A very important development in the intertestamental period is the motif that the true justice of God will be manifest only at the end time. This motif is anticipated in the Old Testament, especially in the "Messianic" oracles of Isaiah 9:2-7 and 11:1-9 in the *Isaiah Apocalypse* (24:1—27:13) where themes like the eschatological judgment, the messianic banquet and the cosmic upheavals will prepare the command "Open the gates that the righteous nation which keeps faith may enter in" (26:2), and in the prophecies of Deutero-Isaiah which look to a time when the conversion of the nations will be due to the justice of God (45:23-25), salvation will be granted (60:18), and the people will be just and possess the land forever (60:21). Such prophetic sayings provide the matrix for the view that justice is no longer something that Yahweh will establish in the sphere of history, but will be reserved to the end time and be characteristic of the new age.[19]

Eschatological justice assumes different forms. One form is the revelation of justice by a final judgment of God. The just will be vindicated and the deeds of evil persons will come to light (Sir. 16:11-14). Characteristic of this period is the "eschatological reversal" (mirrored in the New Testament Beatitudes). The *Book of Enoch* captures this reversal by a juxtaposition of woes on the unjust and exhortations to the community to await final vindication:[20]

> Woe to you sinners, because you persecute the righteous, for you will be delivered and persecuted because of iniquity and heavy will be his yoke upon you (95:7).

The unjust are characterized by a series of actions which destroy the social fabric of the community. They are lying witnesses (95:6); they trust in riches (94:8); they acquire gold and silver unjustly (97:8); they persecute just people (95:7) and they spread evil by making false weights and measures. The world as described by Enoch is a world where injustice is rampant and the just suffer. Coupled with this indictment of the unjust are a series of exhortations. The just are told to "take courage" for sinners will perish (97:1); a bright light will enlighten them and "the voice of rest you will hear from heaven" (93:6). The just will be companions of the hosts of heaven (104:6). The final judgment is simultaneously revelation and vindication. It uncovers the sins of the unjust and vindicates the just. Eschatology does not function simply as speculation on the end time. It provides a double answer: (a) to the problem of theodicy—how a just and loving God can permit the unjust to prosper; and (b) to the problem of salvation history—what the history of God's saving acts means to a people who experience oppression and loss of political power. Therefore, in eschatological thought not only are the faithful "justified" at the end time, but God himself is shown to be just and faithful. The meaning of history is seen not simply from the course of events but from the perspective of the goal or end of history. The "God who acts" of the Old Testament is here the Lord of hope. This type of eschatology is important for understanding Paul's teaching in the New Testament on the contrast between this age and the age to come and his statements that the end time, that is, the judgment on the powers of the age, has come in Jesus Christ.

Allied to this eschatological reversal is the rise of the theology of the double resurrection. The classic text is Daniel 12:2-4:

And many of those who sleep in the dust of the earth shall awake, some to everlasting life, and some to shame and everlasting contempt. And those who are wise shall shine like the brightness of the firmament, and those who turn many to justice like the stars for ever and ever.

The Maccabean martyrs become models of fidelity to the law and they will rise to life everlasting (2 Mc. 7:11, 14, 34-36). This conjunction of a theology of eschatological vindication with a teaching on resurrection indicates that as resurrection faith emerges it is not simply a belief in return to life, but resurrection itself is a form of vindication—of the justice of God and of those who suffer injustice.

3. Justice as Almsgiving

One of the more interesting transformations of older biblical notions of *sᵉdāqāh* during this period is that the word comes to mean "almsgiving" and is translated by the Greek *eleēmosynē*.[21] Justice in the sense of almsgiving is found in Tobit 1:3; 12:8-9 and 14:11, and while the Greek text of Ben Sirach employs *eleēmosynē* in such sayings as "almsgiving atones for sins" (3:30) and "do not be fainthearted in your prayers, nor neglect to give alms" (7:10), the Hebrew original has *sᵉdāqāh* in these places. The change in meaning of the term can be seen from a comparison of Proverbs 10:2 with Tobit 12:9:

Righteousness *(sᵉdāqāh)* delivers from death (Prov. 10:2).

Almsgiving *(eleēmosynē)* delivers from death (Tb. 12:9).

J. Lauterbach describes the significance of this development when he says that in later Judaism charity and concern for neighbor are conceived as justice and not simply as an excess of love.[22] The roots of this view lie in the Old Testament identification of doing justice with concern for the poor, the widow, the orphan and the sojourner. The development lives on in both Christianity and Judaism. In Judaism it produced a large system of care for the poor in the community. In the New Testament it is mirrored in Paul's concern for the poor and for the collection and in the view of the relation of faith and works in the letter of James where true faith demands acts of charity (Jas. 2:16-17). Also in the early Church the command to give alms and share the goods of the earth is seen as a manifestation of justice rather than an act of unselfish charity, crystallized in Augustine's statement: "Assisting the needy is justice *(Justitia est in subveniendo miseris)*."[23]

This development represents a very important facet of biblical thought which was obscured by later distinctions between justice and charity. Concern for the poor and a desire to lessen the inequality between rich and poor either individually or collectively, in a biblical perspective, should not proceed simply from a love for or compassion with the sufferings of others, but is rooted in claims of justice, i.e., how one can be faithful to the Lord who has given the goods of the earth as common possession of all and be faithful to others in the human community who have equal claim to these goods.

III
THE NEW TESTAMENT

New Testament statements on justice are neither as rich nor as direct as the Old Testament witness. Nonetheless justice is central to the New Testament. In Matthew Jesus says "Seek first his [the Father's] Kingdom and his justice" (Mt. 6:33), and Jesus criticizes the scribes because they have neglected the weightier matters of the Law, "justice and mercy and faith" (Mt. 23:23). The early Church proclaims the risen Jesus as the just one (Acts 3:13ff; 7:52). A major emphasis of Paul is the justice of God and the justice given to the world in faith. The Book of Revelation takes up the tradition of justice as the eschatological vindication of the faithful (Rev. 19:11), and the letter of James as well as 1 John is concerned about care for the suffering members of the community. Since the new element in the New Testament is the linking of the revelation of God's justice to the life and death of Jesus, we will make some initial observations about the relation of the Kingdom proclamation of Jesus to the quest for justice. Secondly we will indicate some ways in which justification by faith in Christ, in Paul, which has traditionally been interpreted in an individualistic sense, has a social dimension, and we will call attention to certain aspects of the theology of Matthew and Luke which contribute to a theology of justice.

The Teaching and Life of Jesus

In 1 Corinthians 1:30 Paul says that Jesus has become our wisdom, justice, sanctification and redemption. The question is: How does Paul's theological statement mirror the life and career of Jesus? Answering this question has become increasingly difficult in light of the intense debate on the "historical Jesus." Virtually all scholars admit that the Synoptic Gospels are not biographies of Jesus but presentations of a "faith image" of Jesus which reflect the theological concerns of the evangelists and their traditions. What Jesus actually did and said must be reconstructed by source and form criticism. Such a reconstruction is beyond the scope of the present discussion. What we can do is to indicate certain elements of the Jesus tradition which are agreed on by all scholars as authentic Jesus material and from these elements make certain observations on Jesus as the revelation of God's justice.

1. *The Kingdom Proclamation*

In the Gospels Jesus begins his ministry with a proclamation: "The Kingdom of God is at hand. Repent" (Mk. 1:15; Mt. 4:17). The Kingdom is proclaimed as a present reality active and calling for a response from the hearers (Mt. 3:2; 4:23; 5:3, 10; 9:35; Lk. 10:9; 11:20; 17:21: "The Kingdom of God is in your midst"); at the same time, it is a future reality, the object of hope and prayer: "Thy Kingdom come" (Mt. 6:10).[24] The meaning of Kingdom is much debated. Older exegesis tended to interpret it in a spatial sense—the place where the king dwells—and identified Kingdom with ecclesiastical or political realities. Liberal Protestantism saw it as a purely spiritual reality dwelling only in the hearts of men, urging them to love of the neighbor as brother and God as Father. A certain breakthrough was achieved when Kingdom was understood in the Old Testament sense as the active exercise (Yahweh is king or reigns) of God's sovereignty.[25] While this insight is helpful, it too runs the danger of being overly spiritualized. Kingdom, while denoting the active rule of God, never loses its spatial dimension as active rule calling for a place or area in which this rule finds a home.[26]

The relation of Kingdom to justice may not be immediately apparent, but a connection is suggested by the observation of N. Perrin that, in the New Testament, Kingdom is a "symbol."[27] As a symbol Kingdom carries with it all the overtones of meanings it has in the Old Testament and in the intertestamental literature. As we have seen in the enthronement Psalms, Yahweh's rule and the establishment of justice are closely joined (Pss. 97:1-2; 96:10). In the apocalyptic literature the coming of the time of the Messiah will inaugurate the victory of God's justice and his mercy. By identifying the advent of God's Kingdom with his ministry and teaching, Jesus proclaims the advent of God's justice.

Jesus as the eschatological proclaimer of God's Kingdom and God's justice shows that this Kingdom is to have effect in the everyday events of life. The Kingdom is the power of God active in the world, transforming it and confronting the powers of the world. It is to find a home among the poor (Mt. 5:3) and the persecuted (Mt. 5:4), and only with difficulty will the rich enter it (Mk. 10:23). The person who can summarize the whole Law as love of God and neighbor is not far from the Kingdom of God (Mk. 12:34). The exorcisms of Jesus represent Jesus' confrontation with and victory over the powers of evil and are signs that "the Kingdom of heaven has come upon you" (Lk. 11:20). The Kingdom and therefore the justice of God—his fidelity and his call to fidelity—are to be manifest in history no less than the proclaimer of the Kingdom, Jesus, was incarnate in history.

2. *Fellowship with Toll Collectors*

Jesus manifested the meaning of God's Kingdom by his close association and table fellowship with sinners and toll collectors, the ritual and legal outcasts of his time.[28] He is the one who has come not to call the just, but sinners (Mk. 2:17). By his fellowship with the toll collectors and sinners Jesus makes present the love and saving mercy of God to those whom the social structures of his time would classify as unjust and beyond the pale of God's loving concern. Jesus' association with these groups is a form of symbolic activity which proclaims that those ritual laws which were designed to protect the sanctity and justice of God concealed the revelation of the true God. In associating with these groups Jesus is a parable of God's justice where mercy *(hesed)* and justice *(sᵉdāqāh)* are not in opposition, but in paradoxical agreement.

3. The Call to Discipleship

In the Gospels the proclamation of the Kingdom is followed by the calling of disciples. Response to this call is not simply a hearing of Jesus' teaching but involves following and mission. The disciple is called to be with Jesus, to have the same authority, to preach, heal, and confront the power of evil in the same way that Jesus did (Mk. 3:13). Like Jesus the disciple is not to be a person of power, but is to be a servant of all and give his life for others (Mk. 10:35-45). The disciple is to be a person who is free of the care and anxiety which centers on length of days and wealth (Mt. 6:25-33). Discipleship involves commitment to the kind and quality of life Jesus led as well as dedication to a mission of compassion and mercy to the outcast along with a prophetic stance which confronts the power of evil in the world.

Therefore, as the proclaimer of God's Kingdom, Jesus is also the sacrament of God's justice in the world. In Jesus' life this involved engagement with the social world of his time, the offer of mercy to the outcasts of his time, and the calling of others to continue this mission.

The Preaching of Paul

It is a paradox in contemporary discussions of faith and justice that while the Old Testament and the teaching of Jesus are called on to construct a theology of social justice, Paul, who cites the Old Testament "The just man lives by faith" (Rom. 1:17; Hab. 2:4), and who struggles with the relation of faith and justice in Romans and Galatians, is rarely treated in this context. A variety of reasons explain this neglect. Since the Reformation, Paul's teaching on the justice of God has been seen under the problematic of how the individual sinner can be accepted by a just God. This has led to an exegesis where Paul is, as Krister Stendahl has remarked, "the introspective conscience of the West."[29] Though there is no doubt that Paul's language resonates with a modern quest for personal freedom and a struggle with guilt, much of the individualized and existential study of Paul was based on a misreading of his understanding of justice. Recent exegesis has located Paul's thought not so much in the Pharisaic problem of the just individual, but in the context of Old Testament and apocalyptic thought about the justice of God.[30] Ernst Käsemann captures the significance of this when he describes the justice of God in Paul as follows:

> Even when he became a Christian, Paul remained an apocalyptist. His doctrine of the *dikaiosynē theou* demonstrates this: God's power reaches out for the world, and the world's salvation lies in its being recaptured for the sovereignty of God.[31]

In the following pages we will attempt to locate aspects of a Pauline doctrine of faith and justice in the context of (a) Paul's eschatology, (b) his view of the saving significance of the cross, and (c) the application of his theology to the ethics of the community.

1. *Paul's Eschatology*

In his use of the terminology "this age," Paul shows himself to be an heir of apocalyptic Judaism.[32] Paul asks: "Where is the debater of this age?" (1 Cor. 1:20). He exhorts his community: "Do not be conformed to this age" (Rom. 12:2). The rulers of this age are doomed to pass away, and it was the rulers of this age who crucified Jesus (1 Cor. 2:6-8). The present age is transitory (1 Cor. 7:31); it is an evil age (Gal. 1:4) which is characterized by suffering and tribulation (Rom. 8:18). Paul does not root the evil of this age only in an empirical description of sin, but sees this age as held captive by evil power. The god of this world (2 Cor. 4:4) and elemental spirits enslave man and hold him in bondage (Gal. 4:3). Man is under the power of sin (Rom. 3:9; Gal. 3:22). Sin enters the world and takes it captive (Rom. 5:21; 6:12, 14), enslaves man (Rom. 6:16-17) and finally kills him (Rom. 7:11; 8:10). Death is both the consequence of and punishment for sin. Death is not simply an event but a power which "reigns" in this age (Rom. 5:14, 17).

However, Paul parts company from apocalyptic Judaism in not contrasting this age with the age to come which will bring victory over sin and death, but in locating the sending of Jesus at the turning of the age when this victory is inaugurated:[33]

> So with us, when we were children, we were slaves to the elemental spirits of the universe. But when the time had fully come, God sent forth his Son born of woman, born under the Law to redeem those under the Law, so that we might receive adoption as sons (Gal. 4:3-5).

Jesus "gave himself for our sins to deliver us from the present evil age" (Gal. 1:4). The Christians are those who live in the period of the "eschatological now" and the end of the age has come upon them (1 Cor. 10:11).[34] For the Christian the old has passed away and the new has come (2 Cor. 5:17). Therefore, Paul has in one sense a "realized eschatology." The events of the hoped for end time have arrived in Christ.

While emphasizing the "already" in the event of Jesus, Paul has also an eschatological reservation.[35] Though the evil powers have been broken by Christ who is now Lord of all creation (Phil. 2:10-11), the Christian lives between the times, a period when evil and injustice will continue to exercise their influence until the final victory. For Paul all creation is groaning and "we ourselves who have the first fruits of the Spirit groan inwardly as we wait for adoption as sons, the redemption of our bodies. For in this hope we were saved" (Rom. 8:23). Though Jesus has risen and conquered death, death still reigns and will be the last enemy to be conquered (1 Cor. 15:51-54). In the present time Christians are the body of Christ (Rom. 12; 1 Cor. 12), but "our commonwealth is in heaven" (Phil. 3:20).

This eschatological reservation explains Paul's constant juxtaposition of the indicative and the imperative. He writes to the Galatians:

> For freedom Christ has set us free; stand fast, therefore, and do not submit again to the yoke of slavery (Gal 5:1).

For through the Spirit by faith, we wait for the hope of righteousness (Gal 5:5).

Paul here states the indicative—"Christ has set us free," the hope for freedom—and the imperative—"do not submit again." This juxtaposition of indicative and imperative, of gift and command, is strong in Romans 6. Paul states that we are buried with Christ in baptism and by his resurrection "walk in the newness of life" (Rom. 6:4). This fact of saving history then becomes a command not to let sin "reign" in our lives. He then says that Christians should yield themselves to God, so that they might be instruments of justice (Rom. 6:13) as well as servants of justice (Rom. 6:18). Paul is using here the metaphor of two kingdoms or two sovereign powers. The Christian who has received the gift of freedom from the power and domination of sin now receives the commission to be under the power or Kingdom of justice.

When a discussion of justice in Paul is put in the context of his eschatology certain conclusions are suggested. If the sending of Christ is salvation from the present evil age, and if this is a manifestation of the justice of God (Rom. 4:25), then justice is not simply the quality of God as righteous judge over against sinful man, but a relation of the saving power of God to a world captured by evil. God's justice is his fidelity which inaugurates a saving victory over the powers that enslave and oppress man. Paul's eschatology suggests a Christian response to being in the world. On the one hand, if the world is still under the reign of sin and death, a prophetic stance of opposition to these powers is demanded. Such a stance demands an accurate diagnosis of what the powers are in contemporary experience. Along with the prophetic stance is an eschatological stance which sees that the quest for realization of God's saving justice is always held in hope and anticipation. Paul sees the world in process of transformation and Christians as co-workers in the process. However, precisely because the world is in process, is "groaning," no one crystallization of God's saving justice will be adequate, nor will any system ever be the final system. To hope to find a total incarnation of God's saving justice at any one time would, in Pauline terms, turn gift into Law. The Christian who reflects on Paul's eschatology will realize that the quest for justice always operates between prophecy and vision, between realization and hope.

2. *The Saving Significance of the Cross*

The concrete event which Paul sees as a manifestation of God's justice—his fidelity to himself and his people—is the death and resurrection of Jesus. The cross and resurrection have a two-fold significance. First of all, Jesus' death exposes and unmasks the powers (1 Cor. 1:18). Christ redeemed us from the curse, "having become a curse" (Gal. 3:13). "For our sake he made him to be sin who knew no sin, so that in him we might become the justice of God" (2 Cor. 5:21). In the letter to the Colossians we find the statement that God "disarmed the powers and principalities and made public exposure of them, by giving victory over them in Christ" (Col. 2:15). While these texts betray conceptions which are strange to the modern mind, they convey the idea that the death of Christ revealed the true nature of evil powers. This theology continues the motif from the Old Testament that the suffering of the just one exposes the evil of the unjust people. The suffering and death of the innocent is a sign that the power of injustice is at work.

Secondly, in more positive terms Paul portrays the effect of the cross by four metaphors of salvation, among which is justification.[36] The first of these metaphors we will examine is *apolytrosis* or redemptive liberation.[37] Paul writes:

They are justified by his grace as gift through the redemption which is in Christ Jesus (Rom. 3:24).

We wait for the redemption of our bodies (Rom. 8:23).

God has given you life in Christ Jesus. He has made him our wisdom, our justice, our sanctification and our redemption (1 Cor. 1:30).

By the use of this metaphor Paul alludes to the exodus event of the Old Testament. The cross and resurrection are the new Passover (1 Cor. 5:7), a new leading out of a people from oppression and slavery. Allied to this metaphor from saving history is one from the cultic tradition of Israel, *sanctification* (1 Cor. 1:30). God has called Christians not in uncleanness but "in sanctification" (1 Thes. 4:7); Christians are to yield their members "to justice for sanctification" (Rom. 6:19) and, free from sin, Christians are slaves to God and "the return you get is sanctification" (Rom. 6:22). Allied to this cultic metaphor is the statement of Romans 3:25 that God has made Jesus "an expiation by his blood." By using these terms Paul stresses that what the Old Testament cult hoped to achieve—the creation of a holy people, a people "set apart" for the things of God, a covenant people celebrating the mercy and justice of God—has been accomplished in Christ. Paul therefore uses cultic terminology to describe the Christian life: "Present your bodies as a living sacrifice, holy and acceptable to God which is your spiritual worship" (Rom. 12:2).

Reconciliation is a central metaphor which Paul uses for the Christ event and the effect of the cross:

> For if while we were enemies, we were reconciled to God by the death of his Son, much more, now that we are reconciled, shall we be saved by his life (Rom. 5:10).

> All this is from God, who through Christ reconciled us to himself and gave us the ministry of reconciliation (2 Cor. 5:18).

In its root sense reconciliation means "make peace" (after war); in the religious sense, it means a return of man to God's favor and intimacy after a period of estrangement.[38] The effect of reconciliation is peace—peace with God (Rom. 5:1) and the peace which breaks down the walls of hostility between peoples (Eph. 2:14). For Paul the Christian no longer lives in a hostile world as a hostile person but is reconciled with God and called to be a minister of reconciliation (2 Cor. 5:16-21). When we recall that in the Old

Testament one effect of the realization of the justice of God is that peace *(shalom)*, wholeness and harmony are to reign, we can see that the reconciled world is a world where peace and harmony are to prevail.

The final effect of the cross and resurrection is *justification.* As mentioned in Romans and Galatians this is the leading metaphor and in many senses embraces the other metaphors. The Gospel of the death and resurrection which Paul preaches is "the power of God for salvation to everyone who has faith. For in it the righteousness [justice] of God is revealed through faith for faith" (Rom. 1:16-17). In a programmatic paragraph at the conclusion of the first section of Romans, Paul writes:

> But now the righteousness of God has been manifested apart from the law, although the law and prophets bear witness to it, the righteousness of God through faith in Jesus Christ for all who believe (Rom. 3:21-22).

And later in the same letter he asserts:

> Our Lord Jesus . . . was put to death for our trespasses and raised for our justification (Rom. 4:25).

While this theology of justification is central to Paul, its meaning is complex. There is a definite forensic or juridical aspect of justification, that is, justification is a verdict of acquittal given to the sinful by a loving God, in spite of sin.[39] Realization of this acquittal takes place through faith which renounces all claims on God's love and at the same time surrenders to it with the consciousness that one is at the same time a sinner and a recipient of God's love. Paul's idea of justification is not simply a declaration of acquittal by God pronouncing the sinner upright; it is also the power of God at work in the world.[40] As a manifestation of his justice or fidelity God shows in Christ his saving deeds which conquer the power of evil; he opens people to a new covenant relationship where they can live without seeing the past as indictment or the future as threat; he establishes a new people who are to be "servants of a new covenant" (2 Cor. 3:6). The believer can be a person of faith and trust and live in a community of faith and trust because he or she has been the object of God's fidelity by receiving the gift of the justice of God.

Paul's idea of justification has a social dimension. As noted, the metaphors of salvation deal with those events in the Old Testament—redemptive liberation, sanctification, reconciliation—by which God dealt with a people as a whole. The second Adam theology of Romans 5 and 1 Corinthians 15, as well as the discussion about the salvation of Israel in Romans 9—11, shows that the result of justification is not simply individual acceptance and freedom but incorporation into a new social structure, the body of Christ (1 Cor. 12; Rom. 12:1-8) and the household of faith (Gal. 6:10; cf. Eph. 2:19, "household of God"). Those who are justified by faith are called on to be faithful not only to the demands of the relationship with God, but faithful to the relationships with all people.

3. *Effects of Justification*

The effects of justification in Paul are generally classed as freedom from sin, from the Law, and from death (Rom. 6—8). Freedom in Paul is not simply the absence of obligation or of limitations on human activity. It is a transfer of loyalties:

Having been set free from sin, you have become slaves of righteousness (Rom. 6:18).

For he who was called in the Lord as a slave is a freedman of the Lord. Likewise he who was free when called is a slave of Christ (1 Cor. 7:22).

Sin is not simply bad moral action, but a power which affects all of life. It makes man live for himself, is deceit (Rom. 7:11) and cuts him off from God and neighbor. Bultmann has described sin in the following terms:

Since human life is a life with others, mutual trust is destroyed by a *single* lie, and mistrust—and thereby sin—is established; by a *single* deed of violence defensive violence is called forth and law as organized violence is made to serve the interest of individuals, etc. So everyone exists in a world in which he looks out for himself, each insists upon his rights, each fights for his existence and life becomes a struggle of all against all even when the battle is involuntarily fought.[41]

Sin is then the desire and tendency of man to live for himself alone in a world of social and religious isolation; it is the equivalent of living according to the flesh. Freedom from sin is then found when the believer sees himself as one ransomed, as one who does not belong simply to himself, but lives free of care, and lives open to the Lord:

> None of us lives to himself and none of us dies to himself. If we live, we live to the Lord, and if we die, we die to the Lord (Rom. 14:7).

The one who is free from sin is one who now is called "through love to be servants of one another" (Gal. 5:13) and is "a slave to all" (1 Cor. 9:19). Such a one is now free to walk according to the Spirit (Gal. 5:25) and to live according to the fruits of the Spirit— love, joy, peace, patience, kindness, goodness, faithfulness, gentleness, self-control. Therefore, sin is social isolation, and freedom from sin is openness to others. Those things which characterize life according to the Spirit are the things which make human social life possible.

The Christian is also free from Law (Rom. 6:14; 10:4). No subject in Paul is as difficult for subsequent thought than his understanding of Law and freedom from it. On one level freedom from the Law is simply freedom from the demands of the Jewish Law on Gentile Christians (Gal. 2:11-21). On another level Paul sees the Law as a power which enslaved man. It awakened the consciousness of sin (Rom. 3:20) and put a curse on those who did not obey (Gal. 3:10). The Law functioned then as a series of prescriptions without giving the power to follow these prescriptions.[42] The Christian is in constant danger of falling back into the slavery of the Law. Paul here does not simply mean observance of the Jewish Law, but a legalism which he feels is contrary to Christianity. Paul sees in legalism an exclusiveness which would make Christianity into a set of norms and customs, rather than a gift to be shared. Legalism would make the Church simply into a society rather than into a community where membership transcends all norms and social custom:

> For as many of you were baptized into Christ have put on Christ. There is neither Jew nor Greek, there is neither slave nor free, there is neither male nor female; for you are all one in Christ Jesus (Gal. 3:28, cf. 1 Cor. 12:13).

This indicative of freedom from the Law brings with it also the imperative: "Bear one another's burdens and so fulfill the Law of Christ" (Gal. 6:2). The Christian is to owe no one anything except to love one another, "for he who loves his neighbor has fulfilled the Law" (Rom. 13:8). For Paul freedom *from* the Law is also freedom *for* the law of love.

The Christian is also free of death (Rom. 6:23; 7:5-16; 1 Cor. 15:56). Having died with Christ, the believer shares in his resurrection. Resurrection is not simply the return to life of Jesus, but his victory over the power of death. Paul describes an experience of near death in his own life and then shows that the resurrection is freedom from the fear of death:

> Why, we felt that we had received the sentence of death; but that was to make us rely not on ourselves but on God who raises the dead (2 Cor. 1:9).

The victory over death is a victory over the power of death to destroy hope, to limit and be the lord of human life. Such a view is the ultimate basis of the Pauline paradoxes of 1 Corinthians 4:12 and 2 Corinthians 6:9ff, "dying, behold we live." It is also the basis of those places where Paul glories in his weaknesses that the power of Christ may be evident in him (2 Cor. 12).

4. *Faith and Justice*

There are two sets of texts in Paul which group faith and justice. In the first set justice is joined with faith and Jesus Christ
(e.g., Rom. 3:22, "the justice of God through faith in Jesus
Christ"; cf. Phil. 3:9; Rom. 3:26; Gal. 2:16). In the second set
there is the conjunction of simply faith and justice (Rom. 3:28, 30;
4:5, 9, 11, 13; 9:30; 10:6; 10:10).[43] Since faith in Paul is primarily
faith in what God has done in Jesus, the difference between the
two sets of texts is not significant. What is significant is what Paul
means when he says that justice comes through faith.

In most current discussions the meaning of this statement is
seen in terms of the faith vs. works controversy. Justice or the acceptance of man by God is seen as the result of man's total surrender to the loving God, renouncing all claims on his love and not
boasting in "works" as a way of attaining this love. While it is
true that justification comes not from doing the works of the Law,
but from faith, limitation of these statements to this controversy
misses the richness of the relation of faith and justice.

Like justice faith in Paul is both central and protean. Fitzmyer has described faith in Paul:

This experience begins with the hearing of the "word" about
Christ, and ends in a personal commitment of the whole man
to his "person and revelation." It begins with *akoē* (hearing)
and ends with *hypakoē* (obedience, submission: Rom. 10:17;
1:5; 16:26).[44]

Therefore faith is akin to the *metanoia* or conversion of the Synoptic Gospels which demands a turning to the demands of the Kingdom and engagement in the mission of the Kingdom. Faith looks
to the past: "I live by faith in the Son of God who loved me and
gave himself for me" (Gal. 2:20); it also characterizes the present
life of the individual: "I live by faith" (Gal. 2:20) and of the community: "Your faith is proclaimed in the whole world" (Rom. 1:8),
and, as Paul's description of the faith of Abraham in Romans 4
shows, faith is living under a promise which must prove itself in
the Christian life.[45]

In Paul faith is primarily Christological. Philippians 3:8-11 brings this out:

> Indeed I count everything as loss because of the surpassing worth of knowing Christ Jesus my Lord. For his sake I have suffered the loss of all things, and count them as refuse, in order that I may gain Christ, and be found in him, not having a righteousness of my own, based on Law, but that which is through faith in Christ, the righteousness from God that depends on faith; that I may know him and the power of his resurrection, and may share his sufferings, becoming like him in his death, that if possible I may attain the resurrection from the dead.

The faith which justifies is the faith which leads to knowledge of Jesus Christ—a knowledge which involves personal sharing in the life and death of Jesus. The life and death of Jesus is his emptying (Phil. 2:5-11), his renunciation of grasping and the giving of his life for others. Therefore, the justice of God which comes from faith in Jesus is fidelity to the demands of a relationship—the relationship that the Christian is to have with Christ by being "in Christ" (over 165 times in Paul) and putting on Christ and the mind of Christ. Käsemann describes well this Christological aspect of justifying faith:

> This means that in justification it is simply the Kingdom of God proclaimed by Jesus which is at stake. His right to us is our salvation, if he does not let it drop. It will be our misfortune if we resist him. . . . The Christology inherent in the doctrine of justification corresponds to the existence led in the everyday life of the world. Justification is the stigmatization of our worldly existence through the crucified Christ. Through us and in us he simultaneously reaches out toward the world to which we belong.[46]

Therefore, to be justified by faith is to walk in the trust that God through Christ offers grace and redemption to a sinful world, that God is at work in history. A quest for justice which is from faith proceeds with the faith that the kind and quality of life Jesus lived and proclaimed still has meaning.

5. *The Ethics of the Community*

Neither Paul's doctrine of justification by faith nor his eschatological reservation led him to a flight from concern for the world or to an inactive fideism. In his own life Paul was a minister of reconciliation (2 Cor. 5:18) and a servant of justice (Rom. 6:18). The hortatory parts of Paul's letters turn to everyday concerns of the community. Though these concerns may seem archaic to us today (e.g., discussion of food offered to idols, of appearance before pagan courts—1 Cor. 8 and 6), they show that Paul's deepest theological reflection touched on the problems of how Christians were to relate to each other. In the following pages we will indicate some ways in which Paul's theological insights touch on the lives of the community.

(a) Concern for the Weak in the Community. In 1 Corinthians 8:1-13, 11:17-22 and Romans 14:1-4, Paul is concerned that his Gospel of freedom not be a source of division and a stumbling block (1 Cor. 8:9) for members of the community who do not experience this freedom, especially in regard to the matter of eating forbidden foods. In 1 Corinthians 9:1-23 Paul admits to his own freedom in the situation under which members of the community may live: "For though I am free from all men, I have made myself a slave to all that I might win more" (1 Cor. 9:19). Freedom is thus in Paul contextual freedom where the use of freedom is dictated by the consideration of how much the enjoyment of freedom will contribute to the lack of freedom of a brother or sister in the community. In this sense Paul in addressing the conflicts of the community acts like the prophets of the Old Testament who take the part of the oppressed and of those who have no one to speak for them.

(b) The Bearing of Burdens. The salvation and liberation given in Christ is to manifest itself in a new Law: "Bear one another's burdens and so fulfill the Law of Christ" (Gal. 6:2). In Romans 15:1 Paul writes: "We who are strong ought to bear with

the failings of the weak, and not to please ourselves," and he adds to this the Christological motivation: "For Christ did not please himself" (Rom. 15:3). Justice not only involves fidelity in relationships with God, but is manifest in the way the justified respond to the demands of others. This "bearing of burdens" conveys a unity in suffering: "If one member suffers, all suffer together; if one member is honored, all rejoice together" (1 Cor. 12:26). Paul pictures for his day a form of the Church which the Second Vatican Council calls on to be the form of the Church for our day:

> The joys and the hopes, the griefs and the anxieties, especially those who are poor or in any way afflicted, these too are the joys and hopes, the griefs and anxieties of the followers of Christ (*Gaudium et Spes*, n. 1).

(c) Concern for the Poor and the Collection. One of the earliest commands Paul received as a Christian was "that they [the Jerusalem church] would have us remember the poor" (Gal. 2:10). In his letters Paul continues the tradition of justice as almsgiving by constantly exhorting his communities to share their wealth with the poor, especially the poor of Judaea. In 2 Corinthians 8 Paul writes "for the relief of the saints." In exhorting to liberality Paul cites the example of Jesus "who though he was rich, yet for your sake became poor, so that by his poverty you might become rich" (2 Cor. 8:9), and he goes on to say: "But as a matter of equality your abundance at the present time should supply their want" (2 Cor. 8:14). In what might be a separate collection letter, 2 Corinthians 9, Paul again asks about a collection for the saints (2 Cor. 9:1). As motivation for this Paul cites Psalm 112:9: "He scatters abroad, he gives to the poor, his justice endures forever," and he says that if the community is generous, God who is Lord of creation "will increase the harvest of your justice" (2 Cor. 9:10). The generosity he seeks from the community will be their sign of life in the community of the new covenant.

(d) Concern for Peace and Harmony in the Community. We have already noted that both in the Old Testament and in Paul peace is an effect of justice. Such a view is continued by the later letter of James:

And the harvest of justice is sown in peace by those who make peace (Jas 3:18).

Peace in the Bible is not simply absence of conflict but the harmony and wholeness which flows from the establishment of proper relations between God and his creation and between people in their lives. Many of Paul's letters (1 and 2 Corinthians, Philippians, Galatians, 1 and 2 Thessalonians) are precipitated by a dispute within the community. In writing to Philippi he urges Evodia and Syntyche "to agree in the Lord" (Phil. 4:2). The strongest exhortation to harmony comes in Romans 12:14-21 where Paul exhorts them to live in harmony with one another (Rom. 12:14). Later when addressing their dispute over food laws he writes: "For the Kingdom of God is not food and drink, but justice, peace and joy in the Holy Spirit" (Rom. 14:17). Paul concludes a major section of 1 Corinthians which deals with conflicting claims for preeminence in the community by exhorting the community to a love (agape) which "does not insist on its own way" (1 Cor. 13:5).

These aspects of Paul's ethics of everyday life are not exhaustive but indicative that Paul writes as a pastor for a world he sees in process of transformation, but where the transformation is revealed in the creation of structures of interpersonal relations in the community. Paul's ethics are simultaneously an ethics where decisions are made in response to the felt needs of others and an ethics where the goal of Christian life determines its present shape. Today, no less than in the time of Paul, the justice and freedom which comes as gift through faith must be a gift shared and realized in Church and world.

Summary of Paul

1. Paul's statements on justice and on justification must be seen in a Christological context. Paul sees salvation in the event of the incarnation and the cross and resurrection of Jesus. This is the revelation of the justice of God which is God's fidelity to his creation and the saving victory over the evil in creation.

2. Paul's statements about the salvation and justification of the individual are in a context of the salvation and justification of

the world. Evangelization for Paul is not simply kerygmatic preaching, but involves the ministry of reconciliation, the service of justice, and concern for the suffering members of the community.

3. The metaphors which Paul uses for salvation all convey a nuance of the restoration of broken relationships and the creation of a new people. In this sense they are descriptions of the *sedāqāh* or justice of God.

4. The access to salvation is faith. Faith is the obedient surrender to the love of God manifest in Christ. It is a walking under a promise which frees one from the power of evil. In this sense faith frees both the oppressor and the oppressed.

5. The Christian is to live in the new creation, is to fulfill the Law of Christ by love of neighbor and to be in a union where the sufferings and joys of others are his or her sufferings and joys.

The Jesus of the Synoptics

As indicated, the Jesus of history is elusive. However, the Gospels, though viewed from the perspective of the Christ of faith, present a theology in which an evangelist presents to a community the religious meaning of the life and teaching of Jesus. In this sense the question of the historical Jesus is not as important as how the Jesus of Matthew or Luke may become a "pioneer of faith" (Heb. 12:2) for the contemporary believer. In the following section we will indicate some ways in which the Jesus of Matthew and the Jesus of Luke speak to the concerns of faith and justice.

Matthew: The New Righteousness

While Matthew contains some of the harshest statements in the New Testament against the Pharisees (Mt. 23:1-39), his Gospel is the most Jewish of the Gospels. In Matthew Jesus is a teacher of the new righteousness. Jesus is the New Moses who addresses his community in five large discourse blocks, like the five books of the Pentateuch, and his initial thematic sermon is given from a mountain. Like Moses he is to found a new community *(ekklēsia)* which is to follow the new Torah.[47]

Two examples from Matthew are presented to show that for

Matthew the new righteousness is qualified by mercy which reaches out to the marginal ones in the world. The parable of the unmerciful servant (Mt. 18:23-34) shows justice qualified by mercy.[48] The parable is placed by Matthew at the end of a section where Jesus proclaims a series of regulations for life in the community—a community which is concerned about the problem of forgiveness. The parable is familiar. A man who received remission of a huge debt then goes out and demands payment of a minor debt from a fellow servant. When this action is brought to the master's attention he punishes the first servant and says to him: "Should you not have had mercy on your fellow servant, as I had mercy on you?" (Mt. 18:33). Though on one level the parable seems to be an exhortation to forgiveness, on another level it is a parable of justice qualified by mercy. When the first servant approaches the master for remission of the debt, he thinks that the way to be free of his predicament is to satisfy the demands of strict justice: "I will pay you everything" (Mt. 18:26). Given the size of the debt this is impossible, and the master "out of pity" (literally "out of compassion"—(Mt. 18:27) forgives the debt. When forgiven he meets a fellow servant who owes him a minor debt and makes the same request: "I will pay you" (Mt. 18:29). The dramatic tragedy in the parable hinges on why the first servant acted as he did. Unless he is to be considered as totally unfeeling, the only explanation for his action was that he was a person who thought in terms of strict justice. He uses in his request to the master this language and uses it with his fellow servant. The reason he treated his fellow servant as he did is that he is one who was never able to interiorize the forgiveness he received nor make it a norm of action in his life.[49] He experiences a gift without the conversion which comes with having received a gift. This is therefore not an example of how one should forgive but is a parable about the condition necessary for forgiveness—the realization that one can be merciful because one has received mercy. In the parable also the master emerges as the vindicator of the one who is treated unjustly. He restores true justice, which is justice qualified by mercy. Therefore, in the context of Matthew's theology the new law of the Christian community is that the just are those who meet the demands of fellow men because they live in a covenant relationship with a Lord who has given them mercy.

The dramatic scene of the final judgment in Matthew 25:31-46 shows Matthew's concern for the marginal ones in the community. The location of this scene is significant since it is the last discourse of Jesus before the passion narrative. In this section the reader is taken beyond the passion and death to the return of the Son of Man as vindicator. It looks back to the Matthean interpretation of the parable of the weeds and the wheat (Mt. 13:36-43) where the final separation of the good and bad will take place at the Last Judgment; until then the Church is a mixed state. The scene in Matthew 25 unfolds with dramatic intensity. After the judgment and separation the Lord will say to the blessed (called the just in verse 37): "Inherit the Kingdom." The reason for their inheritance is:

> I was hungry and you gave me food, I was thirsty and you gave me drink. I was a stranger and you welcomed me, I was naked and you clothed me. I was sick and you visited me, I was in prison and you came to me (Mt. 25:35-36).

The just ones seem puzzled about how and when they did these things to the Lord, and he answers: "Truly, I say to you, as you did it to one of the least of these my brethren, you did it to me" (Mt. 25:40). In the second half of the scene the structure of the first part is repeated but now it becomes a structure of condemnation. The unjust are condemned because they did not do those things which the just did. The condemnation does not take place because the goats do not know the commands to feed, clothe, etc. Their response and question in verse 44 presupposes familiarity with these.

In effect, they knew what justice demanded; they simply did not know or recognize where its demands were to be met in the world. In the scene it is the marginal and suffering in the world who reveal the place where the Son of Man, Lord and Judge, is, as it were, hidden in the world. The parable is a warning to Christians of all ages that they must discover not only what the doing of justice is but where justice is to be located. As in the Old Testament the marginal ones become the touchstone for the doing of justice.

The Gospel of Luke

More than any other evangelist, Luke is concerned with the life of the Christian in the world. His Gospel is written at a time when hope of the imminent parousia or return of Jesus had waned, and his two volume work (Luke-Acts) wants to present the ministry of Jesus and the life of the early Church as a paradigm for Christian life.[50] Luke is the evangelist who is most interested in what we could call today "social justice," and the Jesus of Luke is very much a prophet in the Old Testament model.

The infancy narratives in Luke form a diptych where John and Jesus are both compared and contrasted. John is a prophet of the old age. He will walk in the "spirit of Elijah and turn the disobedient to the wisdom of the just" (Lk. 1:17). John is the last of the Old Testament prophets (Lk. 16:16). Jesus is to be the first of the prophets of the new order.[51] Like Hannah, the mother of Samuel (1 Sam. 2:1-10), Jesus' mother, Mary, sings a canticle at the announcement of his birth. In the canticle Jesus is proclaimed as one who is to show the saving mercy and justice of God: he will put down the mighty and will exalt the lowly and fill the hungry with good things. This prophetic motif is taken up by Jesus in his inaugural sermon (Lk. 4:18-19) where he applies to himself the role of the servant prophet of Isaiah 61:1-2 who will proclaim release to the captives, recovery of sight to the blind and liberty to the oppressed. This incident is a combination of a prophetic mandate and a prophetic rejection recalling the rejection of Elijah (Lk. 4:25-27—only in Luke). Jesus says in reference to his own death that a prophet should not perish away from Jerusalem (Lk. 13:33), and, after his death, his disciples speak of him as a prophet mighty in word and work (Lk. 24:19). Like the prophets of the Old Testament Jesus speaks on behalf of God (Lk. 6:7, 20-49); he performs symbolic actions and mighty works (the miracles); he shows concern for a widow (Lk. 7:11ff) and takes the cause of the stranger in the land (the Samaritan—Lk. 10:29-37). The Lukan Jesus speaks to his Church with the same prophetic voice for justice with which the Old Testament prophets spoke.

Allied to this is a prophetic critique of wealth which runs throughout the Gospel of Luke. In biblical thought generally, wealth is evil on two grounds: (a) when it becomes a source of dominating power over others, and (b) when it dominates the one who possesses it. For Luke, wealth seems incompatible with the Gospel. Observation of material which is found *only in Luke* illustrates this special Lukan concern. John's preaching includes an address to special social groups (Lk. 3:10-14). Would-be followers are to give away one of two coats; the toll collectors are to collect only "what is due" and the soldiers are to avoid violence, robbery and greed. As mentioned, Luke cites Isaiah 61:1-2, the good news to the poor, at the beginning of Jesus' ministry. When Levi follows Jesus "he leaves everything" (Lk. 5:28). In his sermon on the plain Luke has the "Beatitudes" in the form of prophetic oracles of blessing followed by oracles of woe (Lk. 6:20-26). The "poor" blessed in Luke are the literal poor, not the "poor in spirit." The first two woes are directed against the rich and those who are full. Luke adds a saying on lending, even to enemies, without hope of return (Lk. 6:35). He places the parable of the rich fool (Lk. 12:16-21) after the saying "Beware of all covetousness, for a man's life does not consist in the abundance of possessions" (Lk. 12:15). The disciple in Luke is one who is to "sell your possessions and give alms" (Lk. 12:33). In the parable of the great supper, those invited after the initial refusal are "the poor, the maimed, the lame and the blind" (Lk. 14:21; cf. Lk. 14:13). Discipleship involves renouncing all that you have (Lk. 14:33). The Pharisees are "lovers of money" (Lk. 16:14). Luke alone has the parable of the unjust steward and the sayings which follow (Lk. 16:1-14), as well as the parable of the rich man and Lazarus (Lk. 16:19-31). Zacchaeus, the chief toll collector, is praised at his conversion as a true son of Abraham because he gives half of his goods away and does not defraud (Lk. 19:1-10). It is to Luke that we owe the picture of the early Church as a group which "held all things in common, and sold their possessions and distributed them to all, as any had need" (Acts 2:45; 4:34-36). Having observed these characteristics of Luke's Gospel, Malcom Tolbert writes:

> Luke was convinced that the Gospel was applicable to the great social issues of his day and his presentation is colored throughout with a compassion for the exploited and despised.

The study of the third Gospel should be a reminder that violence is done to the message of Jesus when it is severed from a concern for man's social problems.[52]

IV
CONCLUSIONS

The Bible proclaims what it means to be just and do justice; it is less interested in what justice is in the abstract. It gives concrete instances of justice and injustice in the lives of people. The task of translation is to make alive in our present age the vision of justice which formed the lives of the biblical writers. Interpretation of the Bible is always determined by the social context of the interpreter. Luther wrestled with the late medieval problem of a just God and sinful creation and translated the God of justice into a God of love. The task of our age may well be the reverse—to translate the love of God into the doing of justice.

The God of the Old Testament is a God who loves justice and righteousness. What he loves, he brings to pass. As a just Lord he is faithful to his covenant by revealing to people how they may turn to him and return to him when they fail. His justice is manifest both in the saving deeds whereby he frees people from slavery and oppression and in his indicting of sinfulness. In God justice and mercy are not in opposition, but, as Heschel states: "God is compassion without compromise; justice, though not inclemency."[53]

To be just is to be faithful to the covenant God as he reveals himself in history, in the Law and in the prophets. Covenant faithfulness means that justice is shown to the neighbor as a sign of the saving justice received from God. Peace and harmony are the fruits of justice as well as its signs.

Particular to Israel's faith is the revelation of God as protector of the helpless, the poor and the oppressed in the community. In order to become a faithful and just people, Israel is summoned to true knowledge and true worship of God which is not simply the recognition that another person has equal rights to the goods of God's creation, but is active engagement in securing these goods for them.

In the development of biblical faith the quest for justice is always present gift and demand, and the full realization of the quest is always future hope. The heir of biblical faith lives "between the times" with a mission both to confront the evils of injustice and to offer to the world visions of justice.

In the New Testament the revelation of God's justice is Christological. God shows his fidelity to creation by the offer of love and mercy in the life and teaching of Jesus. This offer represents the reclamation of the world to the sovereignty of God. The world of human history is God's world. Faith is the recognition of God's claim. It is expressed in love and care for all those claimed by God. Faith frees people to be people of compassion because they have received compassion; it frees them to care for the weak and the prodigal because they have been accepted by God though weak and prodigal.

The cause of the poor, the hungry and the oppressed is now the cause of Jesus. He is the Son of Man, present in the least of his brethren. Christians are called on to bear one another's burdens. This is to fulfill the law of Christ, to be a just people.

Engagement in the quest for justice is no more "secular" than the engagement of Yahweh in the history of his people or the incarnation of Jesus into the world of human suffering. The Bible gives a mandate and a testament to Christians that, in their quest for justice, they are recovering the roots of the biblical tradition and are seeking to create a dwelling place for the word of God in human history.

NOTES

1. G. von Rad, *Old Testament Theology*, trans. D. M. G. Stalker (New York: Harper and Bros., 1962), I, 370.

2. *The Biblical Doctrine of Justice and Law*, Ecumenical Biblical Studies, No. 3 (London: S.C.M. Press, 1955), p. 50.

3. F. Nötscher, "Righteousness (Justice)," *Sacramentum Verbi*, ed. J. B. Bauer (New York: Herder and Herder, 1970), II, 780. Hebrew has two main terms for justice, *sedāqāh* and *mišpāt*, usually translated as "righteousness" and "justice." In this essay we will follow the R.S.V. in its translation of the terms but with the caution that the terms are often used synonymously in the Old Testament and that righteousness has a much wider connotation than moral innocence.

4. J. Pedersen, *Israel: Its Life and Culture* (Vols. I-II; London: Oxford University Press, 1926), pp. 337-340.

5. K. H.-J. Fahlgren, *S^edākā, nahestehende und entgegengesetze Begriffe im Alten Testament* (Uppsala: Almquist und Wiksells, 1932), p. 81. Fahlgren describes justice as *Gemeinschafttreue*, i.e., fidelity in communal life.

6. See Hos. 2:19; Is. 16:5; Ps. 38:4-5.

7. E. Achtemeier, "Righteousness in the OT," *Interpreter's Dictionary of the Bible* (Nashville: Abingdon Press, 1962), IV, 80.

8. *Ibid.*, 81.

9. R. A. F. MacKenzie, "Job," *Jerome Biblical Commentary*, ed. R. E. Brown, J. A. Fitzmyer, R. E. Murphy (Englewood Cliffs, N.J.: Prentice Hall, 1968), I, 533.

10. Achtemeier, "Righteousness," p. 83.

11. S. Mowinckel, *The Psalms in Israel's Worship* (New York: Abingdon Press, 1967), I, 16-17, 62, 68-70.

12. Jose Miranda, *Marx and the Bible*, trans. John Eagelson (Maryknoll, N.Y.: Orbis Books, 1974), esp. pp. 77-106; E. Berkovits, "The Biblical Meaning of Justice," *Judaism* 18 (1969), 188-209.

13. A. Heschel, *The Prophets* (New York: Harper and Row, 1962). On p. 5 Heschel calls prophecy "a voice to the plundered poor"; see also p. 205.

14. Miranda, *Marx*, pp. 44-53. "Know" in the Bible is not simply intellectual awareness but involves intimate knowledge and personal commitment.

15. Fahlgren, *S^edākā*, pp. 89-93.

16. A. Cronbach, "Righteousness in Jewish Literature, 200 B.C.—A.D. 100," *IDB*, IV, 85-91.

17. On Pharisaic notions of justice, see G. F. Moore, *Judaism in the First Three Centuries of the Christian Era* (Cambridge, Harvard University Press, 1963), II, 180-197, and J. Lauterbach, "The Pharisees and Their Teaching," *Rabbinic Essays* (Cincinnati: Hebrew Union College, 1951), 87-159.

18. L. Ruppert, *Jesus als der leidende Gerechte*, Stuttgarter Bibelstudien, 59 (Stuttgart: Katholisches Bibelwerk, 1972), pp. 16-22.

19. "Eschatology" is a general term for statements about the end time when Yahweh intervenes to bring history to fulfillment or conclusion. "Apocalyptic" represents a particular form of eschatology which stresses symbolic revelation of the future and depicts a detailed scenario of the end time and the new age. Jewish eschatological thought in the intertestamental and New Testament periods is very often expressed in apocalyptic categories. See *Journal for Theology and Church*, Vol. 6, *Apocalypticism*, ed. R. Funk (New York: Herder and Herder, 1969), and K. Koch, *The Rediscovery of Apocalyptic*, Studies in Biblical Theology, New Series, No. 22 (London: S.C.M. Press, 1972).

20. G. Nickelsburg, "The Structure of Reality According to I Enoch

92-105," paper presented to the Catholic Biblical Association, August 1976.

21. Cronbach, "Righteousness," p. 86; Miranda, *Marx*, pp. 14-18.

22. J. Lauterbach, "The Ethics of the Halakah," *Rabbinic Essays*, p. 292.

23. Cited by Miranda, *Marx*, p. 16. See also elsewhere in this volume, and M. Hengel, *Property and Riches in the Early Church*, trans. J. Bowden (Philadelphia: Fortress Press, 1974).

24. N. Perrin, *The Kingdom of God in the Teaching of Jesus* (London: S.C.M. Press, 1963), pp. 74-78 and pp. 81-87, discusses the evidence for Kingdom as present and as future in the teaching of Jesus.

25. R. Schnackenburg, *God's Rule and Kingdom*, trans. J. Murray (New York: Herder and Herder, 1963), p. 13.

26. P. Hodgson, *Jesus as Word and Presence* (Philadelphia: Fortress Press, 1971), pp. 181-185.

27. N. Perrin, *Jesus and the Language of the Kingdom* (Philadelphia: Fortress Press, 1976), pp. 29-32.

28. "Toll collector" is used in place of the more familiar but less accurate "publican" or "tax collector," since these men were not the rich publicans of classical antiquity but were petty functionaries. They were scorned because of ritual uncleanliness from contact with Gentiles, because they were thought to be dishonest, and because they were seen as "quislings" of the Roman occupation. See, J. Donahue, "Tax Collectors and Sinners: An Attempt at Identification," *Catholic Biblical Quarterly*, 33 (1971) 39-61.

29. K. Stendahl, "The Apostle Paul and the Introspective Conscience of the West," *Harvard Theological Review*, 56 (1963) 199-215.

30. Miranda, *Marx*, pp. 174-177; E. Käsemann, " 'The Righteousness of God' in Paul," *New Testament Questions of Today* (Philadelphia: Fortress Press, 1969), pp. 169-182; *idem*, "Justification and Salvation History in the Epistle to the Romans," *Perspectives on Paul* (Philadelphia: Fortress Press, 1971), pp. 60-78; K. Kertlege, *"Rechtfertigung" bei Paulus*, Neutestamentliche Abhandlungen, 3 (Münster: Aschendorf, 1967); P. Stuhlmacher, *Gerechtigkeit Gottes bei Paulus, FRLANT*, 87 (Göttingen: Vandenhoeck und Ruprecht, 1965). Miranda and Kertlege are Catholic, and Käsemann and Stuhlmacher are Lutheran, which shows an ecumenical consensus on the social dimension of Paul's teaching on justification.

31. Käsemann, "Righteousness of God," pp. 181-182.

32. V. Furnish, *Theology and Ethics in Paul* (Nashville: Abingdon Press, 1968), pp. 115-116.

33. Kertlege, *"Rechtfertigung,"* pp. 135-143.

34. Paul uses the "eschatological now" to stress that the new era has been inaugurated in Christ; see J. A. Fitzmyer, "The Letter to the Romans," *JBC*, II, 301; "Pauline Theology," *ibid.*, 809-810.

35. Käsemann, "The Righteousness of God," p. 170.

112   THE FAITH THAT DOES JUSTICE

36. W. G. Kümmel, *The Theology of the New Testament*, trans. J. Steely (Nashville: Abingdon Press, 1973), p. 185.
37. Fitzmyer, "Pauline Theology," pp. 814-817.
38. *Ibid.*, p. 814.
39. *Ibid.*, p. 817.
40. Käsemann, "Righteousness," p. 180, sums up his view of the justice of God in Paul as "God's sovereignty over the world revealing itself eschatologically in Jesus."
41. R. Bultmann, *Theology of the New Testament*, trans. K. Grobel (New York: Charles Scribner's Sons, 1951), I, 253.
42. Fitzmyer, "Pauline Theology," p. 821.
43. Kertlege, "Rechtfertigung," pp. 161-166.
44. "Pauline Theology," p. 821.
45. Käsemann, "The Faith of Abraham in Romans 4," *Perspectives on Paul*, trans. M. Kohl (Phila.: Fortress Press, 1971), p. 82.
46. "Justification and Salvation History," p. 75.
47. For a survey of Matthew's theology, see J. Rohde, *Rediscovering the Teaching of the Evangelists*, trans. D. B. Barton, (Philadelphia: Westminster Press, 1967), pp. 47-113.
48. E. Linnemann, *Jesus of the Parables*, trans. J. Sturdy (New York: Harper and Row, 1967), pp. 105-113.
49. Dan O. Via, *The Parables: Their Literary and Existential Dimension* (Philadelphia: Fortress Press, 1967), pp. 137-144.
50. On the theology of Luke, see Rohde, *Rediscovering*, pp. 159-239, and M. Tolbert, "Leading Ideas of the Gospel of Luke," *Review and Expositor*, Vol. 64 (1967), 441-453.
51. See J. H. Yoder, *The Politics of Jesus* (Grand Rapids: Eerdmans, 1972), pp. 26-63.
52. Tolbert, p. 451.
53. *The Prophets*, p. 16.

Patristic Social Consciousness—
The Church and the Poor

**William J. Walsh, S.J. and
John P.Langan, S.J.**

The age of the Fathers was a time in which Christianity, originally perceived as a small Jewish sect, spread throughout the Roman world. Even though it endured external persecutions and internal divisions, it ultimately succeeded in capturing the minds and hearts of the majority of the urban population in the Empire. Many reasons have been suggested for its astonishing success. Today scholars tend to stress the fact that the reasons were social as well as theological.[1] Thus one recent study concludes that the ultimate triumph of Christianity is due (apart from external circumstances over which it had no control) to "a single, over-riding *internal* factor":

[This factor was] the radical sense of Christian community— open to all, insistent on absolute and exclusive loyalty, and concerned for every aspect of the believer's life. From the very beginning, the one distinctive gift of Christianity was this sense of community. Whether one speaks of "an age of anxiety" or "the crisis of the towns," Christian congregations provided a unique opportunity for masses of people to discover a sense of security and self-respect.[2]

An essential part of this sense of community depended on the willingness of Christians to aid those in need and on the teachings of the Christian Church with regard to the right use of material goods. Both Christian theory and practice involved a conflict with the values of the pagan world.

113

This essay will use the teachings of the Fathers on almsgiving and avarice to provide an overview of one important aspect of this conflict of values between Christianity and the pagan world. This overview will trace certain theological themes that are present in what the Fathers say about almsgiving and avarice and that give us an important aspect of the social thought of the Fathers. These themes are: (1) the Christian transformation of the values of the pagan world, (2) the Christian criticism of the desires of the human heart, (3) God as Creator of the material world and the purpose of material goods, (4) Christ and his identification with the poor, and (5) love and sharing in the Christian community.

I

THE TRANSFORMATION OF VALUES

The basic elements of the conflict of values between Christianity and the pagan world are already present in the writings of the apostolic Fathers. At the end of the first century the author of the *Didache* begins by repeating the scriptural teaching that people are faced with two options: they can choose the way of life or the way of death.[3] The Christian who chooses the way of life must first love God and then his neighbor as himself. In practice, this means that if one has material possessions, one must freely give to those who are in need: "Give to anyone that asks, without looking for any repayment, for it is the Father's pleasure that we should share his gracious bounty with all men."[4] The argument of the *Didache* sets the tone for much of the patristic literature on property; it runs as follows: "Never turn away the needy; share all your possessions with your brother, and do not claim that anything is your own. If you and he are joint participators in things immortal, how much more so in things that are mortal?"[5] In other words, our material possessions are not exclusively for our own use. The point is not merely that the things of earth belong to God, but that he has made them available for use in common by the rich as well as the poor. In effect, sharing material goods is to replace possessing them as a value for Christians.

The Shepherd of Hermas is a work of the second century. It is basically an impassioned call to repentance and the practice of penance. It reveals what will become a significant feature of patristic literature: a remarkable concern for the welfare of the rich as well as of the poor.

For Hermas, Christianity is viewed as an enormous construction job. New Christians are like stones being used in the building of a tall tower. The rich are "white round stones"[6] which have to be chiseled into the proper size and shape before they can fit into the building. The rich must become detached from their wealth before they can be genuine Christians. One proves that he is detached from his wealth by his willingness to help all who are in trouble financially, emotionally, and spiritually. In listing the kinds of behavior proper to a Christian, Hermas includes the following directives: assist widows, visit orphans and the poor, ransom God's servants, show hospitality, help oppressed debtors in their need.[7]

Moreover, Hermas insists that, since Christians are strangers in a strange land and not permanent residents of this world, they should not settle in like colonists and amass further wealth for wealth's sake. Their priorities must lie elsewhere: "Instead of fields, then, buy souls that are in trouble. . . . Look after widows and orphans and do not neglect them. Spend your riches and all your establishments you have received from God on this kind of field and houses!" There is only one reason, Hermas believes, why God has permitted some Christians to be wealthy: It is "to perform this ministry [to the poor] for him."[8] Here we can see how the other-worldly orientation of Christians leads them to redirect their concerns from the acquisition of material goods to the use of these goods for the aid of the needy.

Tatian, the choleric Syrian and pupil of Justin Martyr, defended Christianity in the late second century by savagely attacking Greek illusions about philosophy and religion. He rejected pagan fatalism and the ascription of personal and social values to the workings of blind chance or predetermined fate. In strong and succinct terms, he expressed the Christian rejection of the established values and desires of the pagan world:

I do not wish to be king; I am not anxious to be rich; I decline

military command; I detest fornication; I am not impelled by
an insatiable love of gain to go to sea; I do not contend for
chaplets of victory garlands; I am free from a mad thirst for
fame; I despise death; I am superior to every kind of disease;
grief does not consume my soul. . . . How is it that you are
fated to be sleepless through avarice? Why are you fated to
grasp at things often, and often to die? Die to the world,
repudiating the madness that is in it.[9]

Such a categorical rejection of traditional pagan values was in fact
a revolution.[10]

In a much more amicable defense of Christianity, which appeared sometime between 177 and 180, Athenagoras of Athens
reveals a similar reversal of commonly accepted values. He reports
that, in times of persecution, Christians endure with equanimity
the loss of what the general public considers to be matters of
paramount importance: their property, their reputations, and their
freedom from physical coercion.[11]

The Epistle to Diognetus, which dates from the late second or
early third century, is perhaps addressed to Diognetus, the tutor of
the emperor Marcus Aurelius. In it, the author invites the educated pagan reader to consider the question how human beings should
behave toward one another. First he notes that, from all evidence,
God is a God of love. God made the world for man, formed him in
his own image, gave him dominion over the world, sent his Son to
rescue him and promised him a share in his Kingdom. An awareness of what God has done should bring delirious joy. In gratitude
for God's gifts, one should imitate God by loving one's fellow men:

Happiness is not to be found in dominating one's fellows, or
in wanting to have more than his weaker brethren, or in possessing riches and riding roughshod over his inferiors. No one
can become an imitator of God like that, for such things are
wholly alien to his greatness. But if a man will shoulder his
neighbor's burden; if he be ready to supply another's need
from his own abundance; if, by sharing the blessings he has
received from God with those who are in want, he himself
becomes a god to those who receive his bounty—such a man
is indeed an imitator of God.[12]

The repudiation of pagan notions about happiness and the transformation of values that we find here clearly depend on a new conception of God's nature and his activity in the history of salvation. The Greek apologists stress the fact that belief in the existence of an all-bountiful God has resulted both in an astonishing reversal of current values and in a new breed of men and women who refuse to abandon the poor and the helpless to fate, but who rush to their assistance in times of crisis.

Clement of Alexandria, writing in the early third century, expressed the transformation of values in a more moderate and nuanced way that made it possible for the intelligent, the cultured and the wealthy to join the Church as orthodox Christians rather than become Valentinian Gnostics.

Given the nature of his audience, Clement quite naturally addressed himself to the problem of wealth. In *Christ the Educator*, a work devoted to the true basis of Christian morality, Clement reaffirms the scriptural position that the source of all man's troubles is the desire for wealth, not wealth itself. The world, he argues, is for our use; we may therefore use as much as we need, but consider everything else superfluous. There is no inherent value in poverty. What is extra must be shared with those who are in need. Disregard for this principle can lead to an excess of vulgarity. "It is farcical and downright ridiculous," he reported, "for men to bring out urinals of silver and chamberpots of transparent alabaster, as if grandly ushering in their advisers, and for rich women in their silliness to have privies made of gold. It is as if the wealthy were not able to relieve nature except in a grandiose style!"[13]

This line of thought leads Clement to ask how one is to estimate the true worth in any human being. Certainly, he contends, not on the basis of wealth:

To begin with, take ornaments away from a woman, and servants from the master, and you will discover that the master differs in no way from the slaves he has bought, neither in bearing, nor in appearance, nor in voice. In fact, he is very similar to his slaves in these respects. He differs from his slaves in one way only, in that he is more delicate and, because of his upbringing, more susceptible to sickness.[14]

Clement cautions the rich against ostentatious display, "lest some-one say of us 'His horse is worth fifteen talents, or his estate or servant or gold plate, but he himself would be expensive at three cents!' "[15] Clement sees that the Christian transformation of val-ues affects not merely our judgments about the objects that human persons desire but also our judgments about the worth of persons themselves.

The transformation of values that the Christian message brings with it lies behind some of the paradoxes expounded by the great preachers of the fourth century. Thus Basil the Great main-tains that the rich are themselves poor. "Poor you are indeed," Basil observes, "and wanting in everything that is good; poor in charity, poor in faith toward God, poor in hope everlasting."[16] John Chrysostom argues that the rich injure themselves by their neglect of the poor. "Don't you realize that, as the poor man withdraws silently, sighing and in tears, you actually thrust a sword into yourself, that it is you who received the more serious wound?"[17]

Augustine exemplifies the transformation of values when he calls for the replacement of selfish and acquisitive greed *(cupiditas)* by self-denying and generous love *(caritas)*. He urges: "Root out ruthless greed and plant charity. For, just as ruthless greed is the root of all evil, so is charity the root of all good."[18]

Elsewhere Augustine reworks the popular Epicurean slogan and Christianizes it. He rejects selfish hedonism and substitutes the radical Christian love which issues in direct action for the poor. He writes:

Let no one say, "Let us eat and drink for tomorrow we die," but rather . . . "Let us fast and pray, for tomorrow we die." I add . . . a third step . . . that as a result of your fast the poor man's hunger be satisfied; and, should you be unable to fast, that you give him more to eat. . . . Let Christians therefore say, "Let us fast and pray and give, for tomorrow we die." Or if they wish to mention only two points, I prefer that they say, "Let us fast and pray."[19]

II
CONVERSION FROM ATTACHMENT TO THINGS

Parallel to the transformation of values that Christian teaching brought with it was an emphasis on the conversion of the human heart. With regard to material goods, this conversion meant a change from the closed, grasping, and ultimately enslaving pursuit of one's own desires to the open, giving and ultimately liberating concern for the needs of the neighbor. In theological terms this is a conversion from idolatry to the service of the living God. In psychological terms, it involves a criticism of some widespread desires that are destructive of human solidarity and community.

Thus the author of the *Didache* denounces those who leave the main road to life and choose to follow the path of ruthless greed. They are "bent only on their own advantage, without pity for the poor or the feeling for the distressed." They "turn away the needy and oppress the afflicted" and "aid and abet the rich but arbitrarily condemn the poor."[20] Their social sins place them on the main highway to eternal death which is the ultimate disaster insofar as it will exclude them from any share in the true wealth of heaven.

A similar criticism of the selfish frame of mind of the rich is made by Hermas in *The Shepherd*. In his view, the rich themselves are suffering from a form of total self-absorption which makes them oblivious of the needs of the poor. When their own needs are superabundantly satisfied, they seem totally incapable of imagining what it is like to be poor and hence remain untouched by the excruciating sufferings of the poor. The poor, he must remind them, suffer "the same torture and affliction as a prisoner."[21] There are times when their torments are enough to drive them to suicide.

In the middle of the second century, Polycarp, bishop of Smyrna, who was martyred in 156, cites with approval the teaching of 1 Timothy 6:7 that the sum and substance of all evil is the love of money.[22] We come penniless into the world and we shall leave it without a single penny to our name. Any effort, therefore, to amass a fortune in this life is an extravagant waste of energy which should be invested elsewhere. We should first be content with what we need for physical life and then unleash our energies in pursuit of "justice, piety, fidelity, love, fortitude, and gentleness."

In the early third century, Clement of Alexandria points to the need for a similar conversion when he examines the different attitudes that Christians can have to riches. He begins with the man who remains addicted to the pursuit of wealth. What sets the money addict apart from other men is his callousness of heart. When the desire for gold and profits and real estate has reached narcotic proportions, he no longer has any room in his heart for thoughts of the Kingdom of heaven. In fact, where his heart should be he has instead a "piece of property" or "a mine."[23]

Nevertheless, Clement is convinced that it is possible for a wealthy Christian to be "poor in spirit." The Christian must acknowledge that the sum total of his inheritance is a gift from God, given "for his brother's sake more than for his own," so that he might be employed at some "divine and noble task" in the service of others. Further, the acid test whether he is the master and not the slave of his wealth lies in his ability to suffer its loss "cheerfully."[24] In a word, he must be detached.

Any discussion of detachment leads inevitably to the central issue of Christianity: one's relationship to Christ. In Clement's view, every human being is summoned to vote for or against Christ.[25] To vote for Christ demands detachment from family, wealth, and even physical life. Christ expects detachment only from what blocks an ever-deepening attachment to himself. Family, wealth, and the desire to stay alive are spiritually dangerous and are to be renounced when they become an obstacle to total commitment to Christ. Clement points out that although persecution by a hostile state is a formidable threat to a Christian, there is this other kind of persecution—the torment of addiction—whose origin lies in the heart of man.

> Passion and pleasure, unworthy hopes and dreams that perish, the flame, goads, stings, and madness of desire—that is the deeper, severer persecution, arising within, never ceasing, impossible to escape. In this state a man carries his enemy with him everywhere.[26]

What sort of motivation is required for a wealthy Christian to escape the enemy he carries within and become poor in spirit? Clement believes that a man can be both affluent and poor in spirit if he is altogether in love with God, with Christ, and with his fellow man. Consequently, Clement urges the rich Christian to probe more deeply into the mysteries of divine love where he will discover the intriguing fact that God is at once Father, Mother, and Lover.

> In his unspeakable greatness lies his fatherhood. In his fellowship with our experience is his motherhood. The Father takes a woman's nature in his love. It is in token of this that he begot the Son from his own being. The fruit born from love was love. Hence his advent, his incarnation, his suffering humanity. He gave himself as a ransom and left us his new covenant of love. As he gave his life for us, so are we to do for our brethren; and for this reason we cannot be grudging in our distribution of the poor and alien and transitory property of the world.[27]

In Clement we find that the basic change of attitude for the Christian is from the addictive pursuit of wealth to detachment in the use of wealth as a result of the heart's conversion to loving God above all things and one's neighbor as oneself.

In the next generation of the Church of Alexandria, Origen manifests a concern for the salvation of the rich as well as of the poor. In an effort to liberate the wealthy Christian from the passion of acquisitiveness, Origen summons him to self-examination. Let him analyze the desires of his heart and hold himself strictly accountable for them to God.

> God desires in some way to secure for himself those affections in the mind of man, and he knows that what a man loves with all his heart and with all his soul and with all his might—this for him is God. Let each one of us now examine himself and silently in his own heart decide which is the flame of love that chiefly and above all else is afire within him, which is the passion that he finds he cherishes more keenly than all others. You must yourselves pass judgment on the point and weigh

these things in the scales of your conscience; whatever it is
that weighs the heaviest in the balance of your affection, that
for you is God. But I fear that with very many the love of
gold will turn the scale, that down will come the weight of
covetousness lying heavy in the balance.[28]

Here, in a way that anticipates Augustine, we can clearly see how
greed is regarded in the early Church as a form of idolatry.

The combination of the transformation of values and the criticism of the desires of the human heart is clearly illustrated in the
following passage from Cyprian, who served as bishop of Carthage
in the mid-third century. He gives a withering account of the un-
bounded self-interest and the rapacious practices of the rich pagan
property owners in North Africa. In it he voices his deep dissatis-
faction with the social inequalities of the pagan world.

They add forests to forests and, excluding the poor from their
neighborhood, stretch out their fields far and wide into space
without any limits, possess immense heaps of silver and gold
and mighty sums of money, either in built-up riches or in
buried stores—even in the midst of their riches those are torn
to pieces by the anxiety of vague thought, lest the robber
should spoil, lest the murderer should attack, lest the envy of
some wealthier neighbor should become hostile, and harass
them with malicious lawsuits. . . . From him there is no liberality to dependence, no communication to the poor. And yet
such people call that their own money, which they guard with
zealous labor, shut-up at home as if it were another's. . . .
Their possession amounts to this only, that they can keep
others from possessing it; oh, what a marvelous perversion of
names! They call those things good which they absolutely put
to none but bad uses.[29]

Cyprian also discerned the evil effects of greed in the Christian community itself. After the bitter persecution of Decius in
which the faith of many Christians buckled, Cyprian searched out
the reason for the debacle. He pursued his investigation with un-
flinching honesty and concluded that God had allowed his Church

to be tested through persecution because bishops and laity were fortune-hunters and had neglected the interests of the poor.

Because the long years of peace had undermined our practice of the way of life which God had given us, our languid faith— I had almost said our *sleeping* faith—was now quickened by the heavenly visitation. . . . Each one was intent on adding to his inheritance. Forgetting what the faithful used to do under the apostles and what they should always be doing, each one with insatiable greed was engrossed in increasing his own property. Gone was the devotion of bishops to the service of God, gone was the clergy's faithful integrity, gone the generous compassion for the needy, gone all the discipline in our behavior. . . . Too many bishops . . . left their sees, abandoned their people, and toured the market in other territories on the lookout for profitable deals. While their brethren in the Church went hungry they wanted to have money in abundance, they acquired landed estates by fraud, and made profits by loans at compound interest.[30]

It was a scandal to Cyprian that so many wealthy Christians had apostasized in the persecution. Escape would have been easy. "A man had only to leave the country and sacrifice his property," Cyprian writes scornfully. "Since man is born to die, who is there who must not eventually leave his country and give up his inheritance?"[31] There is, moreover, no point in glossing over the true reason for their shocking betrayal of Christ.

What deceived many was a blind attachment to their patrimony, and if they were not free and ready to take themselves away, it was because their property held them in chains . . . chains which shackled their courage and choked their faith and hampered their judgment and throttled their soul. . . . If they stored up their treasure in heaven, they would not now have an enemy and a thief within their own household. . . . They think of themselves as owners, whereas it is they rather who are owned: enslaved as they are to their own property, they are not the masters of their money but its slaves.[32]

Cyprian goes on to urge the apostates to express their repentance by generous almsgiving in reparation for their sins.

But Cyprian knew that the wealthy were obstinate and their spiritual sterility evoked from him a brusque diagnosis of their true condition. "The deep and profound darkness of avarice has blinded your carnal heart. You are the captive and slave of your money; you are tied by the chains and bonds of avarice, and you whom Christ had already freed are bound anew!"[33] The rich who hoard their possessions should be shamed by the generosity of the widow in the Gospel who gave all she had.[34] We see Cyprian's repeated interpretation of greed and avarice as forms of slavery, as denials of the freedom brought by Christ and maintained by generous love of him.

A somewhat different metaphor, which focuses on the addictive character of greed rather than on its inversion of priorities, is used by Basil of Caesarea in the fourth century. He sees the rich as suffering from ruthless greed, which is as enslaving an addiction as gluttony: "Surely what ails his soul is much what ails the glutton, who would burst with cramming rather than give the poor any of his leavings."[35] The danger is that one can become mesmerized by the thought of gold and therefore incapable of compassion.

> The bright gleam of gold delights you. . . . Everything is gold to your eyes and fancy; gold is your dream at night and your waking care. As a raving madman does not see things themselves but imagines things in his diseased fancy, so your greed-possessed soul sees gold and silver everywhere. Sight of gold is dearer to you than sight of the sun. Your prayer is that everything may be changed to gold, and your schemes are set on bringing it about.[36]

Their addiction causes the rich to take advantage of the scarcity of food and hike the price of grain while the poor are starving. Some actually refuse to give away to the poor the grain they have stored in their warehouses, even though they know it will rot tomorrow. It is unconscionable, says Basil, thus to traffic in human misery.

People who are addicted to avarice, Basil contends, suffer a loss of memory. They forget that they are the stewards, not the owners, of what they possess. Borrowing an image from Cicero, Basil explains that the rich are "like a man who, in taking his seat in the theater, would like to keep others from entering, and . . . be the only one to enjoy the show that all others have just as much right to see."[37]

Can the wealthy man ever find relief from his addiction? Basil is convinced he can and suggests positive action. Let the wealthy grain dealers throw open their barns to the starving poor.

As a great river flows by a thousand channels through fertile country, so let your wealth run through many conduits to the homes of the poor. Wells that are drawn from flow the better; left unused, they go foul. So money kept standing still is worthless; moving and changing hands, it helps the community and brings increase.[38]

And so, in addition to repeating most of the earlier patristic themes, Basil reveals a special concern for the wealthy. An experienced man of affairs himself, he reasons calmly with the avaricious rich person as with a sick child, diagnoses the illness with clinical accuracy, and prescribes the remedy that will no doubt cauterize but will eventually heal.

John Chrysostom employs a striking biblical comparison to illustrate the situation of the covetous and greedy. In his view, many wealthy men and women are possessed by the evil passion of ruthless greed in much the same way as the demoniac of Gerasa was possessed by demons. Like him, they burst all the ordinary restraints and enslave themselves to Mammon. "Such men," he says, "live in desert places, even though they dwell in the midst of our cities."[39] The avaricious man is a slave of money, a double agent who masks his real allegiance, a Christian who worships Mammon, not Christ.[40]

In response to the charge of idolatry, the rich demonstrate: "But I've never made an idol . . . nor set up an altar nor sacrificed sheep nor poured libations of wine; no, I come to church, I lift up my hands in prayer to the only-begotten Son of God; I partake of the mysteries, I communicate in prayer and in all other duties of a Christian. How then . . . can I be a worshiper of idols?"[41] Chrysostom replies that it is astonishing how the rich, who once experienced the loving-kindness of God and saw that the Lord is gracious, can forsake him for a cruel tyrant: "You pretend to be serving God, but in reality you have submitted yourself to the hard and galling yoke of ruthless greed."[42] Unfortunately the possession of great wealth is dangerous because it often undermines the virtue of compassion. For Chrysostom, mercy is critically essential to Christian life: "Let us judge that we are not really living at those times when we are not showing mercy."[43]

To avoid exploiting the poor, to hold the avaricious instinct in check, to recognize the hidden identity of Christ in the wretched of the earth and respond to their needs requires a radical enlargement of the human heart. But for this to occur, God must act. In the words of St. Augustine, "If our hearts are open, God moves among us; but for our hearts to be opened, we must let God himself do the work."[44]

III
THE CREATION OF THE MATERIAL UNIVERSE

The first two sections of this paper have dealt largely with the ethical and psychological aspects of patristic teaching on avarice and almsgiving. The next two sections will be devoted to the more strictly theological themes of God's creation of material goods and of Christ's identification of the poor, which in turn will lead us to the ecclesiological theme of sharing in a community of love.

We have already seen that the author of the *Epistle to Diognetus* writing at the end of the second century urges Christians to imitate God's beneficence and greatness in sharing their material goods with their neighbors.[45] A similar view is put forward by Cyprian in his treatise *On Works and Almsgiving* in the mid-third century. There he returns to the example of the apostolic Church "when the faith of believers was warm with a fervor of faith still new." Their practice demonstrates that "whatever belongs to God, belongs to all by our appropriation of it, nor is anyone kept from his benefits and gifts, nor does anything prevent the whole human race from equally enjoying God's goodness and generosity." Let the rich, Cyprian urges, imitate God's generosity and his limitless bounty which touches all the members of the human race: "Thus the day illuminates equally; the sun radiates, the rain moistens, the wind blows, and for those who sleep there is one sleep; and the splendor of the stars and moon is common." Let the rich share what they have with the poor, and they will become "an imitator of God the Father."[46]

In the following century, Gregory of Nyssa reminds his fellow Christians that they are taught "by every syllable" in Scripture to imitate their Father in heaven.[47] Let them be as compassionate as he, and hurry to the aid of their brothers in distress, especially the sick. For Gregory, the right to private property is not absolute; rather it yields to the demands of one's fellow human beings. For rich and poor are all of the same stock.[48] Brother should therefore share the family inheritance with brother in equal portions. But actually brothers have become more savage than wild animals.

If one should seek to be absolute possessor of all, refusing even a third or a fifth [of his possessions]to his brothers, then he is a cruel tyrant, a savage with whom there can be no dealing, an insatiate beast gloatingly shutting its jaws over the meal it will not share. Or rather he is more ruthless than any beast; wolf does not drive wolf from the prey, and a pack of dogs will tear the same carcass; thus man in his limitless greed will not admit one fellow creature to a share in his riches.[49]

Gregory's Western contemporary, Ambrose of Milan (339-397), defended the rights of the poor against the powerful. He first treated the question of justice in a short work devoted to the duties of the clergy. Basic to his thought is the traditional patristic belief that all men have the right to a share of God's gifts—a right that he felt was denied far too many of his contemporaries.

God has ordered all things to be produced so that there should be food in common for all, and that the earth should be the common possession of all. Nature, therefore, has produced a common right for all, but greed has made it a right for a few.[50]

Ambrose also devoted a short work entitled *Naboth* to the question of rich and poor. In the Old Testament it is related how Ahab's greed for Naboth's small plot of land resulted in Naboth's death. Ambrose sadly reports that the episode has a never-failing relevance.

> The tale of Naboth, ancient though it may be, is of perennial application. . . . Ahab is not one person, someone born long ago; everyday, alas, the world sees Ahabs born, never to die out—if one such die, a multitude rises up instead, and the spoilers still outnumber the spoiled. And Naboth is not one person either, a poor man who was once murdered; every day some Naboth is done to death, every day the poor are murdered.[51]

This short work is thus directed not against the rich but against the avaricious. Ambrose uses the story of Naboth to develop the common patristic doctrine that all creation was made available for all mankind and that the rich are essentially its stewards. He deplores the ruthless greed of the avaricious, their heartless exploitation of the poor, and the ostentation of their luxury. As far as the avaricious are concerned, almsgiving is defined as restitution for stolen goods: "You are not making a gift of your possessions to the poor person. You are handing over to him what is his."[52]

In this same period, John Chrysostom recognizes the right to private property, but he too looks upon the wealthy as the stewards of God's gifts. For that reason, he clearly distinguishes between wealth and ruthless greed.

> I am often reproached for continually attacking the rich. Yes, because the rich are continually attacking the poor. But those I attack are not the rich as such, only those who misuse their wealth. I point out constantly that those I accuse are not the rich, but the rapacious; wealth is one thing, covetousness another. Learn to distinguish.[53]

While the wealthy have the right to use their possessions for the necessities of life, what remains belongs in strict justice to the destitute. "The rich are in the possession of the goods of the poor, even if they have acquired them honestly or inherited them legally."[54] If they do not share, "the wealthy are a species of bandit."[55] Chrysostom buttresses his position by spelling out the patristic principle of equality: "Do not say 'I am using what belongs to me.' You are using what belongs to others. All the wealth of the world belongs to you and to the others in common, as the sun, air, earth, and all the rest."[56] Unshared wealth is therefore a form of embezzlement.

Thus we find that in the mainstream of patristic teaching the things of the earth are created by God and so they are good. Human persons then have a right to possess and to use material goods. But these goods are to be used to meet the needs of all human beings, the poor as well as the rich, and their owners have the opportunity and the responsibility to imitate the goodness of God, who is both Creator and Father.

IV
IDENTIFICATION OF CHRIST WITH THE POOR

Christians have a further motive in aiding the poor and the needy, namely the presence of Christ in them. Thus Cyprian addresses the bishops of Numidia after raising one hundred thousand sesterces as ransom money for the release of Numidian Christians from their barbarian captors. He writes:

The captivity of our brethren must be reckoned as our captivity, and the grief of those who are endangered is to be esteemed as our grief, since indeed there is one body of our union. . . . It was the temples of God which were taken captive, and . . . we ought not by long inactivity and neglect of their suffering to allow the temples of God to be long captive. . . . Christ is to be contemplated in our captive brethren. . . .

Our brotherhood, considering all these things according to your letter . . . have all promptly and willingly and liberally

gathered together supplies of money for the brethren. . . .
We have then sent you a sum of one hundred thousand sesterces, which have been collected here in the church. . . .[57]

Gregory of Nyssa reminds the rich that they must recognize the
true identity of the poor and acknowledge their special dignity and
role in the Christian community.

Do not despise these men in their abjection; do not think them
of no account. Reflect what they are and you will understand
their dignity; they have taken upon them the person of our
Savior. For he, the compassionate, has lent them his own person wherewith to abash the unmerciful and the haters of the
poor. . . . The poor are the treasurers of the good things that
we look for, the keepers of the gates of the Kingdom, opening
them to the merciful and shutting them on the harsh and un-
charitable. They are the strongest of accusers, the best of
defenders—not that they accuse or defend in words, but that
the Lord beholds what is done toward them, and every deed
cries louder than a herald to him who searches all hearts.[58]

The claim of the poor is based on their identification with Christ,
and their function in the judgment derives from Matthew 25:31-46.
    John Chrysostom draws similar conclusions from the iden-
tification of Christ with the poor:

You eat to excess; Christ eats not even what he needs. You
eat a variety of cakes; he eats not even a piece of dried bread.
You drink fine Thracian wine; but on him you have not bestowed so much as a cup of cold water. You lie on a soft and
embroidered bed; but he is perishing in the cold. . . . You
live in luxury on things that properly belong to him. Why,
were you the guardian of a child and, having taken control of
his estate, you neglected him in his extreme need, you would
have ten thousand accusers and you would suffer the punishment set by law. At the moment, you have taken possession of
the resources that belong to Christ and you consume them
aimlessly. Don't you realize that you are going to be held accountable?[59]

It is obvious, moreover, that, for Chrysostom, the poor actually represent the person of Christ in a way the rich do not. "Because he is a poor man," Chrysostom argues, "feed him; because Christ is then fed, feed him."[60]

In his reflections about wealthy bequests for church decorations, Chrysostom further develops the principle that the poor represent Christ. Like earlier Fathers, he bases his teaching on the Pauline doctrine of the body of Christ.

Do you really wish to pay homage to Christ's body? Then do not neglect him when he is naked. At the same time that you honor him here [in church] with hangings made of silk, do not ignore him outside when he perishes from cold and nakedness. For the One who said "This is my body" . . . also said "When I was hungry you gave me nothing to eat." . . . For is there any point in his table being laden with golden cups while he himself is perishing from hunger? First fill him when he is hungry and then set his table with lavish ornaments. Are you making a golden cup for him at the very moment when you refuse to give him a cup of cold water? Do you decorate his table with cloths flecked with gold, while at the same time you neglect to give him what is necessary for him to cover himself? . . . I'm saying all this not to forbid your gifts of munificence, but to admonish you to perform those other duties at the same time, or rather before, you do these. No one was ever condemned for neglecting to be munificent: for the neglect of others hell itself is threatened, as well as unquenchable fire. . . . The conclusion is: Don't neglect your brother in his distress while you decorate his house. Your brother is more truly his temple than any church building.[61]

To the rich who imagine that they can make offerings to the Church from money extorted from the poor, Chrysostom quotes Sirach 34:20: "To offer a sacrifice from the possessions of the poor is like killing a son before his father's eyes." He immediately comments: "Write this passage in our minds, on our walls, on our hands, in our consciences—write it everywhere. Extortion is more wanton a crime than murder."[62]

So convinced is Chrysostom of Christ's identity with the poor that he does not hesitate to put words in the mouth of Christ.

> It is such a slight thing I beg. . . . Nothing very expensive. . . . Bread, a roof, words of comfort. [If the rewards I promised hold no appeal for you] then show at least a natural compassion when you see me naked, and remember the nakedness I endured for you on the cross. . . . I fasted for you then, and I suffer hunger for you now; I was thirsty when I hung on the cross, and I thirst still in the poor, in both ways to draw you to myself and to make you humane for your own salvation.[63]

It is because Chrysostom sees Christ in the poor that he made a suggestion which must have startled the rich in his congregation. The rich, he says, should actually invite the poor to live in their own homes.

> Make yourself a guest-chamber in your own house: set up a bed there, set up a table there and a candlestick. . . . Have a room to which Christ may come. Say, "This is Christ's cell; this building is set apart for him." Even though it is just a little insignificant room in the basement, he does not disdain it. Naked and a stranger, Christ goes about—all he wants is shelter. Make it available even though it is as little as this.[64]

Augustine drew his teaching on rich and poor from a close reading of Scripture and from his study of Ambrose and the Cappadocian Fathers. For him, as for the earlier Fathers, the proper use of wealth is based squarely upon the Pauline doctrine of the body of Christ.[65] The risen Christ, Augustine taught, is at the right hand of the Father interceding for us, but he is also present in his followers on earth.

> Hold in awe the Christ who is above; but recognize him here below. Have Christ above granting his bountiful gifts, but recognize him here in his need. Down here he is poor; up there he is rich.[66]

In Augustine's view, there is a real but hidden identity between Christ and Christian which calls for vigorous community action in behalf of the needy.[67] Christ is the head; the Church is the body. Where the body here on earth suffers, Christ the head suffers too. The crisis of a single individual is a crisis for the whole Church.

> For consider, brethren, the love of our head. He is in heaven, yet he suffers here, as long as his Church suffers here. Here Christ is hungry, here he is thirsty, is naked, is a stranger, is sick, is in prison. For whatever his body suffers here, he has said that he himself suffers.[68]

The sound health of the body, moreover, depends on unity and charity. Charity is one of the body's vital signs; if the body grows cold in charity, it becomes feeble and weak. The Dives of the Gospel parable is, for Augustine, the classic example of the rigidity of the human heart. Dives dies and is rightly buried in hell. "He desired a drop of water, though he gave not a scrap of food himself; he did not get it out of righteous judgment, who refused to give out of cruel avarice."[69] Like Chrysostom, Augustine's sharpest words are directed at those who actively exploit the poorer members of the body of Christ.

> A certain exploiter of the property of others says to me, "I am not like that rich man. I give love-feasts, I send food to the prisoners in jail, I clothe the naked, I take in strangers." Do you really think that you are giving? . . . You fool. . . . You must grasp the fact that when you feed a Christian, you feed Christ; when you exploit a Christian, you exploit Christ. . . . If then he shall go into eternal fire, to whom Christ will say, "When naked you did not clothe me"? What place in the eternal fire is reserved for him to whom Christ shall say, "I was clothed and you stripped me bare"?[70]

When the members of the body grow cold and callous, only the head can cure them. Only the head, by an infusion of love, can empower the members to be united to their brothers by the bond of charity.[71]

V

SHARING ONE'S POSSESSIONS WITHIN THE COMMUNITY

When Augustine considers the relation between Christ and the poor in terms of the relation between head and members of the body, he is using a theological doctrine that is at the same time a basis for judgment of our treatment of the poor and a foundation for our understanding of the Church. We can say that in general the Fathers discuss the treatment of the poor in a way that depends on and illustrates their understanding of the Church as a community of love and of sharing. This way of dealing with the problems of the poor goes back even to the time of the New Testament.

There were both well-to-do and poor among the first Christians at Corinth, and St. Paul (1 Cor. 11:17-20) reports that class distinctions were at the root of the disturbances at the agape-meal and the Lord's supper. As J. Hering remarks, "Social inequality was shamefully displayed, and that at a time when brotherly unity should have been stronger than ever. Instead of waiting until all were present and the food brought by each member was fairly shared out, the more affluent hurried to eat their share without waiting for the arrival of the poor, who might have been detained longer by their work."[72]

Later, the Corinthian community was again split into factions and Clement of Rome wrote urging the Church to close its ranks out of a concern for the true well-being of the whole body of Christ. "The strong are not to ignore the weak," he insists, "and the weak are to respect the strong. Rich men should provide for the poor and the poor should thank God for giving them somebody to supply their wants."[73] What is the motive for this mutual sharing? It is the common debt which all men owe God. The Creator brought men into being, as if "out of a tomb"; to God "we owe everything" and are thereby obliged to return thanks "by good deeds and not by words."[74] In a celebrated passage[75] on the power of love as the binding force of the Christian community, Clement echoes the teaching of John and Paul on love (John 15; Colossians 3:14; 1 Cor. 13:4-7). Love is not merely a question of patient endurance, of humility, peace and reconciliation; love must prove itself in action. Christ is the supreme model of love because he gave blood, body and his life's soul for us. Clement believes that Christian love is perhaps best illustrated by those who, for love of their neighbor, have sold themselves into slavery to raise ransom money for others less fortunate than themselves. Clement also mentions many more who "have sold themselves into slavery and given the money to provide others with food."[76]

The community of sharing between rich and poor in the Church is an important concern in *The Shepherd of Hermas*, which uses the parable of the elm and the vine to illustrate how both rich and poor draw profit from almsgiving.

> This vine . . . bears fruit, but the elm is sterile. However, this vine cannot bear fruit, unless it climbs up the elm. Otherwise, it spreads all over the ground. And, if it does bear, the fruit is rotten, because it has not been hanging from the elm. So, when the vine has been attached to the elm, it bears fruit both from itself and from the elm. So, you see that the elm yields fruit also.[77]

In a word, by a kind of spiritual symbiosis, the rich and the poor can help one another: the rich give money and the poor pray for the rich. Thus both "become associates in the just work."[78]

Hermas is also quick to point out the inadequacies of an overly individualistic and self-centered spirituality. He follows the lead of Isaiah 58 and insists upon a spiritual fast which involves keeping the commandments of God.[79] As for actual fasting, he has the following recommendations: "On the day of your fast do not taste anything except bread and water. Compute the total expense for the food you would have eaten on the day on which you intended to keep a fast and give it to a widow, an orphan, or someone in need. . . . Observe this [fast] . . . together with your children and your whole household."[80] This done, he adds, their prayer will be efficacious before God.

The social connections between almsgiving and the life of the

Christian community are relied on by Clement of Alexandria in his resolution of the problem that confronts wealthy Christians in identifying those who are actually poor. Appearances are so misleading that it is almost impossible to distinguish between the deserving poor and the free-loaders. Rather surprisingly, Clement's advice echoes the teaching of *The Shepherd of Hermas*:

> You must not try to distinguish between the deserving and the undeserving. You may easily make a mistake, and, as the matter is in doubt, it is better to benefit the undeserving than, in avoiding this, to miss the good. We are told not to judge. We must open our generosity to all who are enrolled as disciples, paying no attention to appearance or condition, or weakness or tattered clothes. These are but the outer form. . . . But within, in the soul, the Father dwells and the Son, who died for us and rose with us.[81]

What "profits" may a rich man expect to reap from being poor in spirit? Clement's answer is to present a most engaging group portrait of a wealthy Christian surrounded by a band of paupers.

> The aged, the orphans, the widows, the men who wear the uniform of love, you will select to be your spiritual bodyguard, unarmed, unstained with blood, your sure defense against shipwreck or disease or robber's attack or demon's might.[82]

From the poor, the rich man may expect a return of love that takes many forms: nursing care, urgent intercessory prayers in his behalf, instruction, a kindly word of counsel or perhaps even a sharp word of protest. Embedded here is the germ of the idea, to be more fully developed by John Chrysostom, that the protest of the poor can be a positive service to the rich who exploit them. What is fundamental to Clement's resolution of this perennial problem is his sense that both giver and receiver, rich and poor, form one community of support and sharing.

In the next generation Origen resolves this same problem in a different way but with something of the same sense of community.

Origen urges the clergy to be trustworthy and sensible administrators of the community's resources. It is imperative, he says, that they be scrupulously honest and frugal in determining the amount to be set aside for their personal use. Thus, his rule of thumb for allocating funds for the support of the clergy is illuminating: "We must not keep more for ourselves than we give to our hungry or thirsty brothers, or to the naked, or to those . . . oppressed by want."[83] Origen reverts to the teaching of the *Didache*, inasmuch as he feels that it would be shocking extravagance to waste on malingerers what in actuality belongs to the poor. The clergy must therefore consider "the merits of each particular case."[84]

Origen teaches that it is the common duty of all Christians to fast as a way to support the hungry. It is the special duty of the wealthy and the clergy to care for the poor. The rich will be held accountable for the use of their wealth in much the same way as the priest will be required to give an account to God for his use of common Church funds.

Tertullian, the great pioneer of early Latin theology, manifests a similar sense of community and social responsibility in his writings about the Church and its life. Throughout the entire world there is but one authentic and original Christian Church. Its distinguishing marks are three: peace, brotherhood, hospitality. The members of the Church are brothers who live together throughout the world in peace and who welcome each other into their homes with hospitality.[85] Their behavior is in striking contrast to the rest of mankind which is provincial-minded, prone to war, and selfish in the use of its possessions. The Christian attitude toward property, therefore, is one of the three essential characteristics of the Church.

For Tertullian, moreover, the Church is a living organism. "Where there are two together," he wrote, "there is the Church—and the Church is Christ."[86] Whenever one member suffers, the entire Church suffers. Whenever a Christian stretches out his hand to relieve the sufferings of another, he is "in touch with Christ." The sufferer's grateful prayers to God for his benefactor are in effect the prayers of Christ.

Again the practice of the *agape* is an instance of Christian concern. Its name, Tertullian notes, indicates its purpose; it is "a love-meal"[87] where prosperous Christians share food with their hungry brothers and sisters.

In his *Apology*, Tertullian gives more information about another sign of Christian love, i.e., the practice of maintaining a "community chest," which Justin had reported earlier. It signals to the watching world the love with which Christians embrace one another.

> We are a society with a common religious feeling, unity of discipline, a common bond of hope. We meet in gathering and congregation to approach God in prayer, massing our forces to surround him. This violence that we do him pleases God. . . . Even if there is a chest of a sort, it is not made of money paid in entrance-fees, as if religion were a matter of contract. Every man once a month brings some modest coin— or whatever he wishes, and only if he does wish, and if he can; for nobody is compelled; it is a voluntary offering. You might call them the trust funds of piety. For they are not spent upon banquets nor drinking-parties nor thankless eating-houses; but to feed the poor and to bury them, for boys and girls who lack property and parents, and then for slaves grown old and shipwrecked mariners; and any who may be in mines, islands or prisons, provided that it is for the sake of God's school, become the pensioners of their confession. Such work of love (for so it is) puts a mark upon us, in the eyes of some. "Look," they say, "how they love one another" (for themselves hate one another); "and how they are ready to die for each other" (for themselves will be readier to kill each other). . . . So we, who are united in mind and soul, have no hesitation about sharing property. All is common among us— except our wives."[88]

Elsewhere, Tertullian wrote what is perhaps the most beautiful brief sketch of an ideal Christian marriage in patristic literature; in it, almsgiving and the corporal works of mercy rank high.

> How beautiful, then, the marriage of true Christians, two who are one in hope, one in desire, one in the way of life they

follow, one in the religion they practice. They are as brother
and sister, both servants of the same master. Nothing divides
them, either in flesh or in spirit. They are, in very truth, *two
in one flesh* (Gen. 2:24); and where there is one flesh there is
also one spirit. They pray together, they worship together,
they fast together; instructing one another, encouraging one
another, strengthening one another. Side by side they visit
God's church and partake of God's banquet; side by side they
face difficulties and persecution, and share their consolation.
They have no secrets from one another: they never shun each
other's company; they never bring sorrow to each other's
hearts. Unembarrassed they visit the sick and assist the needy.
They give alms without anxiety. . . . Hearing and seeing this,
Christ rejoices. To such as these he gives his peace. Where
there are two together (Mt. 18:20), there also he is present.[89]

It is, therefore, Tertullian's belief that the Christian Church is
a body, one of whose most vital functions is the constant care and
support of all its weaker and ailing members.

The directives on the use of wealth that Cyprian gave to his
flock as bishop of Carthage show a tendency, similar to Origen's,
to regulate the use of wealth by a sense of the needs of the community and its members. Cyprian was, for instance, an enthusiastic
supporter of celibacy and he urged the wealthy Roman women
who had chosen to live as virgins to use their wealth wisely. Wealth
in itself, he argues, is not evil. Just as one may use iron to plow the
earth but not to murder a fellow man, just as one may use incense,
wine, and fire but not to offer worship to pagan gods, so one may
use wealth but not for mere personal gratification. "Let the poor
feel that you are wealthy," Cyprian advises the wealthy virgins.
"Let the needy feel that you are rich. Lend your estate to God; give
food to Christ."[90]

His correspondence as bishop reveals that Cyprian was conscientious about making sure that the poor received adequate aid.[91]
Thus he designated various sums of money for prisoners,[92] widows,
and the sick.[93] Once Cyprian judged that a converted actor was eli-
gible for support from the common Church funds because he could
no longer practice a profession forbidden to Christians.[94] Further-

more, Cyprian instructed his faithful that no special deference is to be shown to the rich merely on the score that they are wealthy. "In the Church," he writes, "he is rich who is rich in faith."[95]

When he confronted the problem of reconciling to the Church wealthy apostates who had weakened under the stress of persecution and who had now repented, Cyprian prescribed generous almsgiving.

A man should not keep and love that patrimony which ensnared him and caused his downfall. Such property must be shunned like an enemy, fled from like a highwayman; those who own it must fear it as they would fear poison or the sword. Let what remains of it serve only to make reparation for the guilt of sin. Let your largess be without delay, without stint; let all your wealth be expended on the healing of your wound; let us use our goods and our riches to make our Lord beholden to us, for he is one day to be our judge.[96]

Their almsgiving should be modeled on the practice of the first generation of Christians: "They gave it once, and generously. They gave their all to be distributed by the apostles—yet they had no such crimes [as yours] to repair."[97]

Cyprian returned to the example of the primitive Church in *The Unity of the Catholic Church* and developed it further.[98] Once upon a time, he argues, there was in the Church a true union of minds and hence a genuine community. What united the early Christians was obedience and charity in Christ. The result was a love community. Today, he writes, the union of minds has grown slack and consequently the community's generosity has disintegrated. Originally Christians sold their houses and their estates and gave the money to the apostles for distribution to those in need. Today Christians do not give even tithes—an unmistakable sign that the faith has withered. The present need, he concludes, is for conversion and an awakening from the "sleep of our past inertia."[99]

In the fourth century, John Chrysostom returns to the task of establishing a religious community of concern between the rich and the poor and of affirming their equality before the judgment and

the grace of the Lord. He assesses the complaints of the rich about
the vices of the poor, beginning with the charge of idleness. Chrysostom admits the truth of the charge, but counters by reminding
the rich of their own spiritual idleness.

> If a poor man comes to you asking for bread, there is no end
> of complaints and reproaches and charges of idleness; you
> upbraid him, insult him, jeer at him. You fail to realize that
> you too are idle and yet God grants you gifts. Now don't tell
> me that you are doing something. . . . If you list earning
> money, business deals, the care and growth of your resources,
> I say, "No, not these, but alms, prayers, the protection of the
> injured and the like are genuine work." And yet God has
> never said to us, "Because you are idle, I refuse to light up the
> sun for you; because you are doing nothing of any real con-
> sequence, I extinguish the moon and paralyze the womb of the
> earth. I hold back the lakes, the fountains, the rivers. I erase
> the atmosphere and withhold the annual rainfall." No, God
> gives everything in abundance. . . . So when you see a poor
> man and say, "It really galls me that this fellow, young and
> healthy as he is, has nothing and yet would like to be fed even
> though he is idle; clearly he is a slave, a runaway who has
> deserted his master," I urge you to speak those words to your-
> self; or rather, allow him the freedom to address them to you
> and he will say with greater justice: "It galls me that you are
> healthy, idle, and practice none of the things which God has
> commanded, you who are a runaway from the command-
> ments of your Lord, settle down in wickedness as in a foreign
> land, in drunkenness and reveling, in theft, in extortion, in
> subverting the houses of other men." You charge him with
> idleness; I charge you with corrupt behavior.[100]

At the same time he scourges the idle rich, Chrysostom makes
it clear that he is not advocating a life of idleness for the poor. He
favors full employment, for sloth is the instructor of every sort of
evil. What he opposes is man's inhumanity: "If you are prompt in
showing mercy," he says to the rich, "the man who is poor will
soon be rid of idleness and you of cruelty."[101]

But, say the rich, the poor are inveterate liars. Chrysostom replies that the poor are the more to be pitied because poverty hardens a man and makes him deceitful. Actually, the wealthy are likewise hardened:

> We are far from feeling any compassion; we even say in our cruelty, "Haven't you already received something time and time again?" That's the way we speak. What sense does it make? He was fed once; does that mean he has no need to be fed again? Why don't you make the same laws for your own stomach and speak to it the same way: "You were filled yesterday and the day before; don't expect anything more"?[102]

Chrysostom then urges the rich to their duty of almsgiving. It is important to remember, that, for him, almsgiving ordinarily meant "not mere giving but lavish giving."[103] What does lavish mean? In the Old Testament the Jews were accustomed to give tithes; in the New Covenant, where they are ordered to give up everything, Christians should give much more than tithes.[104] Further, almsgiving is a useful art which has Christ for a teacher. It is, in fact, far more useful than any other art. Asceticism, it is true, benefits the ascetic, but almsgiving benefits everyone. It covers and quenches sin, for acts of mercy "counter-balance" the weight of sin which each of us bears. Almsgiving, finally, is the "mother of charity,"[105] for, without it, charity is a sham.

Above all, therefore, there must be charity. Love, for Chrysostom, is absolutely essential to the full development of Christian life. The Christian without love is like a ship's rigging without masts, like houses without tie-beams, like the bones of the body without its ligaments.[106]

Thus John Chrysostom recognized the poor as privileged members of the body of Christ and took upon himself the task of defending them against their wealthy oppressors. To their defense he brought the integrity of his personal life, the trumpet voice of an Old Testament prophet, and the clear and direct teaching of the Gospels. Never perhaps had the poor possessed so eloquent a public defender.

Like Cyprian of Carthage, Ambrose of Milan addresses the

problem of almsgiving within a Church community of which he is the episcopal head. Thus he summons his clergy to a leadership role in righting injustice and lists the multiple ways in which they can serve God's poor. Charity should begin at home and then spread out to encompass the entire world.[107] The priest may give to his relatives who are in need, but not too much; they are not to be made rich while the poor remain poor.[108] One should care for orphans, make provision for their education, and provide dowries for orphan girls.[109] Further, one should protect widows and orphans against the powerful, even the officials of the Empire.[110] One should be diligent in seeking out the poor who would otherwise remain hidden: those who are sick or in prison or who are simply too ashamed to beg.[111] One should be willing to tear up the bond of one's debtor without asking for payment.[112] One should ransom those who have fallen captive to the barbarians. The highest form of liberality is "to redeem captives, to save them from the hands of their enemies, to snatch men from death, and, most of all, women from shame, to restore children to their parents, parents to their children, and to give back a citizen to his country."[113]

The Church, Ambrose maintains, has gold in its possession not for hoarding but to spend on those in need.[114] To the objection that the temple of God has its need of ornament, he replies that the sacraments do not need gold; the gold that can be tried, the useful gold, the gold of Christ, is the gold used to redeem (or ransom) long lines of captives.[115] Gold should be used for ransom, he claims, because Christ's blood was used for ransom.[116] Hence it is permissible to break up the sacred vessels, even "the mystic cup," and sell them to ransom captives.[117]

VI

THE CHURCH AND THE SOCIAL SYSTEM

Reflection on the theme of community in the teaching of the Fathers on almsgiving shows that they understand the Church as a community of sharing and mutual support. This view is presented metaphorically in the parable of the elm and the vine in *The Shepherd of Hermas*. More practically, in the teaching of Clement and

Origen, of Tertullian, Cyprian and Ambrose, this view is intended
to be normative both for the Church's use of material goods and
for the transformation in the character and purpose of fasting. But
in general there is very little sense of the issues of social justice as
these affect the larger society of the Roman Empire. The principal
early exception to this generalization is Cyprian. When Cyprian
was bishop of Carthage, Demetrius, the pro-consul of Africa, was
ascribing all the evils of the day to the fact that Christians refused
to worship the gods of the Romans. Cyprian rejects the charge out-
right and in refuting it gives a striking diagnosis of the tragic
social conditions of the third-century Roman Empire.[118] He points
out that were war, famine, and pestilence to cease, the Empire
would still be ravaged from within by spoliation at the hands of the
pagan rich. Crimes of powerful citizens within the Empire are
more to be feared, he wrote, than barbarian assaults from without.
Rapacity causes a greater famine than crop failure. Locked barns
are as serious a threat as skies which give no rain. Those who wait
to pounce upon the property of the dying are as serious a menace
as the plague that is the cause of their death. The arrogance of the
rich, he notes, is astonishing:

> Among thieves there is at any rate some modesty in their
> crimes. They love pathless ravines and deserted solitude; and
> they do wrong in such a way that still the crime of the wrong-
> doers is veiled by darkness and night. Avarice (on the con-
> trary) rages openly, and, safe by its very boldness, exposes the
> weapons of its headlong craving in the light of the market-
> place. . . . The crime is committed by the guilty, and the
> guiltless who can avenge it is not found. There is no fear from
> accuser or judge: the wicked obtain impunity, while modest
> men are silent; accomplices are afraid, and those who are to
> judge are for sale.[119]

Implicit in Cyprian's thinking is the deep-rooted conviction that,
were the pagan landowners to repent and live as Christians, there
would be a drastic improvement in the well-being of the Empire.

The plague which afflicted north Africa in the year 252
prompted Cyprian to write his treatise *On Works and Almsgiving*.

His intention was to spur the members of his flock to liberality in the service of the plague-stricken, whether they were Christians or pagans. He based his instruction squarely on the now familiar teaching of Isaiah 58 and the Gospels that God will show mercy only to the merciful: "He will gain no request from the divine love by his prayers who has not been humane toward the prayer of the poor."[120]

After pointing out that Christ's teaching on the need for almsgiving is clear and unequivocal,[121] Cyprian deals with the various fears which this teaching inspires in the hearts of the rich. Do the wealthy fear that the practice of almsgiving will reduce them to poverty themselves? Let them give generously, Cyprian suggests, and then trust in the Lord.[122] Does a concern for their own children limit their giving? Let them remember that they must hold Christ (in the person of the poor) above members of the family.[123] Do the rich have many children for whom they are responsible? Let them commend their children to the Lord's keeping on the strength of their generous efforts in behalf of the poor.[124] Or, let them commend both their children and their wealth to God the Father; let him be their children's "guardian, caretaker, and protector." The rich, he adds finally, will be guilty of criminal neglect as parents if they work only for the temporal and not the spiritual welfare of their children.[125]

Cyprian developed Tertullian's idea that caring for the weak and ailing members of the Church is a vital function of the body of Christ. The absence of concern for the lower classes was for him a cause of the massive social and economic problems that almost brought the collapse of the Empire in the third century. Further, the malfunctioning of the practical charity in the Church explained for Cyprian both the arrival of the Decian persecution as a divine visitation and the apostasy of so many of the faithful and their bishops. The success of the reform program initiated by Cyprian can be measured by the fact that the majority of the urban population of North Africa became Christian during the third century.[126]

Cyprian's treatment of the issues in both his apologetic against Demetrius and in his exhortations to his own flock shows an awareness that almsgiving and the sharing of material goods does not serve only to manifest and strengthen the inner unity of the Christian community, but also to remedy some of the problems and injustices of the larger society, in which Christians were but a persecuted minority.

VII
CONCLUSIONS

Archaeologists will often run a narrow step-trench up the flank of a mound which marks the site of an ancient city. The work of excavation uncovers a certain amount of the remains. Because it proceeds by steps, it reveals the various levels of occupation and development. Because the trench is narrow, the knowledge gained remains limited and tentative until the excavation of the entire mound is completed. This paper has used a step-trench approach to the massive accumulation of patristic literature. It has dug in search of what some of the Fathers wrote during the first four centuries of the Christian era about the vice of avarice and the virtue of almsgiving. Accordingly, the width of the trench being so narrow, the conclusions of the survey remain limited and subject to modification, but we offer them for further reflection and discussion:

1. Christianity calls on human persons to renounce wealth and power as ultimate values and to find their happiness in the love of God and of their fellow human beings.

2. The problem for Christians is not the use or possession of material goods, but excessive desire for them (avarice) and selfish use of them (exploitation, greed, and waste).

3. Material things are good because they are created by God, and they are to be used to meet the basic needs of all human beings.

4. The poor are identified with Christ in a special way, and this gives Christians a special motive for generosity in meeting their needs.

5. Love and the generosity born of Christian faith are to make of the Church a new people with transformed values and purified desires, a true community of sharing and support.

6. The Christian sense of community, as expressed both in the

teachings of the Fathers and in the life of the Church, played an important part in drawing the ancient world to an acceptance of Christian belief.

7. The social teaching of the Fathers provides certain elements that should continue to shape the social teaching of the Church today. Among these elements are the principle that material goods are to be used to meet basic needs of all human persons, the insistence on the need for conversion of heart and the purification of our desires, the importance of considering issues of distribution and need within the context provided by a community of concern, and the doctrine of the special identity of Christ with the poor. These elements should be combined with a realistic and systematic analysis of the problems of society, an analysis that is almost completely lacking in the Fathers. For these elements constitute a message of solidarity and hope that the Church should strive to realize in its own life and that it can commend to the world as a response to the search for humane social values.

As we conclude our uncovering of the social thought of the Fathers, which dates from the formative experience of Christians as a minority community within the Roman Empire, we should reflect on our need to appropriate their humane and evangelical concern for those who are least well off in society. We need to interpret and develop their teaching in ways that can be persuasive in a world that is socially and economically more complex than theirs but that is still in need of the transforming and unifying effects of *agapé*.

NOTES

1. J. G. Gager, *Kingdom and Community: The Social World of Early Christianity* (Englewood Cliffs, N.J. 1976) 96. See also Martin Hengel, *Property and Riches in the Early Church* (London 1974) 84-88.

2. Gager, *op. cit.*, 140.

3. The actual date of the *Didache* remains uncertain. Scholarly opinion has placed it as early as 70 A.D. or as late as 180 A.D. Edgar J. Goodspeed and Robert M. Grant suggest that it be located at about 90 A.D.; see a *History of Early Christian Literature* (Chicago 1966) 12-13.

4. *Didache* 1.1, 5: *Early Christian Writings*, tr. by Maxwell Staniforth (London, 1968) (= ECW) 227.

5. *Op. cit.*, 1.4.8; *ECW* 229.

6. *Visions* 3.6.5; *The Shepherd of Hermas*, tr. by J. M.-F Marique in *Fathers of the Church* (=FC) Vol. 1; *The Apostolic Fathers* (New York 1947) p. 247.

7. *Mandates* 8.10; FC 1.272.

8. *Parables* 1.8-10; FC 1.288-289.

9. *Address to the Greeks* 11.1-2; Ante-Nicene Christian Library (Edinburgh 1868 ff.) (=ACL), Vol. 3.14.

10. I. Giordani, *The Social Message of the Early Church Fathers* (Paterson, N.J. 1944) 260.

11. *A Plea for Christians* 1; translation based on ACL 2.376.

12. *The Epistle to Diognetus* 10.2; ECS 181.

13. *Christ the Educator* 2.3; FC 23.128-129.

14. *Op. cit.*, 3.6; FC 23.227.

15. *Loc. cit.*

16. Homily on Luke 12.18, 6; PG 31.276; English translation in Walter Shewring, *Rich and Poor in Christian Tradition* (London 1948) 60.

17. *On Matthew: Homily 35, 5:* translation based on LF 15.519.

18. *Sermon 72.4*; translation based on FC 11.289.

19. *Sermon 100.7*; translation based on LF 20.705.

20. *Op. cit.*, 1.5.2; ECW 230.

21. *Op. cit.*, 10.4.2-3; FC 1.350.

22. *Philippians* 4.1.

23. *Quis Dives Salvetur?* translated in R. B. Tollinton, *Clement of Alexandria: A Study in Christian Liberalism* (London 1914) 313.

24. *Op. cit.*, 312-313.

25. *Op. cit.*, 315-316.

26. *Op. cit.*, 316.

27. *Op. cit.*, 319-320.

28. *Homily on the Book of Judges* 2.3, in R. B. Tollinton, *Selections from the Commentaries and Homilies of Origen* (London 1929) 257-258.

29. *To Donatus* 12, quoted in Hengel,·*op. cit.*, 80-81.

30. *The Lapsed* 5-6; ACW 25.16-17.

31. *Op. cit.*, 10; ACW 25.20.

32. *Op. cit.*, 11-12; ACW 25.20-22.

33. *On Works and Almsgiving* 13; FC 36-239.

34. *Op. cit.*, 15; FC 36-241.

35. *Homily on Luke 12.18*, 2; Shewring, 53.

36. *Op. cit.*, 4; Shewring 56-57.

37. *Op. cit.*, 7; Shewring 60-61.

38. *Op. cit.*, 5; Shewring 58.

39. *On Matthew: Homily 28.5*, translation on LF 15.422-423.

40. *On Philippians: Homily 6.5-6*; LF 14-72-74.

41. *On Galatians: Homily 18*.

42. *Loc. cit.*

43. *On Matthew, Homily 52.5*; translation based on LF 15.714.

44. Sermon 113.1; translation based on LF 20.817.

45. *The Epistle to Diognetus* 10.2; ECW 111.

46. *On Works and Almsgiving* 25; FC 36.250-252.

47. *Love of the Poor*; Shewring, *op. cit.*, 85.

48. *Op. cit.*, 66.

49. *Loc. cit.*

50. *Duties of the Clergy* 1.132; translation based on NPNF 10.22. That this patristic commonplace still has currency, see J. Cousteau, "The Perils and Potentials of a Watery Planet," in *Saturday Review*, August 24, 1974, 122; "The riches of the sea must belong to *everybody*, not to *nobody* and not to *anybody*—it is high time to establish a world policy and an international control of the high seas."

51. *Naboth* 1; Shewring, *op. cit.*, 69. See 1 *Kings* 21.1-29.

52. *Naboth* 55; quoted in J. P. Miranda, *Marx and the Bible: A Critique of the Philosophy of Oppression* (Maryknoll, N.Y., 1974) 16. In contrast to Miranda's interpretation of this text, it should be noted that Ambrose defends the right of private property; it is precisely Ahab's violation of Naboth's right to his property that Ambrose attacks. Cf. Shewring, *op. cit.*, 38 n. 5. See also R. M. Grant, *Augustus to Constantine: The Thrust of the Christian Movement into the Roman World* (N.Y. 1970) 268: ". . . only Irenaeus among the early Fathers suggested that the ownership of property was due to avarice. . . . The right to own private property was taken for granted."

53. *Fall of Eutropius* 2.3, Shewring, *op. cit.*, p. 35.

54. *On Lazarus; Himily 11*; quoted in P. Evodokimov, *Theology Digest* (18:1, 1970) 49.

55. *1 Corinthians; Homily 10.3*; quoted in P. Evdokimov, *loc. cit.*

56. *Loc. cit.*

57. *Letter 59*; ACL 8. 199-202.

58. *Love of the Poor*; Shewring, *op. cit.*, 65.

59. *On Matthew: Homily 48.8*; translation based on LF 15.659-660.

60. *On Matthew: Homily 48.9*; LF 15.661.

61. *On Matthew: Homily 50.4*; translation based on LF 15.684-685.

62. *Loc. cit.*

63. Quoted by W. J. Burghardt, "The Body of Christ: Patristic Insights," in R. S. Pelton, ed., *The Church as the Body of Christ* (South Bend, Ind., 1963) 97.

64. *On Acts: Homily 40.2*; translation based on LF 35.612.

65. See Burghardt, *op. cit.*, 98-101.

66. *Sermon 73.4*; translation based on LF 20.522.

67. *Sermon 87.3.*

68. *Sermon 87.1-2*; translation based on LF 20.622-623.

69. *Sermon 128.3*; translation based on LF 20.922.

70. *Sermon 128.4*; translation based on LF 20.922.

71. *Sermon 87.1-2.*

72. *The First Epistle of St. Paul to the Corinthians* (London 1962) 113.

73. *1 Clement* 38.2; ECW 43.

74. *Op. cit.*, 38. 2-4; ECW 43.

75. *Op. cit.*, 49 and 50; ECW 49.

76. *Op. cit.*, 55.2; ECW 51.

77. *Parables*, 2.3-4; FC 1.288.

78. *Op. cit.*, 2.9; FC 1.289.

79. *Op. cit.*, 5.1.1-5; FC 1.292-293.

80. *Op. cit.*, 5.3.7-9; FC 1.295.

81. *Quis Dives Salvetur?* translated in R. B. Tollinton, *Clement of Alexandria*, 318.

82. *Loc. cit.*

83. Commentary on Matthew (Series 61), in Tollinton, *Selections*, 134-135.

84. *Op. cit.*, 135.

85. *Prescription* 20; *The Ante-Nicene Fathers* (Edinburgh 1873ff.) Vol. 15.23.

86. *Penance* 10; *Ancient Christian Writers: The Works of the Fathers in Translation* (= ACW) (Westminster, Md, 1946ff.) Vol. 28.33.

87. *Apology*, 39.16.

88. *Apology* 39.1,5-7, 11, in *Loeb Classical Library*, tr. by T. R. Glover (N.Y. 1931) 175-176.

89. *To His Wife* 8; ACW 13.35-36.

90. *On the Dress of Virgins* 11, ACL 8.341-342.

91. *Letter 5*; ACL 8.20-21.

92. *Letter 4*; ACL 8.18-19.

93. *Letter 35*; ACL 8.100.

94. *Letter 60*; ACL 8.203.

95. *Letter 63.86*; *Nicene and Post-Nicene Fathers of the Christian Church* (N.Y. 1904) (= NPFC), Vol. 10.469.

96. *The Lapsed* 35; ACW 25.41.

97. *Loc. cit.*

98. *The Unity of the Catholic Church* 25-26; ACW 25.66-67.

99. *Op. cit.*, 27; ACW 25.67.

100. *On Matthew: Homily 35.5*; translation based on LF 15.515-516.

101. *Loc. cit.*

102. *Loc. cit.*; translation based on LF 15.516.

103. *On Ephesians: Homily 4*; LF 6.145.

104. *1 Corinthians: Homily 21;* quoted in Shewring, *op. cit.*, 32.

105. *On Titus: Homily 6.2.*

106. *On Colossians: Homily 8.2.*

107. *Duties of the Clergy* 1.169.

108. *Op. cit.*, 1.150.

109. *Op. cit.*, 2.72.

110. *Op. cit.*, 2.149-150.

111. *Op. cit.*, 2.77.
112. *Op. cit.*, 1.168.
113. *Op. cit.*, 2.70.
114. *Op. cit.*, 2.137.
115. *Op. cit.*, 2.138.
116. *Op. cit.*, 2.139.
117. *Op. cit.*, 2.142-143.
118. *To Demetrius* 10-11; ACL 8.431-432.
119. *Loc. cit.*
120. *On Works and Almsgiving* 5; FC 36.231.
121. *Op. cit.*, 7; FC 36.233-234.
122. *Op. cit.*, 9-10; FC 36.235-236.
123. *Op. cit.*, 16; FC 36.241-242.
124. *Op. cit.*, 18; FC 36.244.
125. *Op. cit.*, 19; FC 36.245.
126. I. K. Baus, *From the Apostolic Community to Constantine* (N.Y. 1965) 382-383.

What Jerusalem
Says to Athens

John P. Langan, S.J.

What does Christian faith contribute to our understanding of justice? What can Jerusalem say to Athens about justice in the human city? There are two answers that are attractive in their simplicity but that are hard for a Christian working for justice in a pluralistic society to accept. The first is "everything." This is the theocratic answer. Briefly put, it comes to this. God is supremely just and wills that all human persons live together in justice and harmony. By his law and by his call to men to live in the spirit of the Gospel, by the teaching of his Church, he reveals to human societies what his justice demands of them. Christians by understanding God's revelation know what justice is, and by responding to this revelation in grace they realize it in the world. This answer runs into two problems. First, in a religiously fragmented world it is doubtful how acceptable such a purely theological conception of justice would be. Second, a purely theological conception of justice is confronted with the dilemma of being either so general that it requires independent principles if it is to guide social policy or so specific that it effectively canonizes for all societies and all times the norms and social structures of a primitive agricultural society or of a dissident apocalyptic minority in the Roman Empire. It seems implausible to maintain that norms for the just operation of the Chase Manhattan Bank can be arrived at either from consideration of the Decalogue and the Sermon on the Mount or from application of the prescriptions governing the year of jubilee. Even for those who would commit themselves to a purely theological notion of justice in society, in a spirit of confidence and trust in the Lord, the risk of being relegated to the fringes of society and losing influence on the forming of social policy remains and should remain a problem.

The second answer about what Jerusalem can say to Athens on the shaping of a just society is equally sweeping. It is "nothing." The source for our understanding of the needs of persons in society and of the norms that should govern their interaction is human reason. Political thought is partly philosophical, partly empirical, and not at all theological. God's revelation is concerned with the personal relationship of the faithful to their Lord and Savior. The shaping of a just society is incidental to the coming of the Kingdom of heaven; the vicissitudes of the human city are occasions for the conversion of sinners and for the testing of the faithful. The human city itself is the object of political thought, which is an exercise of practical reason and of human prudence. Moral guidance for the shaping of the human city is to be sought in the natural law which is both applicable to and accessible to members of all human societies. Since the end of the human city is natural and secular, it does not need the guidance of faith. Furthermore, since the human city as we know it is religiously pluralistic, appeals to Christian faith are likely to be divisive and are certain to be ineffective. Justice is a virtue necessary to the attainment of the essentially secular end of the human city, and concern with it belongs not to the shepherds of the people of God but to those who exercise political leadership and to those who possess the requisite political and economic expertise.

As we have sketched this second position, it actually covers two rather different views. The first view regards the human city and its political and economic structure as inherently fallen and corrupted. The human city is effectively beyond the reach of redemption, though individual members of it are not. Involvement in the concerns of the human city is corrupting and dangerous to those who would respond to God's call. Such a view is perfectionist and sectarian; it is dualistic and points to the separation of the city of God and the city of man.

The second view is also dualistic, but it calls for the distinction of the two cities rather than their separation. The ends of the human city are worthy and virtuous but remain inferior to the ultimate end of salvation. Society's attainment of these ends is neither a participation in the ultimate end nor a necessary means to its attainment. The ends of the two cities remain distinct and even separate, and this is the basis for a separation of the virtues conducive to them and of the offices, powers, and social forms appropriate to them. Trying to overlook or override the distinction between the two realms of natural and supernatural, of political and spiritual, leads to both conceptual confusion and practical discord.

I

CLASSICAL AND CHRISTIAN APPROACHES

Attempting to resolve the points of conflict among these positions and offering a comprehensive answer to the question of what the community of faith can say to contemporary political society is clearly a major task, one that would require a series of tomes rather than a slender essay. This would be true, even if the task were limited to examining the bearing of faith on the one political notion which is central to every society's understanding of itself and to every political ideology. Justice is, in Perelman's words, "one of the most highly respected notions in our spiritual universe. All men, religious believers and non-believers, invoke justice, and none dare disavow it."[1] John Rawls, in the most influential recent account of justice, has spoken of the primacy of justice in our assessment of social institutions in the following terms: "Justice is the first virtue of social institutions, as truth is of systems of thought. A theory, however elegant and economical, must be rejected or revised if it is untrue; likewise laws and institutions no matter how efficient and well-arranged must be reformed or abolished if they are unjust."[2]

Rather than offering a comprehensive account of the relationship of faith and justice, or of the Christian community and political society, it is the purpose of the present essay to explore one approach to these large areas of investigation and controversy. By reading some passages from St. Ambrose and St. Augustine against the background of classical political thought, we will consider some ways in which Christian faith has altered the understanding of justice. Such an historical approach which focuses on the period when Christians first began to assume responsibility for the overall structure of civil society may provide us with a helpful starting point for reflection on contemporary problems of Christian participation in the struggle for justice. In our comparison of Augustine and Ambrose to the thinkers of classical antiquity, we hope to avoid implying that the contrasts to be drawn are simply equivalent to distinctions between grace and pure nature or between revelation and unaided reason; for we affirm that the world order that God creates and that we know is a world order of redemption and grace and that its history is a history of revelation and salvation. The contrast between Christianity and classical thought is precisely that, namely, a contrast between historical movements and the epochs they shaped. Reason and faith, nature and grace are found on both sides of such a contrast, as they also would be in a contrast between Christianity and the modern world.

In our reading of Augustine and Ambrose we will not be concerned to offer a full presentation of their thought on justice or on the bearing of faith on the political order, but rather to point to some aspects of their thought that illustrate the transformation of philosophical thought on justice by Christian faith. So this essay is neither strictly historical, nor strictly systematic; it aims to provide historical aids for systematic reflection on the problems that cluster around the question with which we began. The three themes that we will explore will be: (1) the transformation of the vindictive character of justice by charity or love, (2) the transformation of the circumstances of justice by Christian faith, and (3) Augustine's definition of justice in terms of love in his essay *De moribus ecclesiae catholicae.*

II
Justice in Cicero and St. Ambrose

St. Ambrose's treatise *De Officiis Ministrorum* was "the first manual of Christian ethics" and "a favorite textbook" for the Middle Ages.[3] Written after the spring of 386, it was modeled on Cicero's treatise *De Officiis*, but it was directed to the ministers of the Christian faith rather than to a man intending a public career at Rome.

Cicero devotes the first book of his treatise to the *honestum* or the morally good, which he divides into four parts corresponding to the four cardinal virtues of prudence, fortitude, justice, and temperance (I, 15). Of these four, justice has a special place; for on the basis of it men are called good, and the duties that arise from it take precedence over duties arising from the other virtues (I, 153). Justice is necessary for economic activity and for the preservation of society, so much so that it is required even among thieves (II, 40). It is the need for justice that governs the choice of rulers and of laws (II, 41-42).

Cicero lays down two fundamental principles of justice: "The first office of justice is to keep one man from doing harm to another, unless provoked by wrong; and the next is to lead men to use common possessions for the common interests, private property for their own" (I, 20).[4] He later restates the second principle in a somewhat vaguer way: men are to use property in such a way "that the common interests be conserved" (I, 31). He holds that these two principles override more specific principles such as the principle that promises must be kept (I, 31-32). The first principle of justice forbids injury to others, the second requires that people contribute to the common welfare and to the protection of others (I, 28-29). So Cicero says:

> There are some also who, either from zeal in attending to their own business or through some sort of aversion to their fellow men, claim that they are occupied solely with their own affairs, without seeming to themselves to be doing anyone any injury. But while they steer clear of the one kind of injustice, they fall into the other: they are traitors to social life, for they contribute to it none of their interest, none of their means (I, 29).[5]

Such a passage is part of Cicero's polemic against the apolitical tendencies of the philosophical life as envisioned both by Plato[6] and by the Epicureans, but it also represents one of his deepest personal convictions. This conviction of the moral worth of public service takes him beyond the view that justice is to be sought simply as a means to the protection of social order by providing a means for adjudicating and resolving the conflicting claims of individuals and groups. It is not an accident that the same Greek word *dike* refers both to law and to justice and that the development of a notion of justice is normally tied to the establishment of a legal and constitutional system. So Aristotle says, "The just, then, is the lawful and the fair, the unjust the unlawful and the unfair. . . . Evidently all lawful acts are in a sense just."[7]

Cicero sees the preservation of society as the result not merely of justice but also of generosity *(beneficentia)* (I, 20). Although it goes beyond the demands of justice, generosity or kindness is to be regulated by the norms of justice: "By the standard of justice all acts of kindness must be measured" (I, 42). Though kindness goes beyond justice, Cicero is willing to speak of duties or *officia* of kindness. Kindness, however, in Cicero's view, is not fundamentally altruistic. For it supposes a prior love for us in the one to whom we show kindness: "It is the first demand of duty that we do most for him who loves us most" (I, 47). In fact, the most pressing obligation of kindness is the expression of gratitude. Furthermore, it is to be shown to others on the basis of their closeness of relationship to us (I, 50). Cicero's tendency to regard kindness as a means of drawing together the social fabric lies behind his judgment that "when with a rational spirit you have surveyed the whole field, there is no social relation among them all more close, none more dear than that which links each one of us with our country *(re publica)*" (I, 57). In contrast with the clear and peremptory prohibitions and commands of justice, the duties of generosity are to be met by a calculation of the differing needs of individual cases (I, 59).

Cicero's account of justice and kindness can be taken as a benchmark for consideration of the views of Ambrose and for a determination of the transforming effect of Christian faith. Cicero had laid it down that "the foundation of justice, moreover, is good faith, that is, truth and fidelity to promises and agreements" (I, 23). Ambrose takes this up and gives it a theological interpretation:

The foundation of justice therefore is faith, for the hearts of the just dwell on faith, and the just man that accuses himself

builds justice on faith. . . . This means Christ as the foundation of the Church. For Christ is the object of faith to all; but
the Church is as it were the outward form of justice; it is the
common right of all. For all in common it prays, for all in
common it works, in the temptations of all it is tried (I, 142).[8]

Ambrose elsewhere points to justice as the characteristic virtue of
the Gospel.[9] He is willing to speak of justice in terms that are familiar from classical philosophy: "Justice, which assigns to each
man his own, does not claim another's, and disregards its own advantage, so as to guard the rights of all" (I, 115). Ambrose takes
over from Cicero the distinction that he makes between justice and
good will or generosity: "For that which holds society together is
divided into two parts—justice and good will, which also is called
liberality and good will, which also is called liberality and kindness
(beneficentia)" (I, 130). But he then goes on to make the following
criticism of the principles of justice proposed by Cicero:

But that very thing is excluded with us which philosophers
think to be the office of justice. For they say that the first
expression of justice is to hurt no one, except when driven to it
by wrongs received. This is put aside by the authority of the
Gospel. For Scripture wills that the Spirit of the Son of Man
should be in us, who came to give grace, not to bring harm.

Next they considered it consonant with justice that one should
treat common, that is, public property as public, and private
as private. But this is not even in accord with nature, for nature has poured forth all things for all men for common use.
God has ordered all things to be produced, so that there
should be food in common to all, and that the earth should be
a common possession for all (I, 131-132).

Here we find Ambrose moving onto controversial ground, for he
here denies both the right of self-defense and the right of private
property. It is not clear just how strongly Ambrose meant to insist
on either of these denials, for he argues that justice is to be pre-
served even in war (I, 139) and in commerce (III, 66-69), and he

also repeats these denials in a form that applies specifically to priests (III, 59-60).[10]

Furthermore, in a move that anticipates subsequent views of St. Augustine and St. Thomas Aquinas,[11] he includes our relationship to God under the heading of justice:

> But the piety of justice is first directed toward God; secondly, toward one's country; next, toward parents; lastly, toward all. This, too, is in accordance with the guidance of nature. From the beginning of life, when understanding first begins to be infused into us, we love life as the gift of God, we love our country and our parents; lastly, our companions with whom we like to associate. Hence arises true love, which prefers others to self, and seeks not its own, wherein lies the preeminence of justice (I, 127).

As this passage makes clear, Ambrose links justice very closely to charity. Homes Dudden summarizes this tendency in Ambrose's thought thus: "Ambrose's work *De Officiis* is full of charity. In the first book he sets forth charity as a part of justice; but, as has already been explained, the part so preponderates that justice, strictly so called, becomes merely, as it were, a beginning or first imperfect form of charity."[12] This tendency to transform the norms of justice to meet the demands of charity can also be seen at work in the following passage from Ambrose:

> He who is ordinarily wise is wise for temporal matters, is wise for himself so as to deprive another of something and get it for himself. He who is really wise does not know how to regard his own advantage, but looks with all his desire to that which is eternal, and to that which is seemly and virtuous, seeking not what is useful for himself, but for all. . . . The upright man must never think of depriving another of anything, nor must he ever wish to increase his own advantage to the disadvantage of another (III, 11-12).

The transformation of justice by charity may seem to be open to charges of conceptual confusion and of impractical perfectionism. The charge of conceptual confusion is perhaps best put off until we examine Augustine's definition of justice in terms of charity. But the charge of impractical perfectionism should be addressed now.

We should begin by observing that the political world that Ambrose knew in the late fourth century was not less violent and unstable than our own, and that there is no reason to think that Ambrose, who was a former imperial prefect and a shrewd man of affairs, expected the imminent transformation of the Roman Empire into a school of love. It seems best to regard what he says about justice as addressed to the Church and its ministers and to the members of the Christian community, and as providing guidance for their actions. It is noteworthy that he speaks of the Church itself as the form of justice and of Christ as the foundation for our works of justice. The point of this would be that justice as transformed by charity would find its home in the Christian community and from there could exercise some influence on the ideals and practices of the larger society.

There is a certain ambivalence in Ambrose's thought about justice which is found also in St. Paul, when he writes to the Corinthians: "If one of your members has a dispute with another, has he the *face* to take it to pagan law courts instead of to the community of God's people?" (1 Cor. 6:1). Paul was concerned about Christians submitting themselves and their cases for judgment to those who were outside the Christian religious community, but he was also concerned about Christians entering into what modern philosophers would call "the circumstances of justice."[13]

David Hume pointed out the essential aspects of the circumstances of justice when he affirmed as certain the proposition "that it is only from the selfishness and confined generosity of man, along with the scanty provision nature has made for his wants, that justice derives its origin."[14] As Hume saw the matter, the circumstances which make justice necessary for the functioning and the preservation of society are both objective and subjective; they "proceed from the concurrence of certain qualities of the human mind with the *situation* of external objects. The qualities of the mind are *selfishness* and *limited generosity*, and the situation of external objects is their *easy change*, joined to their *scarcity* in comparison of the wants and desires of men."[15] If one imagines a sufficient alteration of either the objective or the subjective circumstances of justice, as is commonly done in utopian fantasies or in speculations about the Kingdom of God, then the need for justice vanishes. As Hume says, "Increase to a sufficient degree the benevolence of men, or the bounty of nature, and you render justice useless by supplying its place with much nobler virtues and more valuable blessings."[16] Here Aquinas would agree, since he holds that, in the condition of the blessed, justice is unnecessary except as an attitude of obedience to God in the will.[17] In the circumstances of justice, persons stand ready to enforce conflicting claims on each other and to defend their competing interests in the name of justice. So Paul writes to the Christians of Corinth: "Indeed, you already fall below your standard in going to law with one another at all. Why not rather suffer injury? Why not rather let yourself be robbed? . . . Surely you know that the unjust will never come into possession of the Kingdom of God" (1 Cor. 6:7-9). Of course, Paul recognizes that even a community of the elect and holy will need means to settle disputes, and he is willing to urge stern measures against transgressors (1 Cor. 5:9-13). Justice and social order are necessary, but it is a fundamental mistake for Christians to conceive of human relations as based simply on the circumstances of justice, and it is a falling short of the ideal for them voluntarily to enter into the conflicts of interest that arise from the circumstances of justice. Likewise, for Ambrose, the preservation of one's interests by self-defense and by private property obscures the fundamental truths that the earth is intended by God to be a common possession of all (I, 131) and that men are made for the sake of other men (I, 134). The conflict situation that is characteristic of issues of justice is unavoidable in the present order of things, and Ambrose has no sympathy for agapistic anarchy. But the situation of justice does not form a situation which Christians accept as paradigmatic for their moral efforts or as exhaustive of their moral ideals. It is also a situation which does not adequately recognize the deeply felt aspirations to and the imperfectly achieved moments of human solidarity and cooperation that are an important part of the universal human experience.

Efforts to base the structure of human society on such aspirations and moments may seem naive and unrealistic in a world of division and conflict, but they are also a response to something very deep and important in human social desires and goals, something that is present in different ways in the quasi-religious force of much contemporary nationalism and Marxism and in various experiments in communal living. The Christian tradition is peculiarly suited to foster such aspirations in a productive way because of its universalism and its realism. For universalism is needed to protect these aspirations from the dangers and corruptions of group egoism, which would restrict the scope of these aspirations and goals to certain favored races, nations, or classes. Realism is needed to ensure the acceptance and effectiveness of norms of justice that, while they fall short of communal ideals, are in advance of existing situations of conflict and institutionalized injustice. Against these contributions of the Christian tradition in fostering the human aspiration to move beyond the circumstances of justice to a situation of solidarity and community must be set the fact that the Church cannot be, in Ambrose's words, "the form of justice" when it falls below the norms of justice in its internal life or when it supports injustice in the larger society.

III
JUSTICE, RIGHTS, AND CHARITY

In thinking of justice as transformed by charity, we are calling attention to two important developments that go beyond the scope of most political theories of justice and that are of particular importance for understanding current discussions about the promotion of justice as part of the vocation of Christians.[18] These are, on the one hand, the transformation of the spirit and the demands of justice, and, on the other, the transformation of the circumstances of justice.

We recall that Cicero's first principle of justice was "to keep one man from doing harm to another, unless provoked by wrong" (I, 20). Justice draws its strength from its appeal to the desire for fairness and from its appeal to the emotions which are concerned with the preservation and vindication of the self's interests and rights.[19]

Thus Gerard Gilleman, in his exposition of the moral theory of Aquinas, remarks: "By its function of mediation the virtue of justice governs the relation between the vindictive instincts and self-defense and the fundamental tendency to communion."[20] Justice both utilizes and regulates the vindictive passions in order to preserve social order and harmony, which will ensure a safer and better life for each member of society.

It would be a mistake to regard the doctrines of justice found in Plato, Aristotle, the Stoics, and Cicero as purely an expression of self-interest and vindictive passion. For, as Plato says in the first book of the *Republic*, "It has been made clear to us that in no case is it just to harm anyone."[21] As the context makes clear, the harm that is in question here is limited to making a person less virtuous, that is, depriving a person of the excellence that is proper to him as a human being. But it remains true that, in nearly all secular theories of justice, both ancient and modern, there remains a strong element of the prudential. Thus the central argument of the *Republic* is to the effect that the just man is also the happy man.[22]

Now in justice as transformed by charity, there are two important moves that can be made to bring justice closer to the ideal of communion and solidarity. The first, which St. Ambrose proposes, is the surrender of one's own claims and interests. This is one way of attaining the freedom from conflict and the condition of social harmony that are aimed at in any theory of justice. It is, we must admit, a policy that is open to abuse and that needs to be applied with intelligence and discretion. The person who slaps my right cheek and my left cheek (Mt. 5:39) may well be emboldened to slap my neighbor's cheeks. It is far from clear that non-resistance to an aggressor really is for his good or for the good of third parties. Paul Ramsey has made this point in the following passage, where he is arguing that the Christian doctrine of the just war is rooted in the ethics of love as well as in the Stoic conception of justice:

While Jesus taught that a disciple in his own case should turn the other cheek, he did not enjoin that his disciples should lift up the face of another oppressed man for *him* to be struck again on *his* other cheek. It is not part of the work of charity to allow this to continue to happen.[23]

Non-resistance and the surrender of rights can lead to social quietism and a passivity in the face of injustice, which causes a deterioration in both the internal cohesion and the moral worth of the social order.

On the other hand, the voluntary surrender of the exercise of certain rights for the sake of a communal life has been a central feature of the way of life of religious orders down through the centuries. Anyone familiar with the history of religious communities would hesitate to say that all the demands of justice have been met in them. But he would also have to grant that willingness to surrender certain claims and interests, when this willingness is effectively present and when the trust that makes it possible is not abused, is a central source of the solidarity and charity of the religious community. The renunciation of claims has, then, been the classic Christian way of achieving a state of community that is a partial embodiment of the notion of justice transformed by charity.[24]

The extent to which the way of life of a religious order can be exemplary for the larger society is obviously limited, but the possibility should not be dismissed out of hand. For religious life stands as evidence of the viability of a form of community that is based, not on the vindication of rights, but on their voluntary renunciation. The continued existence of such a form of life can be of some help to those who wonder whether the renunciation of claims and interests is pure loss and who may also long for the trust that is needed to make such a renunciation of claims possible and endurable. The life of the religious order, when it does not serve as the instrument of collective egoism, can be an example of a distinctive realization of the possibilities of justice as transformed by love and can fit into the progression of forms of society moving toward the ideal of a community of love described by Reinhold Neibuhr:

> The basic rights to life and property in the early community, the legal minima of rights and obligations of more advanced communities, the moral rights and obligations recognized in these communities beyond those which are legally enforced, the further refinement of standards in the family beyond those recognized in the general community—all these stand in an

ascending scale of moral possibilities in which each succeeding step is a close approximation of the law of love.[25]

But the policy for realizing justice as transformed by charity that is of more interest today is the vindication of the rights of others. Gilleman writes of it in this way:

> Under the impulse of charity, of which it is the mediation, it takes a larger vision of the rights of others, who now are loved as brothers in Christ. And charity facilitates any step in this direction by its inspirations of self-forgetfulness. Finally, no longer content with respecting the rights of others, Christian justice positively tends to promote them, for they are the rights of fellow members of Christ.[26]

Working for the promotion of justice in society is not a matter of defending one's own claims and interests, but of working for the effective recognition of the justified claims and interests of those who need support for the vindication of their rights. This is a policy that calls persons forth from their own egoism to action for the needs and rights of others. This policy presupposes as its motive either a devotion to a moral or religious value such as justice or God's will or an altruistic concern for the plight of other human persons. However, since it frequently appeals to the vindictive passions, even though for a social rather than a personal end, it can lead to anger, bitterness, and vengefulness. Precisely because it sets its moral sights so high, it is especially liable to the deceptions and corruptions of self-righteousness. This policy also presupposes a belief in the possibility of significant social improvement brought about by political action. It is optimistic in a way that the previous policy of renunciation is not, though its confidence may turn to desperation should its goals become unattainable. It aims at a transformation of the social order that will assure the rights of those who are presently powerless, and thus it is implicitly and necessarily a political policy, though it need not be committed to a particular political party. It is a policy that does not shrink from the conflicts that usually accompany disputes about rights and the demands of justice. In fact, as Ramsey argues, the policy of vindicating the rights of others can even be used to justify a resort to arms:

> Instead, it is the work of love and mercy to deliver as many as possible of God's children from tyranny, and to protect from oppression, if one can, as many of those for whom Christ died as it may be possible to save. When choice *must* be made between the perpetrator of injustice and the many victims of it, the latter may and should be preferred—even if effectively to do so would require the use of armed force against some evil power. This is what I mean by saying that the justice of sometimes resorting to armed conflict originated in the interior of the ethics of Christian love.[27]

But if it is pursued in a way that avoids the involuntary surrender of rights by those who lack the power or ability to defend them, and that avoids the danger of producing lasting and dangerous social discord, it can lead to the vindication of rights in a stable and harmonious society.

When it falls short of this goal, the policy of vindicating the rights of others is open to criticism in the light of the values of justice and charity. The policy aims at rectifying the injustice as an imperfect social order and so is open to disapproval by those who either on religious or secular grounds commend the acceptance of existing social institutions ("the powers that be") and by those who counsel to Christians a policy of abstention from the world and its cares and conflicts. More deeply, it is open to criticism because it is, in effect, a policy of the second-best. It is this because it urges on other persons the vindication of their rights rather than a policy of voluntary renunciation, and so it seems to fall short of the perfection of love. In reply to such criticism, it can say that in most cases of social injustice the best is the enemy of the good and that appeals to perfect love perpetuate injustice and produce a false social harmony, false both by reason of the injustice that it condones and of the instability that it produces.

Nonetheless the policy of vindicating the rights of others must be subject to the law of love, for the conflict that the policy involves must not degenerate into hatred, and the means that it uses must not be inherently incompatible with the demands of love. For then there is no longer a question of pursuing a policy for achieving the goal of justice as transformed by charity. This restriction requires that Christians who accept a Marxist or neo-Marxist account of the problems of industrial society and of imperialism must, if they are to be faithful to the ideals of justice transformed by charity, be careful not to allow class struggle to degenerate into class hatred. More generally, members of liberation movements must not deny the essential humanity or the basic human rights even of those whom they regard as oppressors. Justice as transformed by love is a norm superior to considerations of revolutionary effectiveness and to the appeals of bloodthirsty demagoguery. Recognition of the human rights of all does not, however, require acquiescence in the indefinite continuation of oppressive regimes or preservation of the interests and positions of those who have benefited from such regimes. In recent American history, Martin Luther King provided a striking illustration of an active, creative struggle for justice that did not shrink from disturbing order and "the system" but that fundamentally respected the law of love.

We may note also that often the measures proposed by those who seek to vindicate the rights of others may be supported on self-interested grounds by those who do not share the same moral perspective but who are concerned to appease the demands of those who might otherwise threaten the stability and harmony of the social order. The promotion of a more just social order normally has important non-moral and non-religious advantages, and it is important to bear in mind that the policy of promoting justice by vindicating the rights of others does not require or presuppose the moral transformation of all elements or aspects of a society. Reform coalitions have characteristically used a mixture of moral and non-moral appeals. Justice, as well as honesty, may indeed be the best policy for a morally imperfect society. Reinhold Niebuhr illustrates this point in his considerations on the advantages that the United States stands to gain from ensuring equal rights for its black citizens:

The fact that the interest of the whole nation is involved in this struggle for human rights is shown vividly in the following ways. First, it is in the national interest of a free nation to have the harmony which only justice can guarantee. For a revolutionary racial minority endangers the harmony of a democratic society. . . . Secondly, an increasing technical culture needs trained manpower. Thus untrained workers do not serve the national interest. . . . Finally, world opinion, especially in this day of mass communication, is important for American power and prestige. The rise of new nations in Asia and Africa relates our solution of this domestic problem to our moral prestige abroad. Thus the national interest is involved.[28]

The policy of vindicating the rights of others is subject to three fundamental limitations. The first is the limitation of power. Not all justified claims can be made good in a given society because of the limited power available to those working to realize justice in the society; their cause can and often does suffer political defeats. Secondly, in drastic situations of scarcity, it may be the case that there simply are not the economic resources available to meet the needs or to satisfy the claims of all. Now those who work in the cause of justice can argue that things might well be otherwise and should actually be otherwise. But it remains true that any realistic policy of working for justice must reckon with political and economic limitations that are not logically necessary but are inevitable, given the world as it currently is. After all, it is the present world which is to be redeemed and renewed. The third sort of limitation is even more fundamental, since it is inescapably characteristic of our world. It is the necessary collision of at least some of our *prima facie* rights with each other. To point to this collision is not to claim that there is no justifiable way of resolving conflicts or rights, but simply to say that, in some cases, some rights which should generally be respected have to yield to other, even more pressing claims—e.g., one's right to know may have to yield to another's right to privacy, one's right to enter into contracts may have to yield to another's right to a living wage, etc.[29] One may restrict the notion of right to those claims which are finally justified in a particular case and so deny that rights really do conflict. But such a move, which offers certain theoretical and linguistic advantages, does not alter the necessity for persons to surrender certain normally justified claims, a necessity that does not arise because of the power or the resources available to others, but because of the justified claims of others. This necessary limitation on the policy of promoting justice by vindication of the rights of others shows that justice cannot be understood simply as the vindication of the rights or normally justified claims of persons. For, since rights or normally justified claims come into conflict, justice would then lead to contradictory practical conclusions. So the policy of promoting justice by vindication of the rights of others must be prepared to come up against certain limit situations in which the realities of the situation and the claims of others require the resignation of rights or normally justified claims.

A final point of comparison between the two policies should be mentioned in this section. The policy of vindicating the rights of others presupposes the circumstances of justice that we have already mentioned and that are familiar in both ancient and modern political thought, and then attempts to add a new altruistic motive of concern for others in order to achieve a just social order. The policy of voluntarily renouncing rights and claims attempts to change the motives and the demands of participants in disputes about justice in such a way that the circumstances of justice no longer apply. The parties take an active interest in each other's welfare and place the formation and development of an agapistic community above the promotion of their own interests.

IV
FAITH AND THE STRUGGLE FOR JUSTICE

It is now necessary to consider the connection between these two policies and the content of Christian faith. First, it should be noted that neither policy strictly presupposes a commitment to Christian faith. A commitment to the value of justice, to the welfare of others, or to the goal of social harmony can lead a person to adopt either of the two policies, and we find that in fact there are many non-Christians and non-religious persons who commend or adopt these policies. For Christians this should not be surprising, for the two policies both involve values that are of fundamental and near universal human appeal, even though they also involve heavy sacrifice of personal interest that few of us, Christian or not, are willing to make consistently. The appeal of the values aimed at in these policies, while universal, is at the same time limited because of the potential opposition to the interests of the self that they involve, and it would be unrealistic to attempt to base an entire polity or social structure on the motivating force of these values alone. But the place and function of the values of justice and love, of solidarity and fairness and of the policies that attempt to realize these values is by no means exclusively religious or religiously exclusive. Adoption of either of the policies of working for justice does not constitute the imposition of an extrinsic religious demand on society but rather calls on society to be more fully what it ought to be and can be.

But there are aspects of the Christian faith that provide special support and a special context for the promotion of justice. Thus, justice is an essential part of what the Lord asks of Israel (Am. 6:24). The commandment of love obliges us to effective concern for the needs and interests of our neighbors (1 Jn. 3:13-24). It is possible to work out a theological understanding of the place of the virtue of justice as transformed by charity in relation to the Christian doctrines of redemption, of grace, of the Church, and of the last things. Here we will confine ourselves to pointing to what we believe to be the central aspect of Christian teaching that sustains both policies, namely, the primacy of religious and moral values as objects of human striving.

> Do not store up for yourselves treasure on earth, where it grows rusty and moth-eaten, and thieves break in to steal it. Store up treasure in heaven, where there is no moth and no rust to spoil it, no thieves to break in and steal. For where your treasure is, there will your heart be also (Mt. 6:19-21).

"Set your mind on God's Kingdom and his justice before everything else, and all the rest will come to you as well" (Mt. 6:33). It might be thought that these admonitions of Jesus represent merely a ranking of one class of goods over another or a piece of sublime moral teaching, or an expression of human idealism that is both impractical and challenging. But, as the context of these sayings make clear, they are part of an entire system of beliefs that discerns the events of this world and the lives of Christians within it as subject to God's loving providence. If this system of beliefs, which is common and central to both the Old and the New Testaments, is taken seriously and is accepted with living faith, then it transforms the circumstances of justice in a radical way. For it proposes an ontological framework that makes sacrifices of thisworldly self-interest reasonable, and that ensures the ultimate coincidences of virtue and happiness that seemed essential even to so austere a moralist as Kant.[30] Of course, we do not want to suggest that acceptance of the biblical belief in a just and loving God transforms our pursuit of moral and religious values into a simple calculation of individual welfare; for to choose the higher goods, to put one's treasure and one's heart in heaven requires a willingness to sacrifice lesser goods that both requires and challenges faith. It redirects the striving for personal identity, security, and recognition of worth from the pursuit of worldly interests to the religious domain where these personal goods are found in a response to God's grace and call. The goods that are of most worth to persons who accept the biblical account of life are not of such a kind that they present problems of distribution or of restoration and rectification in case of involuntary loss, for they are not economic goods. They are essentially interior and spiritual—God's loving favor, loving communion with God and other persons, the virtues that unite us to God and that impart rational order and harmony to our lives as personal agents living in union with other personal agents.

It is to these goods that the Lord offers in the words of Deutero-Isaiah:

> Come, all you who are thirsty, come, fetch water; come, you who have no food, buy corn and eat; come and buy, not for money, not for a price. Why spend money and get what is not bread, why give the price of your labor and go unsatisfied? Only listen to me and you will have good food to eat, and you will enjoy the fat of the land (Is. 55:1-2).

Affirming the primacy of these goods introduces an important new factor into the motivations and preferences of persons in the circumstances of justice. The spiritual and personal character of these goods does not altogether eliminate the need for consideration of the circumstances of justice, as it would if we were dealing with a society of pure spirits. For the partial attainment of these goods in this life requires the existence of a society which meets the minimal needs of its members as incarnate persons and provides that minimum of social harmony and security that is necessary for them to exercise their abilities as moral agents and to develop at least some relations of mutual concern and trust. Also, certain of these goods, particularly the virtues of justice and charity, are exercised and developed precisely in regard to the shaping of society. As Aquinas clearly taught, the active life, which includes the ordering of human society, is itself a part of imperfect beatitude.[31]

Christian faith interprets the promotion of justice not simply as a temporal political struggle but also as a partial realization of the fullness of the communion of love given and received in the Kingdom of God. But it also recognizes the limitations to which our struggle for justice is subject and places the struggle under the sign of the cross, the sign of the self-sacrificial love of one who knew defeat and death and who gave his life as a ransom for many (Mk. 10:45). The ministry that begins with the announcing of good news to the poor and the proclaiming of freedom for prisoners (Lk. 4:16-21) ends with the one who has done no wrong (Lk. 23:41) praying for forgiveness for those who have done injustice (Lk. 23:34). In every Christian life and in every political struggle to which Christians commit themselves, there comes a moment when the claims of justice must grow silent before the response of faith, of hope, and of love: "Father, into thy hands I commit my spirit" (Lk. 23:46). In this moment, the claims of justice are not denied or dismissed; nor is the struggle to realize these claims seen as trivial or unnecessary or extrinsic to the life of faith. But in this moment, the Christian must recognize that the goal of a just society is not to be attained under present circumstances by the resources now available to us and that the loving union of persons is fully realized only in the Kingdom of God. In acknowledging this moment, Christian faith provides the ultimate basis for a realistic acceptance of the limits of political action for justice as of every other human project and achievement. But it also sees the struggle for justice and its moments of failure and defeat as occasions for hope, both because they are moments of the life of the risen Christ in his members and because they make us "fit to share the heritage of God's people in the realm of light" (Col. 1:12). In this way, the circumstances of justice take their place in the history of the salvation of humanity. The context of the Christian struggle for justice is no longer the legislative chamber nor the barricades of the streets but ultimately the paschal mystery itself.

V

THE TRANSFORMATION OF JUSTICE BY CHARITY

In considering the transformation of justice by charity and the new context that Christian faith provides for the resolution of disputes about justice, we have put to one side the question of whether justice can be redefined in terms of charity without producing conceptual confusion and a blurring of natural and supernatural principles of the moral life. The classic example of such a redefinition of justice in terms of charity is offered by St. Augustine in his treatise *On the Morals of the Catholic Church* written in 388 shortly after his conversion and so almost exactly contemporary with St. Ambrose's *De Officiis*.[32] Augustine there makes the following claim about the cardinal virtues of ancient moral thought:

I hold virtue to be nothing else than perfect love of God. For the fourfold division of virtue I regard as taken from four forms of love. For these four virtues . . . I should have no hesitation in defining them: that temperance is love giving itself entirely to that which is loved; fortitude is love readily bearing all things for the sake of the loved object; justice is love serving only the loved object, and therefore ruling rightly; prudence is love distinguishing with sagacity between what hinders it and what helps it.[32]

Augustine then goes on to specify that the object of love that he has in mind is God. Now serious difficulties stand in the way of taking Augustine's proposal as a definition in a strict sense. In the first place, it is difficult to hold that charity or love as specified in the four ways mentioned is what the virtue terms mean. Secondly, it is not clear what defining the cardinal virtues in terms of charity gains for our ethical knowledge, that is, our knowledge of what we should do or how we should act. For our notions of what the various virtues require are more specific than our notion of what charity or love requires.

Rather, what Augustine is doing is pointing to a further entity or state of soul that is operative by way of the various virtues. In proposing this interpretation of Augustine's account of the cardinal virtues in terms of charity, we are employing a suggestion made by Terry Penner with regard to the moral philosophy of Socrates. Penner holds that the "What is X?" question raised about the virtues in the early Platonic dialogues is not "a request for a conceptual analysis" but is rather "the general's question, 'What is bravery?' "—that is, an inquiry about "what psychological state it is, the imparting of which to his men will make them brave."[34] This question, Penner argues, is not a conceptual question, but a substantial question of psychology, akin to Freud's question, "Well, what is hysteria really?" Penner says, "I take the reference of 'bravery' in 'What is bravery?' to be simply that psychological state *which explains the fact that certain men do brave acts*—what we might call a *theoretical entity*."[35] The virtues are "motive-forces or states of soul," and "the same motive-force or state of soul can result in different kinds of behavior."[36] Penner holds that Socrates' view is that "the single entity to which the virtue words refer" is an "explanatory entity . . . identifiable as the knowledge (science) of good and evil."[37]

The interpretation of Augustine that we are putting forward here maintains that, whereas in the Socratic view knowledge produces acts of the virtues, in the Augustinian view it is love or charity that produces the acts of the different virtues. In this interpretation, love or charity is a motivating force of soul and serves as part of the causal explanation of virtuous acts rather than as a separate source of norms for good or virtuous activity or as an element in the cognitive process of arriving at norms. This interpretation of Augustine saves him from the charge of promoting a conceptual confusion of charity and justice, since love is the motive for and cause of just activity and the notion of justice serves to specify right activity in the realm of social relations. The interpretation also accords with Augustine's desire to understand the moral lives of individuals and societies as shaped by the motivating power of a dominant love or desire.[38]

But, it may be asked, where does such an understanding of love leave things that were said earlier about justice as transformed by charity? If we adopt the notion of love as the motive force behind the various virtues, we can readily see how love or charity can have a correcting and transforming effect on our motivations for virtuous activity. Thus, just acts can result from motives characteristic of justice—e.g., the desire to protect one's interests, the desire to retaliate against an aggressor—or from motives that have no logical relation to the notion of justice—e.g., a desire to impress others. When charity or an active concern for the welfare of others serves as a motive, just acts will still result, though certain demands that one may rightly make of others by reason of justice will be passed over (the policy of renunciation of rights) and certain demands that others make in the name of justice will be supported, even though they do not bear on one's own interests (the policy of altruistic vindication of rights). Charity as a motive will still need the cognitive guidance provided by a developed conception of justice, both in order to meet the demands that others make on the charitable person by reason of justice and to avoid actions that, while charitable in intention and motivation, fall short of the demands of justice, for instance, by lending support to an unjust and oppressive social order. Justice as transformed by charity must not be less than justice. Charity, however, also moves the agent to a good that transcends the good of right social order that justice aims at, and so a person who works for justice in a spirit of charity uses and interprets his work for justice as a stage to a more intimate and loving communion with other persons and with God.[39] In this movement to communion and to a more perfect relationship of persons than justice provides, charity is guided both by human ideals of community and by the interpretative resources of faith.

VI
SOME CONCLUSIONS

After this overview of a range of systematic and historical considerations bearing on the connections between faith and justice, we may suggest some conclusions to the questions with which we began. What can Jerusalem say to Athens? What guidance does faith give to the search for justice?

1. It is the task of practical reason and more specifically of law, political philosophy and social and historical knowledge to elaborate a conception of justice and to determine norms of justice for human society in general and for specific societies. This immense task demands careful inquiry, respect for the beliefs and desires of other persons, and the honest and humble examinations of one's own principles and presuppositions. It is not only the matter of inquiry that is of moral importance, but also the manner of inquiry.

2. Christian faith sets love as the supreme and central virtue in our lives as moral agents. This love is to motivate the process of inquiry already mentioned as well as the actions of those who share in a system of social cooperation. It is to produce appropriate acts of all the virtues necessary for the moral life, including acts of justice. While it is an attitude and a state of soul of supreme moral and religious worth, it is bound to respect the norms set for human conduct by the moral virtues. Acts motivated by charity are not to be contrary to justice.

3. Christian faith commits us to the aspiration for a community of love that is deeper and more comprehensive than the order of justice in the human city. This aspiration is both a desire for such a community and a hope that God will, through his providence and its instruments, bring it about in his saving will. This aspiration for a community of love is also the expression of a universal human desire and the source of ideals and policies that can

have beneficial effects on the very imperfect political communities in which we presently live. But the aspiration for a community of love, if it is not to lapse into idle utopianism or sectarian perfectionism, must be tempered by a realistic assessment of the strength of those egoistic human desires that are at variance with the aspiration itself and even with the minimal demands of civic virtue, and of the power of those human institutions and groups that are social objectifications of such egoistic desires. The aspiration to perfect communion with God and with our fellow human beings must be set alongside acceptance of our condition as weak and sinful creatures. The transformation of society, gradual and imperfect as the process is, requires grace as well as human effort and engagement.

4. Christian faith interprets the struggle for justice and the movement beyond justice to a more perfect form of community as part of the history of salvation, as an aspect of the redemption of the entire human reality, both social and individual. More specifically, faith interprets the struggle for justice in the light of the paschal mystery of death and resurrection and on the model of the self-sacrificial love of Jesus Christ. In this way Christian faith does not serve as the ideology of any class or political movement or as the source of a specific conception of justice. Rather, we maintain that Christian faith serves as an interpretative and motivational principle for a universally and characteristically human enterprise, the intellectual search and the political struggle for the fuller realization of justice in society.

In maintaining that Christian faith is not the ideology of a class or political movement, we are pointing to the way in which Christian faith transcends particular political projects and programs, however wise and good these may be. When there is serious reason drawn from consideration of the actual situation of society to think that Christian beliefs are being used in the service of the exclusive interests of some class or political movement, then we are indeed dealing with ideology and not with Christian faith. The thesis that Christian faith is not an ideology should not serve as a means of canonizing the political attitudes and objectives of Christians, but as a call to purify them in a critical and charitable way.

5. The Christian form of commitment to justice in the human

city grows out of hope and faith in a God who both transcends history and is active within it. Alan Paton, the South African writer, has spoken of his hope for the triumph of righteousness in his own divided and fearful land in simple and moving terms that should encourage all Christians in those difficult times when justice seems to have departed from the earth:

> The might and the power of hope must come, and can only come, from a faith that there is a might and a power that is above all, and that rules all, and directs all. It is a faith in the Holy Spirit, that he moves abroad in the world, that he contains all and sustains all; and the inevitable corollary of this faith is that the Holy Spirit is in us, and can use us in the achievement of his purposes. Yet this might and this power are not to be confused with any might or power of this earth; they are totally of another order. This distinction is made clear in the book of the prophet Zechariah, where it is said to Zerubbabel, "not by might nor by power, but by my spirit, saith the Lord." It is not the power of rulers and parliaments and armies, but the power of the Spirit; and when men and women have believed in such a power, they are able, if it is required of them, to defy rules and parliaments and armies. . . . Our task is to be the instruments of the Holy Spirit, knowing in full faith that his purpose also is the triumph of righteousness.[40]

NOTES

1. Chaim Perelman, *Justice* (New York: Random House, 1967), p. 5.
2. John Rawls, *A Theory of Justice* (Cambridge, Mass.: Harvard University Press, 1971), p. 3.
3. F. Homes Dudden, *The Life and Times of St. Ambrose* (Oxford: Clarendon Press, 1935), II, 502-503.
4. *Ibid.*, II, 695.
5. This and other quotations from the *De Officiis* are from the translation by Walter Miller (London: Heinmann, 1913).
6. Cf. Plato, *Republic* VI, 520A-E.
7. Aristotle, *Nicomachean Ethics* V, 1.1129a33-34, b 13.

8. St. Ambrose, *On the Duties of the Clergy*, tr. H. DeRomestin, in *St. Ambrose: Select Works and Letters*, in A Select Library of the Nicene and Post-Nicene Fathers, ed. Philip Schaff and Henry Wace (Grand Rapids: Eerdmans, 1955).

9. St. Ambrose, *Paradise*, 22, tr. John J. Savage (New York: Fathers of the Church, 1967), p. 300.

10. Homes Dudden takes Ambrose's denials of the right of self-defense and of private property to be unqualified, and in fact passages supporting such a view can be found; but there are other passages where the denials are restricted to the clergy, and it should be remembered that the treatise as a whole is addressed to the clergy of Milan. Cf. F. Homes Dudden, *The Life and Times of St. Ambrose*, II, 524-525, 545-550.

11. Cf. St. Augustine, *The City of God*, XIX, 21; Thomas Aquinas, *Summa Theologiae*, II-II, 81.

12. Homes Dudden, II, 531.

13. Important recent discussions of the circumstances of justice can be found in Rawls, pp. 126-130, where they are taken as presuppositions for a form of social contract theory, and in H. L. A. Hart, *The Concept of Law* (Oxford: Clarendon Press, 1961), pp. 189-195, where they are taken as factors determining the content of a minimal version of natural law.

14. David Hume, *A Treatise of Human Nature*, Book III, Part II, ch. 1, "Of the Origin of Justice and Property," in *Hume's Moral and Political Philosophy*, ed. Henry D. Aiken (Darien, Conn.: Hafner, 1970), p. 64.

15. *Ibid.*, p. 63. Emphasis in original.

16. *Ibid.* Emphasis is original.

17. Thomas Aquinas, *Summa Theologiae*, I-II, 67, 1.

18. "Our Mission Today," par. 18. Documents of the Thirty-Second General Congregation of the Society of Jesus (Washington: Jesuit Conference, 1975), p. 21.

19. Cf. John Stuart Mill, *Utilitarianism*, ch. 5, "On the Connexion Between Justice and Utility," where Mill gives an account of the sentiment of justice; and Joseph Butler, Bishop of Durham, Sermon 8, "Upon Resentment," in *Works* (Oxford: University Press, 1850), II, 87-98, where Butler argues for a divinely established connection between resentment and injustice.

20. Gerard Gilleman, S.J., *The Primacy of Charity in Moral Theology*, tr. William F. Ryan, S.J. and André Vachon, S.J. (Westminster, Md.: Newman, 1959), p. 332.

21. Plato, *Republic* I, 335e 3-4, tr. Paul Shorey, in *Collected Dialogues*, ed. Edith Hamilton and Huntington Cairns (New York: Pantheon, 1961), p. 585.

22. Plato, *Republic* II, 367 a-e; IX, 588e-592b.

23. Paul Ramsey, "Justice in War," in *The Just War: Force and Political Responsibility* (New York: Scribner's, 1968), p. 143. Emphasis in original.

24. For an interpretation of the life of religious orders as a community of charity based on voluntary renunciation, cf. Rene Carpentier, S.J., *Life in the City of God*, tr. John Joyce, S.J. (New York: Benziger, 1959), ch. 5, "The Community of Charity Through the Triple Counsel," pp. 42-53.

25. Reinhold Niebuhr, *An Interpretation of Christian Ethics* (New York: Harper, 1935), p. 110.

26. Gilleman, p. 338.

27. Ramsey, *The Just War*, p. 143. Emphasis in original.

28. Reinhold Niebuhr, *Man's Nature and His Communities* (New York: Scribner's, 1965), pp. 104-105.

29. For a discussion of conflicts of liberties, cf. Rawls, pp. 203-205, and for a discussion of conflicts of obligations, cf. Sir David Ross, *The Right and the Good*, ch. 2, "What Makes Right Acts Right?" (Oxford: Clarendon Press, 1930), esp. pp. 28-33.

30. Immanuel Kant, *Critique of Practical Reason*, Book II, ch. 2, sec. 5, "The Existence of God as a Postulate of Pure Practical Reason," tr. Lewis White Beck (Indianapolis: Bobbs-Merrill, 1956), p. 129.

31. Aquinas, *Summa Theologiae*, I-II, 3, 5.

32. Cf. Eugene Portalie, S.J., *A Guide to the Thought of St. Augustine*, tr. Ralph J. Bastian, S.J. (Chicago: Regnery, 1960), p. 47.

33. St. Augustine, *On the Morals of the Catholic Church*, c. 15, tr. R. Stothert, in *Basic Writings of Saint Augustine*, ed. Whitney J. Oates (New York: Random House, 1948), I, 331-332.

34. Terry Penner, "The Unity of Virtue," Philosophical Review 83 (1974), p. 40.

35. *Ibid.*, p. 41. Emphasis in the original.

36. *Ibid.*, p. 45. Emphasis in the original.

37. *Ibid.*, p. 67.

38. The most famous instance of this tendency in Augustine's thought is the passage on the two loves that are basic to the two cities, the city of God and the city of man. Cf. St. Augustine, *The City of God*, XIV, 28.

39. We leave to one side the difficult theoretical question of how charity is to be understood so that it applies both to our relationship to God and to our relationships to our fellow human beings.

40. Alan Paton, "The Nature and Ground of Christian Hope Today," in *Knocking on the Door* (New York: Scribner's 1975), pp. 290, 292.

Tridentine Justification and Justice

Richard R. Roach, S.J.

At their recent Thirty-Second General Congregation which closed on the 7th of March, 1975, the members of the Society of Jesus (Jesuits) solemnly affirmed that Christian faith absolutely requires the pursuit of justice in this world. The Jesuits were not dealing with an intramural matter affecting only their Order; rather, as the largest Order within the Roman Catholic Church, they were striving to affirm something generally valid about the Roman Catholic understanding of faith which they believe links faith with justice. Their concern, therefore, is shared by all Catholics and Christians concerned with the relationship between Christian faith and justice in the world.

Unfortunately, although the affirmation is clear, the reason given for the link between faith and justice is succinct, to say the least. One might even say that it is cryptic. Therefore, it is not surprising that one hears many Jesuits today maintain that their Thirty-Second General Congregation did indeed link faith and justice, but failed to define what it meant by either term. Such Jesuits and other Catholics feel that they could compensate from their own resources for a failure to define faith in the documents, because they have some little experience wrestling with the various significances of that key concept. But some, at least, are not as confident about the relationship between the two terms, a link which their Jesuit brothers maintained was "required absolutely." The Jesuit Congregation, for example, avers:

The mission of the Society of Jesus today is the service of faith, of which the promotion of justice is an absolute requirement. This is so because the reconciliation of men among themselves, which their reconciliation with God demands, must be based on justice.[1]

The reason the Congregation asserts for the link "required absolutely" between faith and justice is that our reconciliation with God demands reconciliation between human persons, which in turn requires justice. Implicitly, therefore, the Jesuits understand faith as at least a part of our reconciliation with God and as exigent of our reconciliation with our fellow human persons which in turn cannot come about save by our acting justly with one another. We cannot be reconciled with persons who continue to treat us unjustly or whom we continue to treat unjustly.

How are we meant to understand this nexus of terms? I suggest that we can understand it properly if we begin with the term believers think they find the easier to understand, with the term "faith," and if we regard the paragraph as representing a development of the traditional and specifically Roman Catholic use of the term "faith." Jesuits are the sons of St. Ignatius of Loyola, founder of the largest Order of the Counter-Reformation. It is appropriate that echoes of the understanding of faith which informed the Counter-Reformation and came to live expression at the Council of Trent should still live in the Jesuit use of the term. That traditional understanding emphasizes intellectual assent to revealed truth (cf. Dulles' essay on the intellectualist meaning of faith) and ties faith to a justification which as such requires good works (included in which, of course, would be works of justice) and is the principle of their merit.

Although the term "justification" is less than common in religious discourse today, we recall that it was the key term in the sixteenth-century imbroglio over the understanding of our salvation, brought about through Jesus Christ. The Tridentine Fathers understood the Reformers' position regarding justification by faith alone as an act or state of being extrinsic to persons in this life. They thought that the Reformers' position was that justification was not truly imparted to persons in this life, nor did it inhere in them in any way. Because of this understanding of justification, the Reformers appeared to the Tridentine Fathers not to recognize the necessity of good works. The Reformers seemed almost to reject the role of good works in the plan of salvation because they rejected their merit. The Tridentine Fathers for their part held that good works were indeed meritorious. Therefore, other things being equal, they were "required absolutely" in the plan of salvation. So, for at least two reasons, Trent taught that one could not rely solely on a fiducial faith—one that consisted essentially, if not exclusively, in trusting God. First, although one's salvation was "inside" one even in this life, nonetheless it had to manifest itself in deeds just as the faculty of will manifests itself in actual choices. Second, as we shall see in more detail later, faith is but part of a plan of salvation in which good works are necessary or "required absolutely." This plan of salvation is the "justice of God" for this world, which justice both God and man exercise in part through the good works of "justified" men and women.

Coming from such a tradition, was it not appropriate that the Jesuit fathers at the Thirty-Second General Congregation spoke of the "service of the faith" when they linked faith with justice, rather than using only the term "faith"? In so doing they reveal that they are developing the Tridentine understanding of faith which linked faith with good works. The "promotion of justice" is a collective term for some of the good works which faith requires. Furthermore, the term begins the job of specifying the nature of the good works which faith requires. Since defense of this doctrine was the Jesuits' apostolate in the sixteenth century, it is fitting that they have continued and developed this tradition in the twentieth century.

In order to understand the development, let us briefly review the essential components of the use of the term "faith" in the Counter-Reformation as found in the documents of the Council of Trent. When placed in that context, the expanded term, "service of faith," denotes not the dead faith described in Chapter XV of Trent's *Decree on Justification*, but rather the faith that is alive with the grace of justification described in that decree[2] (Neuner and Roos, 1967, p. 395). Along these lines we shall see that it is the old doctrine of justification which forges the link between faith and justice today.

Etymologically, the connection between justice and justification is obvious. The equivalent terms in the other languages relevant to this development of Christian doctrine are similarly related: e.g., *justificatio, justitia*; *dikaióō, dikaiosúnē*, etc.[3] Thus, even verbally, the Tridentine problematic and the Jesuits' General Congregation are in continuity one with another.

Fundamental to our review is Trent's specific claim regarding justification by faith. Trent taught that we are justified by faith in the sense that God gratuitously justifies us. This *results* in a faith without which we are not pleasing to God.[4] Therefore, the "service of" this "faith" is really the service of the one who justifies, that is, God. It is "service of faith" in the sense that it consists in all those works which go along with the gift of faith. They are works commanded by the one who both justifies and gives faith; in performing those works, we obey our God who lovingly and gratuitously justifies us.

All this fits in with the plain meaning of the Tridentine *Decree on Justification*. Chapter IX warns against a merely fiducial understanding of faith, Chapter X relates the increase of justification to good works, and Chapter XI states both the necessity and possibility of observing God's commands on the part of the justified person. This Roman Catholic understanding of justification truly gives rise to a faith which requires a whole program of service to live out its meaning.

Thus far our observations are commonplaces of Roman Catholic believing. All Roman Catholics know that their faith must issue in the spiritual and corporal works of mercy or theirs is a dead faith.[5] But there is a more specific teaching in the Tridentine decree which strengthens the link between faith and justice, the working out of which is *the* Jesuit and, analogously, the Christian mandate. That teaching is Trent's account of the formal cause of our justification. I understand formal cause to mean that component of an entity that makes it what it is and not something else. This is the common understanding of formal cause in Thomistic metaphysics. Ultimately, it may disguise a muddle, but it helps get at what the Church wanted to teach when, as in Trent, it spoke of the formal cause of justification: it is the "component" of God's redemptive love received in a person, or in which the person shares or participates, whereby he or she is both justified and enabled to act justly. Let us examine that part of the decree.

Having treated of the final, the efficient, the meritorious, and the instrumental causes of justification, the Council comes to the formal cause of our justification:

> Finally the single *formal* cause *(unica formalis causa)* is the justice of God, not that by which he himself is just but that by which he makes us just, that, namely, whereby being endowed with it by him, we are renewed in the spirit of our mind, and not *only* are we reputed but are truly called and are just, receiving justice within us, each one according to his own measure, which the Holy Spirit distributes to everyone as he wills (1 Cor. 12:11), and according to each one's disposition and cooperation.[6]

Two items of importance for us today stand out in this definition. They are, first, that justification is participation in the justice of God for his creation, and, second, that this created justice is real within us in this life. Oddly enough, because of the state of the question in the sixteenth-century imbroglio over justification, the second item of importance has obscured the first. Because the Tridentine Fathers wished to insist over and over again that the justice of God inhered within us in this life, we in succeeding generations have not drawn out the implications of the first item. When the emphasis falls on the inherence of justification within us, Trent's notion of the "justice of God" loses its "objective" force. Under the influence of this emphasis it can seem that the justice of God by which he makes us just consists solely in a state of personal or subjective being much like a disposition or a virtue. The justice of God, then, need not imply changes in, or requirements for, the objective order of human affairs.

When the justice of God is not seen to require adaptations and transformations of the objective order of human affairs, the tendency is to regard the structure of that order as if it were like a structure of physical nature. How often have societies explained their hierarchical arrangements as modeled after the order of the heavens? In that way societies make a not so subtle claim that their orders are as unchangeable as the heavens. If structures or orders are unalterable, why worry whether they are just? In more modern terms, we distinguish between a subjective emphasis in moral matters that looks primarily at our motives and intentions and an objective component that looks beyond not only motives and intention or even private activity but also beyond what a given individual as such can do toward a social goal which only a community of persons could achieve. Thus, commonly, the distinction we are drawing here between subjective and objective is drawn by distinguishing between the personal and the social or between the individual and the communal. Our distinction between subjective and objective is virtually synonymous with these distinctions and others like them, but we endeavor with our somewhat unusual use of terms to bring out what we consider a terribly important but often overlooked element latent in the distinction. To our mind, the term "subjective" points to the intentions and purposes of human agents as individuals. It points to the structure of their characters, their virtues and vices, and by a slight extension names those choices and activities which have little or no effect in the larger, social world, but do indicate the quality of the subjects performing them. On the other hand, "objective" does better duty than "social," "collective" or "communal" in our opinion because we can use it to name the objective realities created for us by other subjects acting in common or those objective realities our communal actions posit. We use the term to point to the fact that the social, collective, or communal is the objectification of subjects who must necessarily exist communally.

The starkest contrast between the subjective and objective as we use the terms consists in the fact that for the most part we as individuals can reform our subjective being, but we must act communally or politically to change our objective being in the world, for it is part of the objectified order or structure of human affairs. Our belief is that along with and through the efforts of human subjects, God wishes to objectify his justice in the social, collective, and communal order as well as within personal characteristics of human subjects. We can distinguish these dimensions, but not truly separate them.

When we consider the social, collective, or communal as objective in the way that nature is objective, I think by implication the justice of God begins to be conceived of as that which improves persons subjectively only and as individuals only. Then the evils of the objective order are suffered patiently as the effects of sin, much as we have understood physical evil, and we mistakenly think that God's justice here and now contains no "plan of salvation" for the objective social order save insofar as the improvements his grace is able to effect in the individual subjects have as a further consequence the amelioration of that order. In other words, the justice of God improves subjectively and as individuals, having no significance for the order, except for those improvements in carrying out the order of human affairs which flow from the renewed subjective dispositions or virtues of individuals.

I would consider it a moot question whether such an interpretation fulfills the letter of the Tridentine decree. To my mind it clearly does not fulfill the spirit of the decree. One of Jedin's remarks confirms me in my conviction. He has observed that the meaning of the *unica formalis causa* of our justification must not be sought only within the seventh chapter of the decree, but finds its full meaning when we consider the teaching on good works in the sixteenth chapter which corresponds to or "objectifies" the teaching on the formal cause of justification in the seventh chapter.[7] The sixteenth chapter underscores the exhortation of the apostle Paul in 1 Corinthians 15:58 to the justified: "Abound in every good work, knowing that your labor is not in vain in the Lord."[8]

Nevertheless, even in the sixteenth chapter, a narrow reading could result in understanding the justice of God by which he makes us just as effecting merely a subjective change. But such a reading would not exploit such images as Christ the head and we the members or Christ the vine and we the branches, or the body of Christ. Nor would it serve to illumine the full meaning of the divine law or the judgment of God or even the term "justice of God." These images and ideas cry out for an understanding of the justice related to faith which is more than a virtuous disposition or a subjective justification. Nevertheless, we must candidly acknowledge that Trent's teaching on the justice of God, objectively conceived, is ambiguous and by now historically a moot question.

Notwithstanding the ambiguity it is true to the expressed sentiments of Trent that if we the justified fail to promote justice, we fail to express the very principle of our salvation. For according to the Tridentine Fathers, in one sense we are not saved by faith alone; we are saved, rather, by that share which is ours in what they called a *unica formalis causa* (a single formal cause). Faith, if it is living faith, is a manifestation of the gift of a share in this justice.

This fundamental teaching is so clear and strong that it has overshadowed the ambiguity between subjective and objective justice. Furthermore, invoking a sense of history, we may claim that the material conditions (that is to say, the infrastructure, the relationships of production, the actual state of affairs within the economy and in politics, etc.—the historical state of affairs) were such in the sixteenth century as to obviate a clear distinction between the subjective and the objective as we have made it, or an equivalent distinction, and therefore to prevent persons from seeing any ambiguity in our understanding of the "justice of God." Nevertheless, the formal conditions (that is to say, a sufficiently clear understanding of the "justice of God" so as to be able to resolve the ambiguity when it would be noticed) do exist in the Tridentine decree. These formal conditions are implicit in the understanding of "form" or *unica formalis causa* in the decree itself. A form must be the form of something, and, as we observed above, the form exists numerically in as many instances as there are entities which it informs. If the form is unique, there can be only one entity which it informs. If the form is unique as is the form of the "justice of God" *(unica formalis causa)*, and if many otherwise individual entities share or participate in the form, then the form must be the shape or structure of a reality that is more cohesive than a mere aggregate.

The Church has consistently taught in various ways that the nature of human persons is social in such a sense that society as seen is a totality (or kind of entity) which is greater than the sum of its individual parts. In recent social teaching the Church has reflected this awareness in its condemnation of "liberalism," because "the very root of philosophical liberalism is an erroneous affirmation of the autonomy of the individual in his activity, his motivation and the exercise of his liberty."[9]

The redeemed order is a transformation of what is seen to exist in this vision of natural society. The objective order of human affairs and the "justice of God" which is its true form can be no mere aggregate, for a mere aggregate has no single form. Each item in the aggregate has its own form autonomously, that is, to the exclusion of another inclusive form. Were our justification merely a subjective disposition or virtue and our good works merely individual and as such exclusive of a societal form within them, then it would have been more appropriate for Trent to have taught that the formal cause of our justification was multiple, a created form of the justice of God tailored to each justified person and having as many numerical instances as there are justified persons. But Trent taught that the form of our justification is single *(unica)*. From this it follows that our good works ought to have some single structure in common which would unite them. Such a common form in turn would make the promotion of justice and efforts to form a just society appropriate rather than merely calling for efforts to reform ourselves morally within a given society. In this way the "justice of God . . . by which he makes us just" would not seem to be merely a subjective ideal of Christians as individuals, but also in some measure the realizable form of the society informed by and forming such individuals.

After all, as a society we collectively or communally make up the one body of Christ. This image invites us frankly and openly to do what we have been doing in bits and pieces all along—that is, to define form in the classical manner of hylomorphism. From Aristotle on, and especially with St. Thomas, the form which is the referent for an abstract universal term exists insofar as it inheres in a body which it informs and thereby makes the body the specific thing that it is. If we correctly understand hylomorphism, we are not misled by the grammatically singular form of the abstract universal term into believing that the form which it names is single. The definition of man as an animal which is potentially rational is singular in grammatical form, but we know that the form referred to with indefinite variation exists insofar as it inheres in the bodies of an indefinite number of human individuals and in composition with those bodies makes of them unique persons. In the clear terms of hylomorphism, we must choose between two understandings of the single formal cause of our justification. Either it is an abstract universal term which is only grammatically singular and actually plural as it inheres with indefinite variety in indefinite number of individuals, or it is actually singular, in which case it is the objective form of a collectivity, community, or society and inheres in individuals only insofar as they participate in that community. If one takes seriously Trent's insistence on *unica*, the latter alternative is preferable.

The difficulty that stands in the way of the preferable alternative is one of discerning the community so informed by the justice of God. Such a discernment is possible only by faith. In faith we seek God's intent and purpose which transforms individuals and constitutes the authentic objective social order in which we are called to participate "according to each one's disposition and co-operation." Although the biblical record ties God's objective intent and purpose to the legendary accounts of history, as in the exodus or the doom of Jerusalem, and classical theology ties his objective intent and purpose to a metaphysics of providence, as in the *Summa* of St. Thomas, this objective will is not a matter of doubt to believing Catholics. It may need reformulation in a post-critical world, but it is not doubted in the believing community. Standing on this conviction of faith, we may describe the justice of God as the *single (unica)* intent and purpose of God, which actually expresses itself in the human social order although discerned only with the eyes of faith. Take the resurrection which is both actual and actually seen only with the eyes of faith; so also we maintain that the single form of God's justice is actually, and not just grammatically, seen to be the singular form of the objective social order in which we are called to participate actively insofar as we are able.

Evidently, from the history of the Church following Trent, these formal considerations did not resolve the ambiguity, for Trent's teaching on justification did not make of the Church a catalyst of social ferment and change in the socio-economic and political orders. Quite the contrary ensued. The Church, for the most part, became famous (or infamous) as a reactionary force. And this state of affairs may well have resulted, at least in part, from the ambiguity regarding the "objective" nature of the justice of God by which he makes us just. On the other hand, the Tridentine understanding of justification did spur on a massive missionary effort and a truly admirable host of charitable movements and institutions—e.g., an enormous array of hospitals, educational institutions, institutions for direct aid to the poor, and the like.

All that was needed to convert this "service of faith" from corporal and spiritual works of mercy in the private sector to the pursuit of justice in the public sector was a shift in our consciousness about the meaning of justice. That shift has since occurred. *Post factum* this can remove any lingering ambiguity in Trent's teaching regarding the subjectivity or objectivity of the justice of God in this world.

The shift consists in two related convictions: persons are responsible to some degree for more than their own personal acts; they are in some measure responsible for the communal or social activity in which they have a part. Furthermore, the corporate or social acts of persons necessarily proceed from structures, institutions and the like. These structures which are necessary for social or corporate activity are not given once for all, but are in themselves subject to change and therefore objects of human responsibility. Heretofore, many Catholics were inclined to regard basic social structures as virtually a part of nature not unlike the given order of the heavens; now we regard them as human artifacts for which we are responsible. As a corollary, we now perceive that the structures, institutions and the like are a prior condition for the acts of individuals within the structures, and in large measure enter into and even determine the morality (the goodness or badness) of the individual acts. In other words, Trent's teaching on the justice of God by which he makes us just must be seen to have something to do with a "common structure" or plan organizing individual acts. In some measure, the plan must be realized in this world, or the good works which our faith mandates in this life would not be good. Thus, the shift in our consciousness of justice resolves Trent's ambiguity.

Since the point of this shift is of vital importance to our discussion, let us use a classic example to fix the notion in our minds. From the beginning of Christianity until after Trent, the institution of slavery was accepted as a given part of the order of human affairs. Christians from St. Paul onward exhorted both slaves and slave-holders to virtuous Christian living. During this period, Trent's "justice of God by which he makes us just," which inhered in both the justified slave and the justified slave-holder, expressed itself in meritorious good works that we can describe in part as the carrying out of the duties of their respective states in life. It did not express itself in efforts to abolish the institution of slavery. After the shift in consciousness, the same justice was seen to require the effort to abolish slavery. The justice of God by which he makes us just comes to mean a mandate for the structural reordering of human affairs.

Unfortunately for Christians, with perhaps the issue of slavery as an exception, the shift occurred for the most part in non-Christian circles. The Second Vatican Council, the Bishop's Synod on Justice and the Jesuits' Thirty-Second General Congregation are but the beginnings of our efforts as an institutional Church to cope with that shift in our consciousness about the meaning of justice. Thus, we can delineate that shift in consciousness by reference to our exhortations in the matter of justice. Exhortations to just behavior used to stress personal reform; now an exhortation to justice can be a call for public reform and in some circumstances even revolution. Whereas Catholic clergy once counseled people to fulfill the duties of their state in life, some now would question whether the state in life is just.

In the larger secular world the Great Revolution of seventeenth-century England adumbrated the shift; 1776 and 1789 clearly placed revolution over reform. Then many, but especially Karl Marx, began to try to understand what it would take to make the revolutionary ideals of liberty, fraternity, and equality mean something for the poor in this life, and revolution moved from the eighteenth-century phenomena to 1917 and all that has followed in our century. Until very recently the Roman Catholic Church constituted a massive resistance to this shift and harbored the best critics of its excesses. But all that is changing.[10]

A word of caution is required with regard to all that is changing. It is a matter of historical fact that the material conditions (the relationships of production, etc.) which gave rise to the shift in our consciousness also gave rise to the modern phenomenon of revolution. But that fact does not of itself justify revolution as the sole or even the privileged way to realize what we now perceive justice requiring of us. In fact, appearances notwithstanding, the form of revolution through armed conflict which has dominated history from the seventeenth to the twentieth century may no longer be the viable way to strive to build a more just society. Unfortunately, it may seem "ideological" for one like myself to note this possibility since I am numbered among those who enjoy the material benefits of present injustice and have evident reasons to hope that armed conflict directed against them is a thing of the past. Nevertheless, it remains possibly true that in most instances revolution is no longer viable, if it ever was the best route to its stated goals.

From the point of view of ideas, though, the shift is relatively simple. In the foreground it may be seen in terms of changes in the meaning of distributive justice and in a development of the meaning of personal freedom. In the background, one must understand that behind the shift in the meanings of otherwise traditional terms, there lies the profound but subtle change in the primary object of moral evaluation. Until the revolutionary period in Western history, we for the most part accepted social structures as given and hardly noticed them, in much the way that the air we breathe is seldom the center of our attention. While in this pre-revolutionary period, as we saw, the primary object of moral evaluation was the person as individual, now the primary object is the structured pattern of our social existence in community. This change does not imply that we have lost sight of the individual. He or she is secondary only in the sense of being located within the primary object.

The shift in our consciousness about the meaning of justice is reflected in Church documents, such as those produced at the Jesuits' Thirty-Second General Congregation, when the documents speak of our responsibility for structures or refer to persons as being systematically oppressed. The Second Vatican Council acknowledged the shift in the ways just mentioned, but it also and very especially recognized the shift in its recognition of politically realized and guaranteed personal freedom. Putting all these ingredients together requires of us a more complex understanding of justice than our tradition gave us, but one that is no more than a development of that tradition.

One could sum up the tradition at least as articulated from

Thomist sources by saying that distributive justice, the backbone of social justice, consists in rendering to each his due (suum cuique).[11] Distributive justice in turn presupposes a system of laws and one or more lawgivers responsible for seeing that the whole of society pursues the common good. Furthermore, the traditional Roman Catholic teaching on questions of social justice rests on the conviction that persons are by nature social and that both our social nature and the divine law require the organization of a society whose primary task is to see that all human beings are able to provide for themselves humanly, or, if unable to do so, are humanly provided for. This is the minimum due each person. Setting the accommodation to feudalism to one side, the Church has never dictated a detailed system as the only means of carrying out this ideal. So, the problem has always been to determine what is due a person, and what system will best provide the person with what is due to him or her.

In a hierarchical and hereditary system, a person's state in life went a long way toward settling that question. But the shift to revolution introduced a notion of equality and upset the notion of states of life. At first it was equality of citizenship, then an equality of opportunity in a competitive race to acquire the goods to be distributed.[12] Finally, Marx and others introduced a more radically material sense of equality. The adage for distributive justice became "from each according to his abilities, to each according to his needs."

The Second Vatican Council did not settle finally the question of which specific sense of equality is just in a Christian sense, nor which ideal of distributive justice or which system we are to prefer. The Council did lean toward greater material equality, and not just to the minimum condition, as a requirement of justice.[13]

But of greater import for our purposes here, Vatican II recognized our responsibility for the socio-economic and political structures which determine the patterns of distributive justice or injustice. With this recognition along with its endorsement of a civil expression of personal freedom (especially in Dignitatis Humanae), the Council embraced positions hammered out by the deists and atheists of 1776 and 1789. When the Council added to these teachings a preference for a greater material equality, it entered even the territory formerly occupied almost exclusively by the militant atheists of 1917 and following. In short, by explicitly recognizing our responsibility for social structures, the Council requires that Catholics face enormous social problems which have unusual historical and theoretical roots as part of their service of faith.

The Thirty-Second General Congregation takes up the new recognition of the Second Vatican Council especially in paragraph 27 of "Our Mission Today":

Finally, among the seemingly constant factors of our world particularly significant to our mission of evangelization is this: it is now within man's power to make the world more just— but he does not really want to. His new mastery over nature and himself is used, often enough, to exploit individuals, groups, and peoples rather than to distribute the resources of the planet more equitably. It has led, it is leading, to oppression and domination rather than to a greater respect for the rights of the individual or of groups, and a more real brotherhood among men. We can no longer pretend that the inequalities and injustices of our world must be borne as part of the inevitable order of things. It is now quite apparent that they are the result of what man himself, man in his selfishness, has done. Hence, there can be no promotion of justice in the full and Christian sense unless we also preach Jesus Christ and the mystery of reconciliation he brings. For us, it is Christ who, in the last analysis, opens the way to the complete and definitive liberation of man. From now on, therefore, it will not be possible to bring Christ to men or to proclaim his Gospel effectively unless a firm decision is taken to devote ourselves to the promotion of justice.[14]

I think the key sentence is: "We can no longer pretend that the inequalities and injustices of our world must be borne as part of the inevitable order of things." Join to this the recognition embedded in the use of language about oppression and domination in the same paragraph, and even more clearly in paragraph 29, where we read of "the enslavement not only of the oppressed but of the oppressor," and we clearly see the shift in our consciousness whereby we have come to acknowledge that there are socio-economic and political structures which, as systems, systematically distribute this world's goods *unjustly*.[15]

If our Catholic consciousness had been developed to this point in the sixteenth century, the Tridentine doctrine on justification would have led us not to necessarily greater, but to different works by which we would have lived with and lived out the form of justice in which we participate. Today we have the consciousness which I have sketched, so the living out of faith requires the work of evaluating and transforming structures in the socio-economic and political field. In some ways it will be new work because it demands evaluation and work for the transformation or replacing of unjust structures. But it will be the same "service of faith" expressing the same formal cause of our justification which gives the new works their shape and purpose as it gave shape and purpose to our works in the past.

One further theoretical issue should complete this essay on the relationship between faith and justice in our day. There are two families of theories whereby theologians have attempted to understand justification. These theories have profound implications for the relationship between faith and justice. One "family" undermines a constructive relationship between faith and justice, the other reinforces the relationship. We shall characterize the "good family" as the "redemptive" theory of justification, although unfortunately we must introduce the name for this family in quotation marks because there is no agreed upon term to designate it.

The "redemptive" understanding of justification is best described in quite anthropomorphic terms, rather than defined. God the Father is seen as striving to rescue his people from the evil into which they have fallen. The evil comes from our own doing, but because it has grown into something greater than we can manage, it is often viewed as personified, superhuman forces. To these forces human persons are enslaved. God the Father comes up with a plan to save his beloved creatures from the prison we have made for ourselves. He sends his Son in human likeness into the prison house of this world. But, instead of rejoicing over the advent of our Savior, we are so enthralled in evil that we reject him. We, the enslaved, unjustly put the Just One to death.

At least three things result from the execution. In the first place, the Just One *freely* undergoes the penalty of death, which in its present form is a penalty we, the enslaved, have brought on ourselves as the fruit of our sins. In sinful blindness we impose death on him, which he freely accepts in a spirit of loving forgiveness toward us who so unjustly treat him, thereby breaking the deterministic hold which evil has over us by meeting our evil with good. Secondly, he reveals to human beings the true nature of our moral evil—it is our rejection of God's love. This is shown clearly when we kill those whom God loves. Finally, through the passion and death of Jesus, the Father is able to complete his salvific plans by resurrecting Jesus from the dead as the first of the reborn. Through the resurrection the Father overturns the evil judgment of this world and declares that it is not his judgment; therefore, it shall not stand.

Nevertheless, we still ask: Since it was the passion and death of his beloved Son which was at stake, why did not God overwhelm evil? Why did he not suppress evil before it could wreck havoc on his beloved Son? What little glimpse of the mysterious answer to this question we may have, we see in terms of God's love for us sinners as well as his love for his Son, and God's firm decision to love us as free beings and thereby elicit a freely given love in return. In other words, had God the Father sent the legions of angels which Jesus mentioned while being arrested in the garden of Gethsemane, God would have been violating our freedom and changing us from creatures who can freely return his love into something else. Therefore, God permitted evil in order to protect personal freedom, and *not*, as the vindictive theory would have it, to restore a balance of justice or to compensate himself for injuries suffered.

This "redemptive" theory of justification which we have tried to describe in an anthropomorphic and narrative style is a variant of an ancient, and I think correct, view of justification. It was, perhaps, Gregory of Nyssa who gave it its most colorful and mythic form. In the 22nd to 24th chapters of his *Great Catechism*, this outstanding patristic figure has God ransom us back from the devil and catch the devil in the bargain.[16] God is like a clever fisherman who gives the devil what he wants by giving him dominion over the flesh of Jesus as he has won dominion over all human flesh through sin. But in this case the flesh is but bait over a divine hook which catches the devil himself, and fairly too, for the devil did have his way with the Christ in the flesh.

Our intellectual distaste for strong anthropomorphisms should not put us off when it comes to Gregory's account of justification. It belongs to a better tradition than the alternative theory, variously called vindictive or retributive.[17] Although never officially embraced by the Roman Catholic Church, the vindictive theory of justification has harmfully influenced our piety. Although this theory may hide itself in abstract language, it comes down to Jesus through his passion and death paying a debt to the Father on our behalf in order to restore the balance of divine justice. The governing metaphor behind the theory is that of a divine scale of justice in God tilted by an infinite offense (infinite because an offense takes its magnitude from the majesty of the one offended). In the vindictive theory, Jesus in his passion and death freely suffers the retribution which human beings owe the divine majesty. But, Jesus' freedom notwithstanding, divine justice exacted those sufferings as punishment (i.e., retribution) in order to *vindicate* itself. Hence the governing image, for when fundamentally justice is vindictive, the need to weigh or measure the retribution, which pays off the offended, becomes fundamental too. The cosmic version of vindication and retributive payment is a vision in which an offense is seen as a dislocation of something in the universe. But since the order is a balance or harmony, the scale metaphor reappears and a painful "payment" commensurate to the dislocation or imbalance must be exacted from the offender. Since the true personhood of Jesus is of infinite, divine worth, the human sufferings he bears are sufficient to pay infinite retribution to the Father on our behalf and tilt the scale back to equilibrium. The sufferings are able to restore the equilibrium because they have infinite value. As the offense took its magnitude from the one offended, so the punishment takes its worth from the majesty of the person who bore the sufferings.

By understanding punishment in this way, the vindictive theory of justification implicitly endows not the initial evil or original sin nor all subsequent evil, but at least some evil with a value in itself. Some evil comes to have at least the value of a needed means. Since, initially, evil is seen as upsetting a balance or scale, then the evil which functions as retributive punishment, even if it has no medicinal, rehabilitating or social value, somehow restores the balance. It is as if an injured person, in this case God, received compensation from the injuries inflicted on the one who did harm in the first place, and this later evil of retribution is somehow necessary to God.

As we shall see, this has the effect of deadening our sense of justice with regard to the objective order of human affairs. From it we learn to tolerate evil and injustice rather than challenge them and strive to transform them. Thus, the vindictive theory of justification blocks the effects of Trent's teaching on justice and good works and thereby would seem properly to belong to what the Tridentine Fathers, rightly or wrongly, took to be the Reformers' teaching rather than their own.

The fundamental problem confronting the vindictive theory is that although it involves a payment, it makes nonsense of the metaphor in the term "redemption." To redeem means to buy back from slavery. A ransom or redemption is paid to a slave-holder so that he will manumit a slave. In the vindictive theory, the obedient sufferings and death of Christ are retribution. If they are then in addition seen as a ransom or redemption, to whom are they paid? If the redemption is paid to the Father, then it would seem that the Father is the evil slave-holder. Gregory of Nazianzus in the fourth century saw that this was not only nonsense but outrageous. He summarily rejected the notion that Christ paid a ransom to the Father. As he wisely said, "We were not held captive by him [God]."[18] Thus, Gregory of Nazianzus joined with Gregory of Nyssa in rejecting the vindictive theory. Nazianzus did so by explicitly denying what the vindictive theory implies about who receives the ransom paid in redemption. Both he and Gregory of Nyssa held that we were redeemed from the power of an Evil One, the devil, although Nazianzus would not follow the operative metaphor to its logical conclusion, as did Nyssa, and conceive of Christ paying a ransom to the devil. For Nazianzus that may not have been nonsense within the terms of the metaphor, but it was certainly outrageous. It sounded to Nazianzus that the payment would consist in handing over God himself to the devil. To avoid this

Nazianzus has God overwhelm the tyrant by force.

The significance for us of this patristic lore lies in the fact that these Church Fathers conceived of the redemptive process, in the first place, as freeing us from bondage to a fellow creature or created reality and forgiving us for our active share in the evils of slavery; then, as the all-important corollary, of that deliverance as freeing us *for* a return to the loving and forgiving Father. The vindictive theory muddles this vision by seeming to make the Father's attitude toward us problematic. In addition to redeeming us from evil and bringing the Father's forgiveness, Jesus must pay the Father retribution before he opens his arms to take us back. Jesus as the Christ in offering the retribution that opens the Father's arms seems to make of the evil of his unjust execution not a revelation of our sin and slavery from which the Father redeems us, but a "good." The cross is not embraced because, although an evil, from rejecting it greater evils would ensue. Somehow, by the alchemy of retribution, the cross itself becomes good.

Both the vindictive and the "redemptive" theory (i.e., Nyssa and Nazianzus) admit of spiritualized interpretations which draw us away from social concerns—the vindictive theory does this of itself and the older theory does it through the somewhat mythic language the Church Fathers used in casting the theory. When evil is personified as the devil, the danger arises that Christians will conceive of the evil from which we are redeemed solely in terms of the inner man. We, then, may attend exclusively to spiritual struggles and entirely forget the larger social arena. We may even claim that all evils in the larger arena derive exclusively from the spiritual and moral failure of individuals as such and can be cured only through the regeneration of such individuals as individuals.

But there are very healthy antibodies in the Church tradition that militate against such Gnostic tendencies embodied in the exaggeration we have just sketched. The Church does not deny—on the contrary, it affirms—that there are dimensions to the evil that enslaves us which can be overcome only by the direct action of God in our hearts, often acting through prayer and the sacraments. What the Church does deny is that prayer and the sacraments and personal virtue represent the only ways God would have us deal with evil. It denies this exaggeration through its social teaching, especially from the *Rerum Novarum* of Pope Leo XIII until the present. It thereby teaches what is true and profound in the "redemptive" theory: the redemptive process seeks to free us from bondage to created evil in all its forms. The Father's arms are already open. His power is on our side to extricate us from created evils. We need not try to make a virtue of the evils and sufferings of this world as if our suffering these evils were somehow necessary to God in order to right our relationship with him, as the vindictive theory would lead us to think.

Sufferings and evil in this world are "necessary" for salvation in a different sense. We understand that "necessity" only imperfectly. We see that they are "necessary" because they resulted from the misuse of human freedom and could not now be fully suppressed without suppressing human freedom, which remains a greater good than the evils tolerated. We see that they are "necessary" because there is a profound wisdom in God's plan for overcoming evil which implies love, patience, faith, and hope, as opposed to a despairing and rebellious attitude toward evil which can and does lead from anger to hatred and even to a rejection of life.

Nonetheless, this latter rebellious position may be closer to Christian faith in a loving, just, and forgiving Father than a position that is ambiguous about the Father's attitude toward our sufferings and evil in this world. The vindictive theory leads to such ambiguity. Suffering and evil may be disguised goods because they provide the retributive punishment that makes up what is lacking in the sufferings of Christ and furthers our restoration to God. Such confusion about the evils of this life leads to resolutions of the ambiguity in Trent's teaching about the justice of God and to misuses of the symbolization of evil in the Church Fathers which clearly undermine a Christian determination to fight evil in this world and to seek freedom from its oppressive bondage. By requiring retribution, "god" would make political reactionaries of us all.

We have not the space to comment further on the understanding of a "god" who would require such retribution in order to restore justice. Suffice it to say, it is incompatible with the Christian vision of a Father who can forgive. Our concern, rather, must lie with the effect that this vindictive theory can have and has had on our response to the evils of this world. It can and has had the effect of encouraging us to tolerate evil passively as what we deserve from God's justice. Often our consciences do tell us that we deserve some chastisement, maybe even serious chastisement, *but* the use of evil merely as retribution never brings good out of evil. Furthermore, it must seem absurd if not blasphemous to the thinking people of this dark century to suggest that the victims of the Holocaust, the wretched in the Gulag Archipelago, the bombed and burned in Vietnam, the sufferers in Chilean concentration camps, and millions of the hungry (to scratch the surface of a list of this century's horrors) are suffering those just penalties which restore proper balance to God's offended, retributive justice. I think that we immediately and rightly prefer to understand the sufferings of the Just One as a revelation of the meaning of the evil that is all around us and as the occasion of coming in faith to know God's determination through the resurrection to completely wipe out the evil and sin that engulfs human beings. This latter view prompts not to passivity, but to action. When we turn from executing the Christ to accepting the forgiving love we in no way deserve, our response is supposed to be an effort to overcome with good the evil revealed in the execution of Christ, not merely to tolerate it.

Secondly, the view which we take of justification emphasizes personal human freedom, as is obvious from theodicy latent in the "redemptive" understanding of justification. God the Father "suffered" the evil of his beloved Son's passion and death because of his love for us as *free* beings. To protect his beloved Son, he would have had to destroy our freedom. Therefore, the passion and death of Jesus reveals the extraordinary value which God places on human freedom. In *imitatio Dei*, we may tolerate evil properly insofar as the toleration serves the greater good of human freedom, and a promotion of justice in this world which is in "the service of Christian faith" must strive to promote authentic human freedom, as the Second Vatican Council so clearly saw. Through the Council, Roman Catholicism has affirmed that the widespread exercise of authentic personal freedom is an essential part of the common good (e.g., *Gaudium et Spes*, n. 17). Therefore, authoritarianism is an improbable means to the common good and certainly not a part of any achieved instance of that good.

Guided by these notions and the ideas we have already expounded, we shall see that "the service of faith" requires promoting just systems which distribute "the benefits of culture" with some measure of equality so that at the very least each human person may creatively exercise his or her personal freedom in the process of providing for himself or herself and for dependents, or, if that is impossible, being provided for. From the development in the meaning of justice through our "revolutionary" period, we realize that merely formal freedoms do not guarantee to real men and women the possibility of exercising authentic freedom to the full. In promoting justice we must strive for the conditions in which persons can exercise their freedom as fully as possible. This exigency of Christian faith precludes totalitarianism as a means of solving other problems associated with building a just social order. But, just as there is an understanding of justification, the vindictive theory, which perverts our vision of God and deadens the call to the loving justice that comes from our faith, so there are understandings of "freedom" which serve only to sap courage and block efforts to make the necessary changes in present structures which even a minimalist's view of justice requires. Usually these false uses of freedom come down to the claim that we cannot change our economic structures significantly without losing what freedoms we now enjoy. The effect of this claim, which I regard as false, is not only to deaden efforts to promote justice through fundamental structural changes in the economic and productive systems, it also curtails the free discussion and debate required to understand the reasons why some believe such changes are necessary. A pall of fear is cast over the discussion. Therefore, we must affirm freedom with the painful awareness that our affirmation can be used for reactionary purposes and do our best to prevent that misuse of our conviction.

Finally, the understanding of the link between faith and justice that comes from our Catholic view of justification by faith, although it does not prescribe the one system of distributive justice which is best, does incline us always to that system which best guarantees a real equality between persons. The dignity God's love for each one of us gives us tends to undermine arbitrary social stratification and even to lead us through the sharing which love inspires to structure our relationships as between equals. The repeated call of *Gaudium et Spes* to greater participation in decisions and more equal sharing of the benefits of culture is but one expression of this tendency in our faith.

Although it took us a dreadfully long time, we Christians finally did see that the institution of slavery was incompatible with the dignity which God's love bestows on persons. Therefore, we may hope that faith will continue to inspire us to seek not a bogus egalitarianism, but an ideal of distributive justice which expresses the equal dignity of persons before God. My preference would be for the ideal which was not original with Marx, "from each according to his ability, to each according to his needs," as understood in conjunction with a democratic ideal.[19]

It is not necessary to stress that this principle is an ideal and does not function as a proximate principle with which we can settle daily matters of distribution. But even when remote, ideals have their place in thinking practically about justice.

The ideal provides remote justification for what may well be *the* task of social justice in our day: to change our economy from one built on the principle of organizing production in order to meet social needs.[20] The secondary task, then, becomes how to engineer the latter, which is really the pursuit of the common good, without losing what few real freedoms remain for the privileged minority within an economy that is organized to maximize profits. It is not a small task, but it is the expression of the justifying love of God within us.

I have attempted to show that the link that the delegates to the Thirty-Second General Congregation of the Society of Jesus saw as required absolutely between faith and justice is but a contemporary expression of the traditional Roman Catholic understanding of justification by faith formulated at the Council of Trent. Justification is a participation in the *unica formalis causa* which is God's justice for the creation of which we are a part. Thus, the reconciliation with God which begins when we are justified requires that we be reconciled with our fellow human persons in the single form that is God's justice for us all. Reflection on that justice which we have in the passion, death and resurrection of our

Lord leads us to hold that no matter what specifications we give to the plan of justice as we actively work it out under grace in this life, we must see to it that all persons are able to provide for themselves humanly, or are provided for when necessary, in and through the workings of a free society so organized that persons exercise their authentic freedom as fully as possible. Such a vision, it would seem, is not only a specific mandate for Jesuits, but is also the challenge of our Christian faith in and for our world today. "For in the Gospel is revealed the justice of God which begins and ends with faith" (Rom. 1:17).

NOTES

1. Jesuit Fathers, "Our Mission Today: The Service of Faith and the Promotion of Justice," *Documents of the Thirty-Second General Congregation of the Society of Jesus (An English Translation)* (The Jesuit Conference: Washington, D.C., 1975), p. 17.

2. J. Neuner and H. Roos, eds. (further edited by Karl Rahner), *The Teachings of the Church*, trans. Geoffrey Stevens (Staten Island, N.Y.: Alba House, 1967), p. 395.

3. Cf. Donahue essay in this volume.

4. Neuner and Roos, *op. cit.*, p. 389. The Tridentine Fathers cite Hebrews 11:6.

5. *Ibid.*, p. 389. The Tridentine Fathers cite James 2:17.

6. *Ibid.*, pp. 387-388. The Fathers at Trent chose *"unica"* to qualify *"formalis causa"* in order to obviate doctrines of two-fold justice which seemed to them to render us somewhat less than really justified when in a state of grace in this life. In this article we do not explore these historical reasons for Trent's choice, but instead attempt a systematic interpretation. Acts we perform because we are informed by God's justice are God's acts in a way that the acts occurring as a result of other, created formal causes, like the human soul, are not. The acts we do because we are informed by the justice of God are attributed directly to God in a way that acts which occur because of other, created forms are not.

7. H. Jedin, *A History of the Council of Trent*, Vol. II, trans. E. Graf (London: Thomas Nelson and Sons, 1961), p. 284.

8. Neuner and Roos, *op. cit.*, p. 396.

9. Pope Paul VI, *Apostolic Letter of His Holiness Pope Paul VI on the Occasion of the Eightieth Anniversary of the Encyclical Rerum Novarum* (A Call to Action), Section 35, p. 18.

10. E.g., cf. Rahner, *The Shape of the Church To Come*, trans. E.

Quinn (New York: Seabury Press, 1974), pp. 123-132.

11. Cf. Hollenbach essay on modern Catholic social thinking in this volume.

12. Cf. T. H. Marshall, *Class, Citizenship, and Social Development* (Garden City, N.Y.: Doubleday and Co., 1965).

13. Cf. W. M. Abbott, ed., *The Documents of Vatican II* (New York: America Press, 1966), pp. 206-207, 274-279; *Gaudium et Spes*: "The Pastoral Constitution on the Church in the Modern World," Nos. 9 and 26-29.

14. Jesuit Fathers, *op. cit.*, p. 25.

15. Cf. *Gaudium et Spes* as a whole.

16. For compact reference, see Bettenson, *The Later Christian Fathers* (London: Oxford University Press, 1970), pp. 141-142.

17. Cf. B. Lonergan, *De Verbo Incarnato* (Rome: Pontificia Universitas Gregoriana, 1964), pp. 486-593.

18. Bettenson, *op. cit.*, p. 122.

19. William K. Frankena provides an example of such an understanding. Cf. his *Ethics* (Englewood Cliffs, N.J.: Prentice-Hall, Inc., 1963), pp. 38-42; Karl Marx, *Critique of the Gotha Programme* (Peking: Foreign Languages Press, 1972), p. 17.

20. Barry Commoner, "A Reporter at Large (Energy—III)," *The New Yorker*, Feb. 16, 1976, 97-103.

Modern Catholic Teachings Concerning Justice

David Hollenbach, S.J.

The 1971 Synod of Bishops of the Roman Catholic Church introduced its reflections on the meaning of justice in world society with a statement which has become the platform and legitimation for a whole series of new initiatives in socio-political life by Roman Catholics. The bishops stated:

> Actions on behalf of justice and participation in the transformation of the world fully appear to us as a constitutive dimension of the preaching of the Gospel, or, in other words, of the Church's mission for the redemption of the human race and its liberation from every oppressive situation.[1]

In the several years since it was made, this statement has been quoted repeatedly in the discussions about the role of Christians in the social and political spheres. These discussions have frequently been heated, and sometimes rather confused. Several crucial issues are at stake in the continuing debate.

First, how is the justice which is "constitutive" of the mission of the Church to be understood? Political philosophers from Plato to John Rawls have proposed a wide array of definitions of justice.[2] Many of these rather technical theories of justice are implicitly present in the contemporary debates over the proper role of the Church in the formation of public policy. Justice can be described most generally in the ancient phrase *suum cuique*—to each what is due. This principle, however, can be specified and concretized in quite different ways, leading to quite different notions of justice. The principle can be interpreted as a call for respect toward a structured system of *roles, offices*, and *powers* in society, usually unequal ones. (Plato: "You remember how when we first began to establish our commonwealth, and several times since, we have laid down, as a universal principle, that everyone ought to perform the one function in the community for which his nature best suited him. Well, I believe that principle, or some form of it, is justice."[3]) The same general norm can imply obligation to respect some form of *excellence, achievement,* or *merit.* (Aristotle: "Everyone agrees that in distributions the just share must be given on the basis of what one deserves, though not everyone would name the same criterion of deserving: democrats say it is free birth, oligarchs say it is wealth or noble birth, and aristocrats say that it is excellence *[arete].*"[4]) *Suum cuique* can be interpreted as a principle of respect for what belongs to each person, namely for *property.* (John Locke: "The great and chief end, therefore, of men's uniting into commonwealths, and putting themselves under government, is the preservation of their property."[5]) The principle can lead to a call for affirmative action by individuals and society aimed at meeting the basic *needs* of all. (Marx: "From each according to his ability, to each according to his needs."[6]) Finally, it can be interpreted, as it perhaps most commonly is by contemporary North Americans, as demanding equal *liberty* and *opportunity* for all. (John Rawls: "First, each person is to have an equal right to the most extensive basic liberty compatible with a similar liberty for others. Second, social and economic inequalities are to be arranged so that they are both (a) reasonably expected to be to everyone's advantage, and (b) attached to positions and offices open to all."[7])

The pluralism of interpretations of justice, moreover, is not simply a diversity of theoretical accounts produced by philosophers. It is a problem which arises within Christian moral theology and Christian life. Men and women within the contemporary Church who consider themselves agents of justice both act and understand their action in quite diverse ways. The experience, motives and goals of a Christian American lawyer or politician, a curial monsignor promoting Vatican *Ostpolitik*, a North American feminist theologian and a Brazilian worker priest lead to conceptions of the promotion of justice which are at least functionally different if not substantively so. This pluralism of definitions of justice is not resolved in any simple way by stating that the promotion of justice is an integral part of the Christian faith. If the Synod's statement is to be saved from falling into the limbo reserved for slogans and platitudes, there is an urgent need to clarify the meaning of justice which it presupposes.

Second, recent debates among theologians, bishops, and activists of various ideological hues have also revolved around the fear that this statement may lead some to identify action for justice with the preaching of the Gospel and the mission of the Church in an illegitimately reductive manner. The fear is voiced in a number of ways: concern that some are confusing the development of a more just society with the radical newness of the Kingdom of God which comes only from grace and the redemptive action of God; dismay that too close an identification of the virtues of justice and faith will lead to an attempt to re-establish a clericalist control of society in an updated version of medieval Christendom; distress over an alleged confusion of the "values of the Gospel" with the orientations of a social-political ideology. These fears are met with counter-claims that any attempt to drive a wedge between commitment to the alleviation of injustice and the life of Christian belief destroys the integrity of Christian life, saps the prophetic power which Christians are called by God to evince, and denies the inseparability of the two great commandments of love of God and love of neighbor.[8] If further light is to be brought to these contemporary debates among Christians, a clarification of the relation between belief in the Gospel and the meaning of justice is sorely needed.

This essay will attempt to clarify both the meaning of justice and its relation to Christian belief by placing the Synod's document in the context of discussions of social justice in the Catholic tradition during the last one hundred years. The bishops' statement represents only the most notable development in a long tradition of Catholic reflection and teaching on social and political questions. The modern phase of the Catholic social ethical tradition, from Leo XIII to the present, is especially rich in refined and critical thought on the nature of justice and its relation to Christian belief.

This tradition's understanding of these questions has grown, developed and changed in significant ways during the past hundred years. A study of these developments may be of considerable help in clarifying both the meaning of the Synod's statement and the basic social and political obligations of Christians.

In 1891 Leo XIII issued his encyclical *Rerum Novarum* and initiated a new phase in social and political self-understanding of the Roman Catholic Church. The years immediately preceding the publication of this document were in many ways like our own time. They were years in which the Church was gradually coming to an awareness that major social change was under way—the transformation of traditional patterns of social life by the process of industrialization. Leo XIII's stated goal was to specify the "principles which truth and justice dictate" for dealing with the "misery and wretchedness" caused by these changes. This goal was to be pursued by an effort "to define the relative rights and mutual duties of the rich and the poor, of capital and labor."[9]

The discussion of justice in terms of relative rights and mutual duties is characteristic of the entire modern Catholic tradition. It is based on the conviction that one cannot specify the meaning of *suum cuique* without examining the social relationships, patterns of mutuality and structures of interdependence which bind human beings together in communities. The normative notion of justice adopted by the modern tradition, which has its historical origins in biblical, Augustinian, and Thomistic thought, is an essentially social concept—it is relational and mutual. Though justice demands respect for human rights as the imperious claims of individual dignity and worth, these rights are always "relative." More precisely, they can be neither specified nor understood apart from the web of social interdependence which entails mutual obligation and duty. This apparently innocuous affirmation is in fact highly significant. For example, Leo XIII's approach immediately distinguishes modern Catholic social thought from the liberal natural rights tradition of the eighteenth century which so much influenced the drafters of the United States Constitution. The mutual interdependence of persons on each other in family life, in work, and in political life is viewed as the foundation and matrix for the realization of human freedom and dignity. Respect for freedom and dignity, therefore, involves more than not interfering with the activity of persons. Obligations of justice include positive duties to aid persons in need, to participate in the maintaining of the public good and to share in efforts to create the kinds of institutions which promote genuine mutuality and reciprocal respect.

This more positive approach to the meaning of justice is rooted in the tradition's acceptance of the Aristotelian and Thomistic view of the essentially social nature of persons. The major encyclicals from Leo XIII to the present make frequent appeals to both philosophical and empirical arguments to establish such a social definition of human nature. The documents, however, also make frequent appeals to a bond of love which lies at the root of the obligations of justice. The stress on mutuality as intrinsic to the meaning of justice is a clear evidence of the influence of a Christian morality of love in what often appear to be thoroughly philosophical discussions of justice. The effect of this presence of the norm of love in the papal writings has been twofold.

First, it has led to continuing stress on concern and respect for individual human persons in their uniqueness and their concrete needs. The fundamental norm of the tradition, as John XXIII put it, is that "individual men are necessarily the foundation, cause, and the end of all social institutions."[10] Within the Catholic tradition respect for human dignity, human rights, and human need cannot be adequately understood without reference to the Christian moral norm of agape and its concern for concrete persons, especially those in need. The demands of justice are thus not primarily the conclusions drawn from a general philosophical principle expressed in propositional form. They arise from the claims or call which the dignity of persons makes on the freedom of others. Justice is rooted in the fact that "man himself is a certain 'ought' with respect to his fellow man. An age-old tradition calls the execution of this 'ought' 'love' and it understands this love as the acceptance, the willing, supporting and fostering of the other's subjectivity, selfhood and freedom."[11] This is not to identify justice with love. It seems clear from a number of recent discussions that the principle of justice has a different role to play in moral argument than does the principle of love.[12] This theory of justice, however, seeks always to remain attentive to the particularity of

persons because of the presence of this agapeistic grounding. The
statement of Augustine that "justice is love serving only the loved
object, and therefore ruling rightly"[13] is paralleled closely by Pius
XI's claim:

> According to the Apostle, then, all the commandments, in-
> cluding those which are of strict justice such as those which
> forbid us to kill or to steal, may be reduced to the single
> precept of true charity. . . . Both justice and charity often
> dictate obligations touching on the same object but under dif-
> ferent aspects.[14]

Thus both philosophical arguments about the social nature of the
person and religious appeals to the Christian norm of love of
neighbor together rule out all individualistic standards of justice
and all those which do not take into account the special claims of
persons in need.

Second, the influence of the norm of agape has caused the
tradition to place special emphasis on interpersonal and social mutuality in its discussions of justice. Justice is viewed as a norm
which calls for social relationships and a kind of social organization that open the way to the fulfillment of the person which can
only occur in unity and solidarity with others. Mutual interdependence is not merely a physical, psychological or economic fact. It
is a moral obligation. This interdependence can only be realized in
that form of solidarity and mutuality that Pius XI called "social
love."[15] Again, though love is not a substitute for justice, without
it justice becomes a lifeless theory and can neither be adequately
conceptualized nor effectively realized in action. As *Quadragesimo
Anno* put it, echoing Thomas Aquinas:

> Justice alone can, if faithfully observed, remove the causes of
> social conflict but can never bring about union of minds and
> hearts. Indeed all the institutions for the establishment of
> peace and the promotion of mutual help among men, however
> perfect these may seem, have the principal foundation of their
> stability in the mutual bond of minds and hearts whereby the
> members are united with one another. . . . And so, only then

will true cooperation be possible for a single common good when the constituent parts of society deeply feel themselves members of one great family and children of the same heavenly Father; nay, that they are one body in Christ, but severally members one of another.[16]

This emphasis on the social role of love has exerted an important influence in the tradition's discussions of the concrete claims of justice.

In all the documents of the tradition, then, the theory of justice is rooted in a philosophical view of the nature of the person as essentially social and simultaneously in an explicitly Christian notion of love as mutuality and as response to persons in the concrete, especially those in need. These theological and philosophical foundations thus point toward the definition of justice in terms of mutually and reciprocally binding obligations. What is *due* to a person or a group is to be determined by the kinds of relationships which shape and influence the life and action of that person or group. Human dignity—the fact that human beings are not things or mere means—always exists *within* these various concrete relationships. The justice or injustice of these relationships is to be judged in terms of the way they promote human dignity by enhancing mutuality and genuine participation in community or, put negatively, by the way they abuse human dignity by reifying persons and excluding or marginalizing them from the relationships without which humanity withers. This vision of mutuality and participation was at the basis of Leo XIII's moral protest against an industrial economy in which "a small number of very rich men have been able to lay upon the teeming masses of the poor *[infinitae proletariorum multitudini]* a yoke little better than slavery itself."[17] It is also the foundation of the 1971 Synod's perception of the present international socio-economic situation:

Serious injustices . . . are building around the world of men a network of domination, oppression and abuses which stifle freedom and which keep the greater part of humanity from sharing in the building up and enjoyment of a more just and more fraternal world. . . . These stifling oppressions constantly give rise to great numbers of "marginal" persons, ill-fed, inhumanly housed, illiterate and deprived of political power as well as of the suitable means of acquiring responsibility and moral dignity.[18]

The notion of justice present in the tradition appeals to the mutuality characteristic of agape in its negative judgments on these patterns of proletarianization and marginalization.

The foundation of the concept of justice in mutuality and love is extraordinarily attractive, especially to contemporary Christians predisposed to be highly critical of the present social configuration of power and wealth. It is a vision capable of inspiring participation in efforts to bring about radical change. It is also, however, a very general and abstract norm, so general as to provide little more than an attitudinal orientation toward the complexities of social, economic, and political activity. Important as this attitudinal orientation undoubtedly is, the *vision of the foundation of justice* in interdependent responsibility and mutual love needs to be differentiated into a *theory of justice* which determines the relative rights and mutual duties of persons with some degree of specificity. In the words of Paul Ramsey, this vision needs to be "in-principled."[19]

The willingness to specify such differentiated and relatively concrete norms of justice is one of the characteristics which has distinguished Roman Catholic social thought from the social ethics of much of twentieth-century Protestantism. The popes and their theological advisors achieved this specificity by an appeal to natural law, that is, by a claim to be able to determine the essential dimensions of the human person and of life in society. By an appeal to rational reflection, the tradition has proposed certain specific human rights, such as the rights to life, food, housing, assembly, etc., as concrete demands of justice and as equally binding on all persons regardless of their religious convictions.[20]

The writings of the popes from Pius IX to Pius XI, however, have also proposed a number of relatively specific moral norms of natural law which are much less attractive to most contemporary Christians. For example, Leo XIII and Pius XI made a very strong defense of social inequality as a characteristic of the natural structure through which human mutuality and interdependence should be realized. In their view some form of social, political and economic inequality was a necessary element in any order of human relationships which could hope to protect human dignity through stable patterns of mutual dependence.

The appeal to mutuality and response to concrete persons only becomes operative as an ethical standard for social life when it is, so to speak, filtered through a model of society which is used to interpret the causes and effects of possible forms of social and political action. The difference in the model of society employed in different phases of the tradition has led to radically different conclusions about the concrete actions demanded by justice. In trying to determine the meaning of that justice which is a proper expression of Christian faith and love, it is thus necessary *both* to keep in full view the social anthropology and norm of love which has been a constant throughout the tradition *and* to rethink the way this basic norm is to be made concrete through an interpretation of the structures of social interaction. To see the difference in the kinds of conclusions regarding equality to which the tradition has come during the past hundred years, one need only contrast the statement of Vatican II that "with respect to the fundamental rights of the person, every type of discrimination, whether social or cultural, whether based on sex, race, color, social condition or religion, is to be overcome as contrary to God's intent" with Leo XIII's belief that "inequality of rights and of power proceeds from the very author of nature 'from whom all paternity to heaven and on earth is named.' "[21]

The disrepute into which "natural law" arguments have fallen in recent years among a fair number of Roman Catholic ethicists and theologians is in part traceable to a rejection of some of the conclusions which have been drawn by the tradition on the basis of its interpretation of social interaction through appeals to right reason. Such recent Catholic criticism of natural-law thinking frequently echoes one of Reinhold Niebuhr's strongest objections to the traditional Catholic approach to social ethics:

It rests upon an untenable faith in the purity of reason and it is merely another of the many efforts which men make to find a vantage point of the unconditioned in history. The effect of this pretended finality of "natural law" is obvious. It raises "ideology" to a higher degree of pretension, and is another of the many illustrations in history of the force of sin in the claim of sinlessness.[22]

The lessons that contemporary representatives of this tradition have learned from some of the exaggerated claims made in the past have led to a new caution in claims concerning the possibility of identifying the concrete demands of justice with precision. A kind of epistemological humility has been characteristic of more recent Church statements. For example, in his most recent major writing on political issues, Paul VI observed:

[Christian social ethics] no doubt will see its field restricted when it comes to suggesting certain models of society, while its function of making critical judgment and taking an overall view will be strengthened by its showing the relative character of the behavior and values presented by such and such a society as definitive and inherent in the very nature of man.[23]

This is a rather remarkable statement coming from the chief spokesman for the tradition which more than any other has claimed to base its moral teaching on the ability to identify at least some of the moral norms which are "definitive and inherent in the very nature of man."

The new cautiousness and humility in the attempt to specify what is just and what is unjust has come about for *several* reasons, all of them evident in Vatican Council II's *Pastoral Constitution on the Church in the Modern World*. Chief among these was the Council's recognition that persons "can come to authentic humanity only through culture, that is, through the cultivation of natural goods and values. Wherever human life is involved, therefore, nature and culture are intimately connected."[24] "Nature" understood as a pre-given structure of human existence and social life does not, therefore, provide a norm of authentic humanity. It must be "cultivated," developed and enriched through the exercise of human freedom.

The stress on the *development* of moral norms through cultural activity raises a second major question in the most recent Catholic statements on the meaning of justice. At the Council the Catholic tradition came to a new recognition that the basic openness characteristic of human freedom implies a plurality of possible concrete norms of behavior. Moral norms, including the norms of justice, cannot be determined apart from careful scrutiny of the cultural milieu in which they are affirmed to be normative. No cultural or societal arrangement can contain or exhaustively realize the drive toward transcendence which is the fundamental characteristic of the human person.[25] On this basis the Council acknowledged that the cultural and social realization of human transcendence and dignity "necessarily has a historical and social aspect" and that "in this sense we speak of a plurality of cultures."[26]

This recognition of pluralism as an expression of the transcendence of the human spirit is the basis of a redefined understanding of the role of reason in the most recent Roman Catholic social statements. These statements acknowledge that scientific thinking, including that of the human sciences, is governed by plural methodologies, and that various insights which can be gained from the use of social analysis, political theory and social philosophy are necessary but not sufficient components in the enterprise of determining the meaning of justice. No single method for analyzing the problems of social interaction can produce a concretely normative set of conclusions about the demands of justice. Sociological and political analysis, contrary to the implicit assumptions of Leo XIII and Pius XI, cannot provide a model of society which will in some way fully embody the norm of justice in a definitive way.[27] This rules out, at least in principle, claims such as those made by earlier popes that a social system based on private property or on a hierarchical distribution of authority and power is the only rational arrangement and therefore the only just arrangement. The same holds true for similar claims made for any concrete socialist system.[28]

This conclusion is reinforced by the acknowledgement that one's class, status, race and social role have important influences on what one admits to be a conclusion of reason. In public argument about social, economic and political questions, "the very words by which key concepts are expressed take on quite different meanings in diverse ideological systems."[29] In short, in the most recent phase of the official Catholic tradition, the pluralization of reason and the constant danger of ideological and self-protective definitions of justice are recognized.

This new caution clearly represents an advance beyond the tradition's past proclivities to identify the patterns of historically conditioned social arrangements with unconditional obligations of justice. This development presents major problems, however, for it threatens to paralyze action by placing all decisions about social policy under the shadow of relativism. An opposite but correlative danger is that the frustrations induced by the difficulty of discerning concrete norms of justice will lead to uncritical and ultimately counter-productive responses to urgent problems. The task which this places before the Church, and especially before moral theologians, has been well stated by James Gustafson:

> The task of theological and ethical work becomes that of finding a justification both for religious belief and for moral decisions which do not deny the relativities of history, but which provide an objectivity short of absolute claims. In ethics the task is to find some degree of order, continuity and structure within historical change.[30]

The attempt to discover such order, continuity and structure indicates a way of reading the modern Catholic social tradition which may be of help in the present difficult situation. It has been suggested that the tradition's conclusions concerning the concrete demands of justice have drawn from the social-relational concept of human existence, interpreted in particular ways because of the presence of an historically conditioned social model. It seems clear that Christian faith has no stake in defending a specific social model, be it feudal, capitalist, socialist or liberal democratic, unless this model either especially promotes or especially threatens the basic Christian ethical conviction concerning the normative character of social interdependence and reciprocal love. The remainder of this essay, then, is an attempt to distill ethical norms from the tradition's fundamental ethical stance which are as specific as possible but not totally historically relative due to the undue influence of conditioned social theories and models.

The centrality of the tradition's concern for the mutual claims of concrete persons is evident in its distinction of three modes or types of justice: commutative justice, distributive justice, and social justice.[31] These three modes of justice are distinguished by the different types of human relationship and interdependence to which they refer. Commutative justice concerns the claims which exist in relations between individual and individual or between groups which are essentially private and non-political, such as voluntary associations. Commutative justice is the form of justice which demands fidelity to agreements, contracts, or promises made between persons or groups outside the political or public process. The obligation of commutative justice is one of fidelity to freely formed mutual bonds and of fairness in exchange. It is rooted in the fundamental equality of persons, an equality which implies that no one may ever presume an arbitrary sovereignity over another by setting aside contracts or promises which have bound two free beings into a relation of mutual interdependence. It implies further that if contracts or agreements are to be just, they must be genuinely free. This latter condition of commutative justice is used extensively throughout the tradition to argue that wage agreements cannot be in accord with commutative justice when a worker is compelled to accept an insufficient wage simply because the only alternative is no wage at all.[32] Commutative justice, then, is an expression in the sphere of private interaction of both the genuine dignity of all persons and the need for a mutuality based on equality in their relationships and agreements.

The other two types of justice—distributive justice and social justice—concern the relative rights and mutual duties which obtain between persons and public societies, especially the state and civil society as a whole. Distributive justice specifies the claim which all persons have to some share in those goods which are essentially public or social. Such goods as the fertility of the earth, the productivity of an industrialized economy and the security provided by advanced systems of health care and social insurance are seen by the documents of the tradition as the products of the social system as a whole. They are not the property of any individual or class in an exclusive sense, for all members of society are at least indirectly involved in their production through membership in public society. Even though participation in the creation of these public goods may be minimal, or, in the case of children, infirm or aged persons, presently non-existent, the tradition claims that membership in the human community creates a bond between persons sufficient to ground a right for all to share in the public good to the minimum degree compatible with human dignity. Distributive justice thus is the norm which states the obligation of society and the state to guarantee this participation by all in the common good.[33] The norm of distributive justice, then, specifies the demands of mutuality and interdependence in those relations which determine the opportunity of every person to share or participate in essentially public goods. It establishes the equal right of all to share in all those goods and opportunities which are necessary for genuine participation in the human community. It establishes a strict duty of society as a whole to guarantee these rights.

The third modality of justice (social) concerns institutionalized patterns of mutual action and interdependence which are necessary to bring about the realization of distributive justice. Within the Roman Catholic ethical tradition, social justice has a meaning somewhat more technical than that in contemporary common usage. It refers to the obligations of all citizens to aid in the creation of patterns of societal organization and activity which are essential both for the protection of minimal human rights and for the creation of mutuality and participation by all in social life. In other words, social justice is a political virtue. It is distinguished from the other forms of justice because it is based on that form of human interdependence which occurs through the state. Citizens have a personal obligation, mediated through political obligation, to those activities necessary for the creation of a society in which the concerns of agape can be made effective, namely concern for concrete needs of all persons and for the creation of reciprocal interdependence. Social justice also states the obligation of the state both to promote distributive justice and to make those legal claims on all citizens which are entailed by this task.

These three forms of justice are evidently interrelated and mutually limiting. All three are an attempt to express the demands of agape. All three contain an egalitarian core: equal claims to mutual freedom and fidelity to contracts in the case of commutative justice, equal rights to mutual participation in the public good in the case of distributive justice, and equal obligation to aid in the creation of social and political structures for participation and mutuality in the case of social justice. These common elements are the foundation of the way the tradition attempts to establish preference rules by which the conflicts between the prima facie claims of the three types of justice can be reconciled. Precisely because commutative justice cannot be realized in situations of drastic economic or social inequality between the partners to a contract or agreement, distributive justice is invoked to set limits to the kind of agreements which can be justly made regarding wages, for example, or to the legitimate accumulation of title to property. When economic or social power is distributed in a grossly unequal way, commutative justice in the economic sphere becomes a factual impossibility. Thus property rights and the operation of a free labor market are morally limited by the interrelated demands of commutative and distributive justice. In addition, the creation of the conditions necessary for both commutative and distributive justice depends on concerted action by society as a whole through its public institutions, especially government. These institutional and political dimensions of the obligations involved are expressed as the claims of social justice.

This distinction between types of justice together with the common root of all three types of agape and mutuality has provided the tradition with a relatively refined language and conceptual framework for the discussion of complex social problems. It is a framework which is at once rooted in the distinctively Christian moral norm of agape and refined through critical human reflection on the diverse dimensions of human interaction. It is an approach which provides a degree of "objectivity short of absolute claims" within the relativities of history which Gustafson sees as one of the goals of Christian ethical reflection.

The employment of these three interrelated concepts of justice during the last hundred years of the tradition has been influenced by the tradition's understanding of the power of human reason to identify those social and political structures through which mutual interdependence is most adequately realized. As noted above both Leo XIII and Pius XI were convinced that an unequal distribution of power, authority, status and wealth was essential to the preservation of a just social order. Because of his identification of the anticlerical and terroristic tactics of Bakuninist anarchism in Italy with the growing egalitarian spirit of his time, Leo XIII frequently adopted arguments based on a hierarchical, semi-feudal social model in spelling out the concrete meaning of justice.[34] The hierarchical model of society thus serves as a kind of mold into which the insights of the tradition concerning mutuality and participation are poured. The potential which the norms of justice and love have as sources of major social reform or even revolution were thus severely curtailed in Leo XIII's writings. For example, in *Rerum Novarum*, Leo XIII stated that neither distributive justice nor social justice could demand that persons sacrifice possessions appropriate to their proper place within the stratified social hierarchy. In his words:

> No one is commanded to distribute to others that which is required for his own needs and those of his household, nor even to give away what is reasonably required to keep becomingly his condition in life, "for no one ought to live other than becomingly." But when what necessity demands has been supplied and one's standing fairly been taken thought for, it becomes a duty to give to the indigent what remains over.[35]

Thus Leo XIII does not interpret the demands of distributive justice in a way which leads to basic changes in the distribution of status and role which are seen as necessary to the protection of social harmony.

In the more recent phases of the tradition, from Pius XII to the present, this commitment to a basically paternalistic framework for the realization of justice has been gradually abandoned. Especially since John XXIII, official Roman Catholic social teaching has been willing to challenge the adequacy of *any* social model or social structure which denies to persons that minimum level of well-being or degree of participation in the social good which is necessary for the realization of *reciprocal* interdependence and *mutual* human dignity.[36] For example, John XXIII abandoned Leo's XIII's reference to what is "becoming" or suitable to one's social status in determining what wealth is superfluous and thus subject to the legitimate claims of the poor. "The obligation of every man, the urgent obligation of the Christian man, is to reckon what is superfluous by the measure of the needs of others."[37] Human need takes priority over claims which derive from a stratified system of role-distribution in society.

The same willingness to judge social models and systems by the standards of mutual human dignity is evident in the 1971 Synod's affirmation that social and political participation for all is a genuine demand of justice. Justice cannot be realized in a society in which some citizens are prevented from sharing in the decisions that shape the basic structures which determine their fate. "Participation constitutes a right which is to be applied both in the economic and in the social and political field."[38] The realization of participation will take different forms in different social political situations. In this context it is clear, however, that any appeal to the exigencies of a particular social arrangement as grounds for excluding some persons or classes from the process of social decision-making is ruled out by distributive and social justice.

In summary, then, the tradition has made a major shift over the last hundred years in the normative status which it grants to particular social models. In Leo XIII the hierarchical model of society served as a framework for the interpretation of the demands of mutuality and reciprocity. This framework entered into the definition of the meaning of justice and the specification of relative rights and mutual duties. Since John XXIII—especially in *Octogesima Adveniens* and *Justice in the World*—the situation has been reversed. The norms of agape—mutuality and concern for persons in their particularity and uniqueness—are used to evaluate critically both social models and social systems.

In the newer framework, commutative, distributive and social justice remain indispensable for the specification of the claims of love. Justice demands equality and fairness in all private transactions, wages, and property ownership. It demands equal opportunity for all to participate in the public goods generated by society as a whole, such as social security, health care, and education.

It demands that all persons share in material well-being at least to a level which meets all basic human needs, such as those for food, clothing, shelter, association, etc. And finally it demands that all persons are under an obligation to share in the creation of those public institutions which are necessary for the realization of these other claims of justice.

Viewed in the framework of this analysis it becomes clear that the theory of justice presented in the tradition is a *Christian* theory of justice. Though Catholicism makes no claim to have insight into the nature of justice which is inaccessible to non-Christians, the theory it advocates comes out of the fundamental norm of Christian love. Commitment to the hierarchical model of social order as a demand of reason surely prevented the standard of agape from having its full impact in earlier years. The unwillingness of the recent statements to adopt *any* social model as in itself normative has brought the norm of agape into the forefront of the discussions of justice. By retaining many of the insights of Leo XIII and Pius XI concerning the relationships between commutative, distributive and social justice, however, the tradition has been able to avoid falling into the kind of appeal to love which shapes attitudes but has little to say about the complexities of social policy and economic life.

The tripartite notion of commutative-distributive-social justice, understood in this way, does not provide immediate answers to the complex problems of social existence, but it does provide principles of discernment and quite specific guides for judgment. Justice explicates the response which love calls for in the differentiated but related relationships of social and interpersonal interdependence. Discernment and judgment concerning the concrete actions called for in particular situations depend, therefore, on the mutuality and concern for individual persons which is love and on the analysis of interaction of different types of human relationships expressed in the tripartite principle of justice.

The position adopted at the 1971 Synod pushes the argument for an explicitly Christian notion of justice to an even deeper level. The affirmation that the doing of justice is constitutive of Christian faith is rooted in the way the bishops developed the relationship which exists between faith and love. The God in whom Christians believe is a God of love. Out of love he established his covenant and committed himself to be forever "the liberator of the oppressed and the defender of the poor." Thus the call to respond to this God of the covenant is "a permanent call to man to turn away from self-sufficiency to confidence in God and from concern for self to a sincere love of neighbor." Because God has identified himself with all persons through the covenant, especially with the "least brethren,"[39] and because every person is a true image of God, response to God in faith and response to the neighbor in love and solidarity are inseparable. Therefore, "the Christian finds in every man [and woman] God himself and God's absolute demand for justice and love."[40]

This theological and religious framework is at the very root of the Christian vocation to justice and the Christian definition of the meaning of justice which is elaborated in the most recent phase of the modern Catholic tradition. The tradition has recognized the problematic and pluralistic definition of justice present in contemporary social and political philosophy. It also recognizes the profound problem of apathy and abulia that afflicts contemporary society. Its answer to both the definitional and the motivational problems is an appeal to Christian faith—to the biblical story of Jesus and its continuation in the redemptive presence of grace in time:

> The uncertainty of history and the painful convergences in the ascending path of the human community direct us to sacred history; there God has revealed himself to us, and made known to us, as it is brought progressively to realization, his plan of liberation and salvation which is once and for all fulfilled in the paschal mystery of Christ.[41]

The paschal mystery of Christ is the very core of Christian faith—belief in the redemptive and exemplary significance of Christ's death and resurrection. The Synod's statement that action for justice is constitutive of the preaching of the Gospel can thus be inverted without doing violence to its substance: faith in the paschal mystery of Christ is a constitutive dimension of both Christian action on behalf of justice and of the effort to formulate a Christian definition of justice.

This Christian pursuit of justice will be action rooted in soli-

darity with all persons, especially the poor. It will be action conformed to the demands of mutuality and reciprocal interdependence expressed in the norms of commutative, distributive and
social justice. It will be action which acknowledges the claim of
every unique individual to those material and social goods necessary for the satisfaction of basic human needs: food, clothing,
housing, health care, social security, decent working conditions,
etc.

These claims of justice are not known only by Christians. But
Christian faith, as interpreted by the developing Roman Catholic
tradition, implies that these obligations of justice are religious
obligations for all who profess this faith.[42] The norms of justice we
have been discussing are not primarily derived from a natural
philosophical ethic, nor are they of peripheral concern to the
Christian community as an organized institution. There is, in
short, a Christian theory of justice and an explicitly Christian
obligation to seek this justice, both of which are rooted in the covenant love of God for all persons and in the fulfillment of this love
in the death and resurrection of Christ.

The roots of this approach to justice in the paschal mystery
suggest one final reflection on the developing Catholic social tradition. This view of the possibility of achieving mutuality and reciprocal interdependence in society clearly calls for significant
changes in both individual behavior and institutional arrangements. Solidarity and concern for concrete persons implies a kind
of self-surrender and self-sacrifice which is contradictory to the
self-interest which is the linch-pin of so much modern political
theory. This norm of justice may appear to be utopian, idealistic
and even naive. It need not be interpreted this way, however.

First, this theory of justice grants the equal claims of all persons to those goods and the kind of participation in society which
are essential to their dignity as persons. The call to self-sacrifice
touches only privilege and superfluity, not essentials and basic
human needs. The call to self-surrender is not a call to self-
immolation but rather a call to a form of solidarity and reciprocity
in which the true fulfillment of self is to be found. Those who dis-
agree that fulfillment is to be found in this way are unjustified in
calling this theory naive or utopian. They may call it wrong or un-

true if they wish. Such an objection, however, is an objection based on an ultimate interpretation of the meaning of human fulfillment, not a judgment of whether such a community of mutuality is possible or not.

Second, Christian faith affirms that the full achievement of this mutuality and reciprocity is an eschatological hope, to be realized only in the Kingdom of God. Human sinfulness and the finiteness of persons make the historical realization of justice always imperfect and partial. Thus this theory of Christian justice can concede that it is in a certain sense utopian.[43] Christian faith is eschatological faith and the Christian pursuit of justice involves an eschatological hope. The movement from the imperfect justice of the present to the perfect justice of the Kingdom is thus a movement sustained and guided by faith. This faith, however, is not simply a formless trust. It has a content and shape: that of the paschal mystery of Jesus Christ. The movement of history toward its culmination in the Kingdom of God is a movement which follows the pattern of death and resurrection.[44] The pursuit of justice is itself part of this movement.

Eschatological hope, therefore, does not weaken the obligations of justice. Precisely the opposite is the case. Christian faith in the ultimate coming of God's Kingdom is a call to share in the death and resurrection of Christ. Christian justice is a specification of how this sharing is to be made present in the relations between persons in history. This implies that the struggle for justice—for a justice both defined and motivated by Christian faith in the paschal mystery—is an expression of the presence of grace and eschatological hope. By the very nature of their faith Christians are called to be continually attentive to the emergence of new possibilities for reciprocal mutuality. They are called to continue this struggle in the face of setbacks, discouragement and even defeat. These are the consequences of the definitional and motivational links which related faith and justice to each other internally. Efforts toward the fulfillment of minimum human needs and the realization of structures of genuine mutuality are consequences of faith in Jesus Christ. They are religious obligations of all Christians and of the Church as an organized actor in society.

NOTES

1. Synod of Bishops, *Justice in the World*, (Washington, D.C.: United States Catholic Conference Publications Office, 1972), p. 34.

2. For an illuminating discussion of alternative definitions of justice, see Chaim Perelman, *The Idea of Justice and the Problem of Argument*, trans. John Petrie (London: Routledge and Kegan Paul, 1963). See also Gene Outka, *Agape: An Ethical Analysis* (New Haven: Yale University Press, 1972), pp. 88-92. This analysis, though different from Outka's in important ways, is heavily indebted to him.

3. *The Republic of Plato*, trans. Francis MacDonald Cornford (New York: Oxford University Press, 1945), no. 432.

4. *Nicomachean Ethics*, trans. Martin Ostwald (Indianapolis: Bobbs-Merrill, 1962), no. 1131a.

5. *Second Treatise on Civil Government*, in *Social Contract: Essays by Locke, Hume and Rousseau*, ed. Sir Ernest Barker (New York: Oxford University Press, 1962), no. 124.

6. "Critique of the Gotha Program," in Lewis S. Feuer, ed., *Basic Writings on Politics and Philosophy: Karl Marx and Friedrich Engels* (Garden City, N.Y.: Doubleday Anchor, 1949), p. 119.

7. *A Theory of Justice* (Cambridge, Mass.: The Belknap Press of Harvard University Press, 1971), pp. 60-61.

8. Some of these concerns are summarized by Avery Dulles in his article in this volume. They are also treated in Peter L. Berger and Richard John Neuhaus, eds., *Against the World for the World: The Hartford Appeal and the Future of American Religion* (New York: Seabury, 1976).

9. *Rerum Novarum*, trans. in Etienne Gilson, ed., *The Church Speaks to the Modern World: The Social Teachings of Leo XIII* (Garden City, N.Y.: Doubleday Image, 1954), nos. 1-3.

10. *Mater et Magistra*, trans. W. J. Gibbons (New York: Paulist Press, 1961), no. 219.

11. William A. Luijpen, *Phenomenology of Natural Law* (Pittsburgh: Duquesne University Press, 1967), p. 180.

12. See, for example, William Frankena, *Ethics*, second edition (Englewood Cliffs, N.J.: Prentice-Hall, 1973), pp. 56-59; Joel Feinberg, *Social Philosophy* (Englewood Cliffs, N.J.: Prentice-Hall, 1973), p. 89; Gene Outka, *Agape: An Ethical Analysis*, ch. 3.

13. *On the Morals of the Catholic Church*, ch. 15, in *Basic Writings of St. Augustine*, vol. I., ed. Whitney Oates (New York: Random House, 1948).

14. *Quadragesimo Anno*, trans. in Terrence P. McLaughlin, ed., *The Church and the Reconstruction of the Modern World* (Garden City, N.Y.: Doubleday Image, 1957), no. 137.

15. *Quadragesimo Anno*, no. 88.

16. *Quadragesimo Anno*, no. 137.

17. *Rerum Novarum*, no. 3.

18. *Justice in the World*, pp. 33, 36.

19. See Ramsey's discussion of in-principled love in, for example, *War and the Christian Conscience* (Durham, N.C.: Duke University Press, 1961). The same need for moving to a more concrete level of normative discourse is made in the writings of James Gustafson, most recently in his *Can Ethics Be Christian?* (especially pp. 148-164). My reading of the Catholic documents has been influenced in important ways by both Ramsey and Gustafson.

20. There are parallels to this type of quest for specificity in modern Protestant theology. The orders of creation, the ordinances of the Creator, the formed references to the ethical and the mandates of God in the world are counterparts to the notion of natural law to be found in the writings of Brunner, Barth, and Bonhoeffer. Catholicism, however, has exhibited a much greater confidence in its ability to identify these specific moral demands in detail.

21. *Gaudium et Spes*, trans. in Walter M. Abbott and Joseph Gallagher, eds., *The Documents of Vatican II* (New York: Guild Press/America Press/Association Press, 1966), no. 29; *Quod Apostolici Muneris*, trans. in Gilson, ed., *The Church Speaks to the Modern World*, no. 5.

22. *The Nature and Destiny of Man* (New York: Scribner's, 1943), vol. II, p. 253. Charles Curran makes the same point from within the Catholic tradition: "There was always the danger of identifying a particular order or structure as the immutable order of God when in reality it was only an historically and culturally conditioned attempt to respond as well as possible to the needs of a particular period and very often manifested the desires of the dominant power group in the society rather than the eternal order of God"—*Catholic Moral Theology in Dialogue* (Notre Dame, Ind.: Fides, 1972), p. 121.

23. *Octogesima Adveniens, Letter of His Holiness Pope Paul VI to Cardinal Maurice Roy, on the Occasion of the Eightieth Anniversary of the Encyclical Rerum Novarum* (Washington, D.C.: United States Catholic Conference, 1971), no. 40.

24. *Gaudium et Spes*, no. 53.

25. On this point the recent developments of the Catholic tradition again seem to have come fairly close to accepting one of Reinhold Niebuhr's most basic points. *Gaudium et Spes* views human beings as both boundless and at the same time radically limited. The tension between these two aspects of humanity is seen as one which leads to sin and injustice (nos. 10 and 13). This anthropology could fittingly be expressed by a well-known passage from Niebuhr: "Man is tempted by the situation in which he stands. He stands at the juncture of nature and spirit. The freedom of his spirit causes him to break the harmonies of nature and the pride of his spirit prevents him from establishing a new harmony. . . . The Christian view of human nature is involved in the paradox of claiming a higher stature for man and of taking a more serious view of his evil than

other anthropology"—*The Nature of Destiny of Man*, vol. I, pp. 17-18.

    26. *Gaudium et Spes*, no. 53.

    27. Paul VI puts the matter this way: "These sciences are a condition at once indispensable and inadequate for a better discovery of what is human. They are a language which becomes more and more complex, yet one that deepens rather than solves the mystery of the heart of man, nor does it provide the complete and definitive answer to the desire which springs from his innermost being"—*Octogesima Adveniens*, no. 40.

    28. *Octogesima Adveniens*, nos. 36ff.

    29. *Gaudium et Spes*, no. 4. See *Mater et Magistra*, no. 206.

    30. "The Relevance of Historical Understanding," in Paul Deats, Jr., ed., *Toward a Discipline of Social Ethics* (Boston: Boston University Press, 1972), p. 67.

    31. For discussions of these three types of justice see the following examples of the extensive literature on Catholic social thought: Charles Antoine, *Cours d'economie sociale*, 4th ed. (Paris: Felix Alcan, 1908), Chap. V, "Justice et Charité"; Johannes Messner, *Social Ethics*, revised edition, trans. J. J. Doherty (St. Louis: B. Herder Book Co., 1965), pp. 314-324; Thomas Gilby, *Between Community and Society* (London: Longmans, Green and Co., 1953), Chap. VIII; John A. Ryan, *Distributive Justice* (New York: Macmillan, 1927), Chap. XVI; Oswald von-Nell Breuning, *Reorganization of Social Economy*, trans. Bernard W. Dempsey (New York: Bruce, 1939), pp. 170-191; Thomas E. Henneberry, "On Definitions of Social Justice," S.T.D. dissertation, Woodstock College, 1941.

    32. *Justice in the World*, p. 38.

    33. In the words of Leo XIII: "As regards the state, the interests of all, whether high or low, are equal. The members of the working class are citizens by nature and by the same right as the rich; they are real parts living the life which makes up, through the family, the body of the commonwealth. . . . Among the many and grave duties of rulers who would do their best for the people, the first and chief is to act with strict justice—with that justice which is called distributive—toward each and every class alike"—*Rerum Novarum*, no. 33.

    34. For discussion of the tension between the hierarchical and egalitarian aspects of Leo XIII's thought see John Courtney Murray, "Leo XIII: Two Concepts of Government," *Theological Studies* 14 (1953), pp. 551-567; *idem*, "Leo XIII: Two Concepts of Government. II. Government and the Order of Culture," *Theological Studies* 15 (1954), pp. 1-33; Arturo Gaete, "Socialism and Communism: History of a Problem-Ridden Condemnation," *LADOC*, September, 1973, IV, 1, pp. 1-16.

    35. *Rerum Novarum*, no. 22.

    36. A major exception to this statement is the tradition's continued adherence to a hierarchical conception of the relations and roles of men and women. For an excellent treatment of this question see Margaret A. Farley, R.S.M., "New Patterns of Relationship: The Beginnings of a Moral Revolution" *Theological Studies* 36 (December 1975). Farley's

general approach to the definition of justice, as expressed in this article and elsewhere, has been influential in shaping the analysis presented here.

37. Quoted in *Gaudium et Spes*, no. 69, note 233 in the Abbott-Gallagher edition of *The Documents of Vatican II*.

38. *Justice in the World*, p. 38.

39. Mt. 25:40.

40. The quotations are from *Justice in the World*, pp. 41-42.

41. *Justice in the World*, p. 34.

42. This way of stating the distinctiveness of a Christian ethic is parallel to that argued for by James Gustafson's *Can Ethics Be Christian?*

43. Paul VI acknowledges the utopian dimensions of a Christian vision of justice and notes that such dimensions are especially important in a world starved for the imagination necessary "both to perceive in the present the disregarded possibility hidden within it and to direct itself toward a fresh future"—*Octogesima Adveniens*, no. 32.

44. See *Populorum Progressio*, no. 79.

Part III
New Directions Envisioned

A Prophetic Church and the Catholic Sacramental Imagination

David Hollenbach, S.J.

In recent discussions of the relation between Christian faith and the effort to create a just society, the question of the social role of the Church has been central. This paper will address the question of the relation of Christian faith and social justice from the perspective of this Church/society interaction. The faith of every believer is born, nurtured and sustained (or perhaps, threatened and even destroyed) through membership in the human community which is the Church. The essentially communal character of belief is axiomatic to the sociologist of religion, who views belief as the result of the interiorization of the ultimate values and commitments which give shape to the living traditions of historical communities. For the Christian theologian this communal character of belief is part of the content of Christian faith itself. In the words of the Second Vatican Council:

> At all times and among every people, God has given welcome to whosoever fears him and does what is right. It has pleased God, however, to make men holy and save them not merely as individuals without any mutual bonds, but by making them into a single people, a people which acknowledges him in truth and serves him in holiness.[1]

What is more, the question of the relation between Christian faith and social justice is a question that concerns the relation between communities—the community of the Church and its various subgroups on the one hand and the economic, political and national communities which structure human society on the the other.

234

Christian faith, though an eminently personal act which relates the believer to God, is never an act of an individual apart from the Church. Thus it is evident that the Christian vocation to do justice will be illuminated in important ways by reflection on the ecclesial dimension of the experience of faith and its relation to those other dimensions of experience which are shaped by the secular communities in which the believer participates.

The first part of this essay briefly outlines some of the ambiguities which make theological efforts to clarify the relation between Church and society quite difficult. These ambiguities have their roots in the tension between the secular and sacred dimensions of human existence. The second section will provide a critical review of some recent theological proposals concerning the scope and limits of the corporate role of the Church in the social sphere. This review concludes that recent discussions have focused too exclusively on the Church's ability to translate general ethical principles of Christian morality into concrete political imperatives. These efforts have given insufficient attention to the social resources present in shared religious experience. In the third and concluding section, the sacramental character of distinctively Catholic forms of religious experience will be briefly explored as an energizing and directing source of common Christian action for justice. More specifically, I will contend that the Catholic sacramental imagination can be a rich resource for the prophetic action of the Church in the social and political spheres.

I
SOURCES OF AMBIGUITY

Illumination of the corporate dimensions of the action of Christians in the spheres of social and political justice has been in scarce supply in the writings of recent theologians. Theological opinions are plentiful, but they conflict with each other or emphasize only a single aspect of the problem. The cause of the relatively confused state of theological reflection in this area is twofold.

First, the question of the proper scope of communal Christian action in the social sphere contains within itself a number of other extremely thorny theological questions which are urgently being debated within the Church today. A partial list of these other, more fundamental issues includes the following: the scope and limits of pluralism with the Church; the role of the teaching office; the internal structures of participation and decision-making; the distinction of various ministries in the Church; the relation between universal Christian beliefs and the particularities of diverse cultures; the relation of general moral rules and individual conscience, and the relevance of the social sciences to the development of Christian ethics. All of these problems converge in the discussion of the Church's role in the promotion of justice.

It seems unlikely that all of these theological questions will receive definitive answers in the near future. Therefore, if we are to shed some light on the corporate dimensions of the action of Christians for justice, it will be necessary to seek a perspective which does not demand that we wait until all these other issues are fully resolved.

The second source of the present uncertainty about the communal and institutional dimensions of the contribution of faith to the realization of justice is the result of structural and historical factors in modern Western society. For the past several hundred years, approximately since the Enlightenment, the assumption that Christian faith is the primary integrating and organizing principle for Western social institutions has been gradually losing its plausibility. The activities and patterns of thinking necessary to keep our society running have become progressively more specialized and differentiated from each other. Max Weber has called this differentiation a process of "rationalization" leading to the "disenchantment of the world." It is a process by which "the ultimate and most sublime values have retreated from public life either into the transcendental realm of mystic life or into the brotherliness of direct and personal human relations."[2] One of the consequences of increasing specialization in both thought and action has been the differentiation of corporate religious associations from the political and economic spheres. This is most evident in the demise of Christendom and the separation of Church and state, though this political phenomenon is but the tip of a much larger social, economic and cultural iceberg.

The differentiation of the institutional Church from other areas of social organization creates problems which must be addressed positively if Christianity is to fulfill its mission of justice. Secularization, in Karl Rahner's words, signifies "the growing influence of 'world' (as the outcome of human ingenuity) and the process by which it becomes increasingly autonomous and separates itself more and more from the Church considered as a social entity in the world."[3] The legitimate autonomy of the political arena, expressed in the principles of religious liberty and separation of Church and state, raises serious questions about the possibility of common Christian action for justice. If common action is to be effective in a bureaucratic society it must be organized action. There is a strong cultural bias present in our society which results in the misinterpretation of any public or political activity by the Church as a violation of the separation of Church and state. Thus the secularization of the state, the economy and the broader sphere of culture can be read as a powerful source of the privatization of religious belief—the withdrawal of religious experience into the spheres of personal salvation and the immediate interpersonal relationships of the family and the primary group. Cultural pressure to keep the Christian community's action in society non-institutionalized also leads to the fragmentation of Christian efforts to bring greater justice to social organizations. It often leads to the view that religiously motivated actions by individuals are legitimate expressions of religious liberty while such actions by organized groups or churches are attempts at re-establishment. Thus both of these tendencies of the contemporary Western structural relation between religion and society—the privatization and the fragmentation of religious influence in society—seem undesirable if one is convinced of the essentially communal nature of Christian faith and its internal demand for the promotion of justice in society.

Recent attempts to find a way around these tendencies toward privatization and fragmentation without moving back to a kind of neo-Christendom tend in two directions.[4] The first emphasizes commonly shared ethical principles and universalizable imperatives. It views the public role of the Church as a prophetic one, and describes the content of the prophecy as both general ethical principles and specific social imperatives derived from a combination of theological and social analysis. This approach stresses argument and analysis as the base of the prophetic role which the Church can play in addressing problems such as war, disarmament, economic exploitation, political oppression and racism.

The second approach emphasizes the lived reality of Christian identity and experience. It attempts to describe the prophetic function of the Church by beginning with the self-identity of the Christian community and the experience of Christians who are engaged in efforts to overcome injustice. The emphasis here is on the resources for public action which arise from the Christian's experience of life as shaped by the Church as a community of belief in Jesus Christ. In recent Roman Catholic literature this second emphasis has been crystallized around the ancient theological motif of the Church as the fundamental sacrament of Christ's active presence in the world. The living experience of Christian community is the fundamental sign of God's gracious intentions for the whole of humanity, not just for those who are formal members of the Church.[5] This sacramental approach has parallels in modern Protestant theology. For example, Karl Barth has argued that the identity of the Church as a community which exists to serve the Kingdom of God is an identity which calls Christians "to regard the existence of the state as an allegory, as a correspondence and an analogue to the Kingdom of God which the Church preaches and believes in."[6] Both the recent Catholic sacramental approach and Barth's allegorical approach presuppose that the living experience of grace realized within the community of the Church is in some way analogous to and correlated with the fundamental normative structure of social life.

These two theological approaches to the prophetic role of the Church, that of principles and imperatives and that of identity and experience, are attempts to gain a perspective on the social roles of the Christian which avoid the twin pitfalls of privatism and individualism. They presume that either commonly shared ethical principles and generally plausible social analysis or common Christian identity and shared experience can counteract the cultural tendencies toward privatization and fragmentation. The disagreements in the recent theological literature reveal that both approaches contain serious difficulties.

II
SOME RECENT APPROACHES TO THE
PROPHETIC ROLE OF THE CHURCH

Recent discussions of the prophetic role of the Church in society have been especially concerned with the common voice of the Church as exercised through official statements and public moral teaching. In the Roman Catholic Church, the questions of the teaching role of bishops, the pope, national and regional conferences, synods, and ecumenical councils have largely set the agenda for the discussion. This public teaching function has also received considerable attention from Protestant theologians, for what is at stake here is not simply the particular conception of moral and doctrinal authority found in recent Catholic tradition. More basically the question is that of the possibility of any Christian communion coming to that level of consensus on social and political problems which is necessary if prophetic statements are to be made in the name of the Church as a whole. None of the participants in the discussions doubt that the Church can and should speak to the moral values, attitudes and general principles involved in public life. The disagreements concern the ability of the corporate voice of the Church to propose concrete and particular actions as morally obligatory. There is also significant divergence of opinion on the way the Church as a corporate body should come to conclusions about the demands of justice in society.

Paul Ramsey's writings, especially his polemical critique of the 1966 World Council of Churches' Conference on Church and Society,[7] present a vigorous argument against the drive toward detailed and particularized ethical prescriptions in public Church statements. Ramsey regards the attempt of Church bodies to prescribe concrete solutions in areas such as disarmament policy, nuclear strategy and the Vietnam war as the result of a misinterpretation of the nature of political decision. It also stems from an overestimation of the practical wisdom of the Church. The Church does not have the political and technical competence to know either what is possible or what is best in such complex areas of international political life. Political decisions and policy-making are prudential decisions demanding knowledge of the real alternatives and the likely consequences of various courses of action

Though political decisions involve fundamental values and principles, in the end the formation of policy and the choice of concrete
action are always the result of practical decision rather than of theoretical knowledge. Because of this prudential and contingent nature of political decisions, concrete directives for action cannot be
unambiguously deduced from Christian faith. The possession of
Christian faith does not give persons any special skills in international economics or diplomacy. In Ramsey's words: "Prudential
political advice comes into the public forum with no special cre-
dentials because it issues from Christians or from Christian religious bodies."[8]

Thus the Church's attempts to recommend policy and specific
action are based on a confusion about the nature of both politics
and the Church. In Ramsey's view, the Church's public function is
the more limited but no less important task of providing perspectives on social and political issues which are rooted in and warrant-
ed by the Christian faith.[9] These perspectives, Ramsey is careful to
note, must be more than pious generalities such as "feed the
hungry" or "abolish war." They must be action-oriented and decision-oriented principles or directions (as opposed to specific directives) which positively illuminate the kinds of public decisions that
in fact must be made. The public task before the Church is the development of "decision-oriented or action-oriented (relevant) social and political analysis" which will serve to cultivate the political ethos of a nation and inform the consciences of its statesmen.[10]
In Ramsey's view, therefore, it will only be on the rarest occasions
that the Church is in a position to advocate a specific and concrete
form of social action as the only Christian alternative. The ordinary and more important function of its prophetic role in society
is that of developing the principles and advocating the Christian
perspectives which should shape the day-by-day decisions of citizens and public figures.

Ramsey believes that the move toward concrete and particularized statements in recent World Council of Churches documents has been the result of a rather superficial attempt to achieve
ecumenical consensus on individual policy issues. This effort has
distracted the churches from the more fundamental and important
attempt to achieve consensus on basic ethical principles and action-oriented theological perspectives.[11] In Ramsey's view, the tra-

ditional Roman Catholic emphasis on general norms is more likely to produce genuine ecumenical consensus in the sphere of social justice. It is also more likely to have a lasting impact on perduring patterns of social relationship.

James M. Gustafson has written concerning the documents of the World Council of Churches in a similarly critical vein. Gustafson, with Ramsey, is dissatisfied with the lack of sufficient theological warrant for the particular moral judgments contained in these documents. The legitimacy of advocating any policy proposal or decision as Christian depends on showing how it fits into a moral vision of the world that is shaped by the central religious symbols and convictions which form the identity of the Christian community. As Gustafson put it, "If there is any common faith and loyalty in the Christian community, that faith and loyalty is the center from which moral outlooks and opinions ought to be formed."[12]

This stress on the theological center of Christian social opinions and strategy which is common to both Gustafson and Ramsey speaks not only to the Protestant churches but also to Roman Catholicism. In the modern Roman Catholic social tradition before the Second Vatican Council the chief warrants for specific ethical conclusions were drawn from a form of natural law theory. This theory was used in a way which frequently reinforced traditional ethical conclusions. For example, the right to private property, the necessity of political inequality, the illegitimacy of contraception, and the subordination of woman to man in both family and society were all justified primarily by non-theological appeals to the law of nature. Theological and biblical appeals were then used to reinforce these non-theological arguments. It does not seem to be an accident that since Vatican II the more direct appeal to the central religious symbols of Christian faith have opened up Catholic social thought to a new period of creativity and moved many groups within the Church toward a positive commitment to social change.[13] The use of biblical teachings concerning the love commandment, the actions and teachings of Jesus, the motifs of covenant and liberation and the doctrine of Christian freedom have stimulated a new dynamism and critical spirit in Catholic social ethics.

The need for an explicitly Christian foundation for the

Church's public activity called for by Ramsey and Gustafson has been addressed in the writings of a group of European theologians, both Catholic and Protestant, who have come to be known as "political theologians." The three leading members of this group are Jurgen Moltmann, Wolfhart Pannenberg, and Johannes B. Metz. The eschatological promise of the final coming of the Kingdom of God is the central theological motif which they use in interpreting the Church-society relationship. Neither Church nor society can be identified with the Kingdom. Neither Church nor society can be expected to be transformed into the Kingdom on earth. The Church, however, is the bearer of a vision of the ultimate and absolute future of all humanity—a vision of the Kingdom of God which, "far from being a merely formalistic idea, is the utterly concrete reality of justice and love."[14] In the eschatological perspective of these writers this concrete justice and love has its reality as promise, a reality known through faith in the resurrection of Christ. Christian faith sees the world's ultimate meaning as based on the trustworthiness of this promise. The Church's mission is that of pointing toward the Kingdom which has not yet been fully achieved and offering humanity the hope that God will remain faithful to his promise of justice and love. The Church's prophetic role, therefore, is to keep history open to the fulfillment of this promise. Its task is "to resist the institutional stabilizing of things, and by 'raising the question of meaning' to make things uncertain and keep them moving and elastic in the process of history."[15]

Consequently, Moltmann, Pannenberg and Metz view the Church's role as essentially that of offering a public critique of the institutions of society in the light of the Kingdom. "The Church must always witness to the limitations of any given society. The very existence of the Church depends upon its playing this critical role. When this critical witness is abandoned, the Church becomes superfluous."[16] Prophecy, then, is the largely negative task of criticizing the ideological tendencies of all political and historical attempts to capture the transcendent meaning of justice and love within a political program or social system. The importance of this negative task, Metz maintains, should not be underestimated.

There is to it an elementary positive power of mediation. Even if we cannot directly and immediately agree as to the positive content of freedom, peace, and justice, yet we have a long and common experience with their contraries, the lack of freedom, justice, and peace. This negative experience offers us a chance for consensus, less in regard to the positive aspect of the freedom and justice we are seeking, than in regard to our critical resistance against the dread and terror of no freedom and no justice. The solidarity which grows out of this experience offers the possibility of a common front of protest.[17]

Moltmann, Pannenberg and Metz, therefore, have produced a strong theological argument for the engagement of the Church in the struggle for the transformation of the structures of society. Because of the link they see between the Kingdom of God and the future of all humanity, their theologies are strong arguments against the privatization of religion. It is not clear, however, that they provide a view of the Church/society relationship that resists the pressure toward the fragmentation of Christian action which is exerted by modern institutional differentiation and specialization. This differentiation has revealed the relativity and partiality of all social roles, institutional structures and specialized methods of social analysis. The recognition of this relativity is a prime source of the fear of ideology which runs through the new political theology, the fear of attaching even quasi-absolute significance to any concrete social institution. The stress on social critique as the primary public role of the Church is a manifestation of this fear. Though the fear is legitimate, Metz's confidence that the corporate solidarity of Christian action in society can be built and sustained on this negative base seems unjustified. Corporate solidarity necessarily entails some positive intra-historical loyalties. In other words, communal Christian action in society demands the presence of commitment to some norms for social life which concretize the Christian vision of social existence even though they do not provide a total description of the Kingdom of God.

Both James Gustafson and Gustavo Gutierrez have voiced a somewhat similar criticism of Moltmann, Pannenberg and Metz, though from two quite different perspectives. Gustafson believes that if the theological insights of this political theology are to have a genuine public relevance, its advocates must assume the intellectual responsibility for showing their positive social and political implications. The new political theology must be converted into a Christian social ethics. The critical approach is not enough, from either a pragmatic or theoretical point of view. Gustafson calls on the political theologians to recognize "the necessity of persuasive rational moral discourse which would convert what is said into terms and arguments that would be more effective in giving directions and control to various social policy proposals."[18] Gutierrez, from a different point of view, believes that this conversion of theological perspective into positive social commitment demands both experiential engagement in conflicts and struggles of society and a greater employment of the analyses of these conflicts provided by the social sciences.[19] Both Gustafson and Gutierrez argue that a theological perspective, though essential to the elaboration of the positive role of the Church, must be correlated with philosophical and social scientific reflection on the lived experiences of contemporary social struggles and problems.

Edward Schillebeeckx and Karl Rahner are in agreement with Gustafson and Gutierrez that human experience of the social struggle for justice must be correlated with philosophical and social scientific reflection if the theological vision of Christianity is to have public influence.[20] They raise a number of questions, however, about the relation between the experiential and the theoretical components of this correlation. With Ramsey, neither Schillebeeckx nor Rahner conceives this correlation as a relation of logical entailment or rational deduction. One cannot produce a concrete and specific ethical conclusion about social policy by beginning with theological principles and then arguing syllogistically to an unavoidable decision for a specific action. The relation of theory and practice is not a relation between axioms or first principles and their necessary corollaries. Such a conception, Rahner states, is the foundation of a theological "integralism" or religious hegemony which is insufficiently aware of the freedom and creativity of all truly human action. In Rahner's words:

Integralism in this sense implicitly presupposed that in his acts man simply puts his theory into practice, and that the world and its history, considered as the material field in which these acts of his are posited, is sufficiently predicable, malleable and submissive to his will, to make such a procedure possible. Integralism in this sense, therefore, entails a failure to recognize that the "practical intellect" has an element of the autonomous in it. Its act of apprehension can be achieved only within the context of the free decision as actually posited in hope.[21]

The acknowledgement of the presence of freedom within the practical intellect implies that the correlation of the theological, philosophical and sociological theories with lived human experience is a synthetic art involving the creativity of human imagination. It is not an analytic act of dissection and deduction. The need for synthesis does not arise simply from the inadequacy of theological principles to produce specific determinations of concrete action. The same inadequacy is present in the principles of social theory and moral philosophy. In Schillebeeckx's view, theoretical formulations, whether theological, philosophical or sociological, are always partial explications of the reality which is at stake in social interaction and the struggle for justice—the human person created and redeemed by God. It is precisely because the person has a worth and individual uniqueness which transcends the categories of theoretically elaborated principles that the decisions of practical reason are both necessary and possible. From this Schillebeeckx draws the following conclusion about the limited usefulness of general ethical principles in the public teaching of the Church:

Abstract pronouncements cannot seize hold of the reality simply *by themselves*; if they nevertheless possess a realistic value, this can only be derived from our total experience of reality. . . . Only and exclusively as intrinsically individualized is "being human" a reality and can it be the source of moral norms (which, in religious parlance, we can rightly describe as the will of God). Therefore, there is only one source of ethical norms, namely, the historical reality of the value of the inviolable human person with all its bodily and social implications. That is why we cannot attribute validity to abstract norms as such.[22]

Both Rahner and Schillebeeckx, therefore, affirm that the correlation of the theological, philosophical and social scientific insight must take place within the broader context of living experience of the social situation and of the dignity of the persons who live within this situation. For the Church, moral principles retain an important role in shaping the decisions reached by practical reason, for they represent a theoretical crystallization of theological reflection on the past experience of the Christian community. In the present, however, the function of these principles is almost exclusively negative. They set limits for Christian action, but do not define a unique path of conduct for all Christians.[23] Moreover, many of the struggles of the human race which call out to the Christian conscience today are genuinely new. The need for common action in addressing problems such as world hunger, rapid population growth, nuclear warfare, and the changing roles of women in society will not be met by a simple reiteration of moral principles formulated in a world where such problems did not exist. Schillebeeckx has observed that these principles "are the tail end of a preceding history, while the future must be prepared by historical decisions and moral imperatives."[24]

Rahner and Schillebeeckx are concerned, then, with broadening the debate about the social role of the Church beyond the theoretical domain where theological doctrines, philosophical analysis and social scientific theories can be interwoven without leading to a sense of direction for the Church. Their concern is the same as Ramsey's, though they are much less confident than he that such a sense of direction can be discovered without some form of positive corporate commitment of the Church to particular historical options. In Rahner's view, the development of any genuine ability to engage in common action depends not only on rational analysis but on "creative imagination" which engages freedom and affectivity.[25] It is through a kind of corporate creative imagination that the Church is enabled to carry out its mission to the world.

Because of its creativity, imagination is a notoriously elusive notion. Its activity cannot be fully captured by theoretical reflection. Rahner sees the corporate creative imagination as the locus of the Holy Spirit's action within the Church as it grapples with decisions about actions in society. It is the corporate counterpart to the charismatic "discernment of spirits" through which an individual person discovers his or her unique vocation and existential obligations.[26] Schillebeeckx stresses that this charismatic element in the Christian imagination is not an intervention of God which guides human action in a totally invisible or non-experiential way. Rather, charismatic guidance and the creativity of the imagination emerge from the very heart of human experience. The charismatic insight arises from the simultaneous experience of the social situation and the call of Christian faith. In situations where injustice is being done, this occurs in what Schillebeeckx calls a "contrast experience." The contrast is between the concrete reality of what is occurring and the concrete reality of one's experience of the Christian life. The creative insight comes in a concrete act of personal and affective synthesis, not simply on the rational level of principles and analysis. As Schillebeeckx describes the process, "the absence of 'what ought to be' is experienced initially, and this leads to a perhaps vague, yet real, perception of 'what should be done here and now.' "[27] The prophetic insight and voice of the Church has its origin in the contrasts which exist within the living experience of those who are touched by actual injustice and who are struggling against it. Within the pre-theoretical experience of those so engaged, concrete "moral pointers begin to stand out."[28] Prophetic insight, therefore, arises in the midst of practice. It is only after this experience has been weighed and tested that the theoretical reflection of theology, philosophy and the social sciences can formulate the prophetic insight into ethical principles and coherent plans for social and political change.

These appeals to creative imagination, charismatic insight and the lived experience of social struggle are all attempts by Rahner and Schillebeeckx to point the way toward a more positive and concrete approach to the Church's prophetic role in society. Their arguments quite rightly emphasize that the prophetic function belongs not only to the individual Christian, but also to the Church as a socially organized body. Within the institutional and corporate context, however, the appeal to imagination, charism and experience must be given more clarity than either Rahner or Schillebeeckx has given it. In particular, the translation of their approaches from the individual to the corporate level depends on being able to identify some dimensions of the experience which are shared by all who are members of the community of belief. Without this identification of commonality, the appeal to experience and identity is a one-sided appeal to subjectivity. If a contrast experience of some persons is to be taken as the basis of an action proposal normative for all, then it must be shown that the proposal emerges from an identity which is normative for all. This clarification is essential if prophetic appeals are to have both communicative and persuasive power. Neither individual Christians, nor corporate bodies, nor official Church leaders can expect their prophetic claims to be accepted as normative for other Christians unless they are prepared to advance reasons why they should be. On this point, Gustafson has remarked:

> It is, however, legitimate to engage prophets in non-prophetic discourse; some testing of their perceptions and of the theological convictions which both justify and empower their utterances is legitimate. Indeed, it is necessary if those who are not inclined to be moved by prophetic rhetoric are to be persuaded of its moral and theological validity. In a time of prophecy from the right and from the left it is even more important to engage in such discourse.[29]

From this review of some of the theological literature on the prophetic role of the Christian community several conclusions can be drawn. First, concrete proposals for social policy cannot be deduced from the general principles of Christian morality. These principles are useful for providing a direction for Christian action, but not for providing the specificity necessary if there is to be actual common action. Second, negative critique of society is an insufficient basis for the common engagement of the Church in society. Third, some positive linkage between the fundamental structure of

Christian identity and positive proposals for action must be shown if these proposals are urged as normative for the community as a whole. And, finally, this link between shared identity and shared action will be a link forged in a creative act of synthesis which occurs within the living experience of those who share a common Christian identity. The concluding section of this essay will argue that the sacramental life and the sacramental imagination which shape the living religious identity of Christians are also a very important basis for common prophetic action in society.

III

THE SACRAMENTAL CHURCH AS A SOURCE OF CREATIVE IMAGINATION AND PROPHECY

If creative imagination, charism and experience are the sources of both individual and corporate prophetic action for justice, then the public role of the Church will be further clarified by reflection on the shape of the Christian imagination. The appeal to imagination and experience which has emerged in recent discussions of this question has a suggestion of irrationalism and subjectivism about it, especially to those who have been educated either in the Catholic tradition of neo-Scholasticism or in those forms of Protestant thought heavily influenced by the Enlightenment. This suspicion points out a genuine danger to which this kind of appeal could lead. But this fear would be justified only if imagination and experience are regarded as shapeless and uncontrollable. Such, however, is not the case. Neither the human mind nor the human heart is a *tabula rasa*, whimsically poised to move in any and every direction without preference. Human experience is shaped by the history of the person who experiences, and by the symbols or "root-metaphors" that provide identity and a means of communication within the community to which the person belongs.[30] The contrast between reason and experience is not a contrast of two contraries. The heart, too, has its reasons. As Iris Murdoch has stated: "A deeper realization of the role of symbols in morality need not involve (as certain critics seem to fear) any overthrow of reason. Reason must, however, especially in this region, appear in her other *persona* as imagination."[31] Imagination has a structure, a logic or a kind of rationality which makes the claims of Rahner and Schillebeeckx far from antinomian irrationalism.

The moral imagination of Christians is shaped by all the fundamental symbols and doctrines of the Christian faith. The other essays of this collection have examined a number of the ways in which these symbols and doctrines influence the basic understanding of justice. Here, however, I want to suggest that the dimensions of this living imagination are most concretely shaped and revealed in those moments where the symbolic enactment of Christian belief is at its most intense—in the sacraments which are at the very heart of the Church's life as a worshiping community. Sacraments are ritualized communal actions which not only express but also embody and realize religious meaning in the life of those who receptively and actively participate in them. Moreover, it is not simply "meaning," in the cognitive sense of this term, which is expressed and embodied in the sacramental event. It is the religious reality itself—God's saving grace and love—which enters into the life of the community of worshipers through a sacrament. Sacramental worship engages not only the mind but the heart. It touches the worshiper on the level of experience and concrete imagination. It is formed activity which, to borrow Bruno Bettelheim's phrase, creates and expresses an "informed heart." The initiation of a new member of the community at baptism and the celebration of the communion of faith at the Eucharist, for example, are not simply illustrations of statements of the content of Christian belief. They are enactments of faith and experiential participation in faith. As David Power has put it:

> One can talk forever of the love of God in Jesus Christ but it takes a parable to make me ask whether this love is present in my daily actions and conduct. This is relevant to liturgy's claim to mediate reality. It claims not only to talk about it but to make it. It purports to allow the subject to express his relation to reality in a self-involving action. To be truly self-involving it must not only express the horizons of faith but must also involve the daily self in their pursuit.[32]

This simultaneous representation and realization of the all-pervasive reality of grace in the sacraments is expressed by Karl Rahner when he calls the sacraments "intrinsically real symbols."[33] It is also the meaning of the Council of Trent's statements that a sacrament is "the visible form of an invisible grace" and that sacraments contain the grace that they signify and signify the grace that they contain.[34] Sacraments, in other words, are an experienced synthesis of the ultimate reality in which Christians believe with the concrete life of a community. This synthesis occurs in the imaginative actions of baptism, the Eucharist, reconciliation, etc.

Thus the Roman Catholic sacramental principle suggests that the normative structure of Christian experience and Christian imagination is concretely expressed in symbolic actions of the Church's sacramental life. I want to argue, therefore, that the structure of the Church's sacramental life can serve as a touchstone for discerning the authenticity of prophetic statements which claim to be calls from God discovered by Christian imagination. More than this, both participation in and reflection on the structure of the sacramental life should be expected to stimulate such charismatic sensitivity. Such participation can orient the Christian community as a whole toward normative interpretations of the social process as, in Barth's terms, an allegory and analogue of the Kingdom of God which is both anticipated and promised by God's already present grace.

This analogy between the internal life of the community, the structures of society and the Kingdom of God is not a relation which collapses into identity, as Barth forcefully argued. The Catholic sacramental principle does not imply that baptism and the Eucharist are realizations of the Kingdom without eschatological remainder. The sacramental principle, however, serves as an important counterweight to the expressively futurist and critical approach of a purely eschatological theology or spirituality. The Kingdom is already present, even though not definitively so. The shape (though not necessarily the extent) of this presence is given its clearest expression in the sacramental life of the Church.[35] Thus whenever the Kingdom becomes visible it will have the shape outlined by this sacramental life. The claim that there is an analogy between the inner sacramental life of the Church and the public life of society is not an argument for the re-establishment of Christendom. It is simply a claim that though neither Church nor secular society is the Kingdom, both can be *loci* in which the reality of the Kingdom becomes visible and actual in human experience. It is to maintain that the Church and secular society can both be the partial realization in history of the Kingdom of God. Whether this realization occurs in the ecclesiastical or political spheres it will have the same imaginative contours. These contours are expressed in the sacramental symbols which give form to the Church's life of worship.

Recent Catholic discussions of the sacramental dimensions of Christian life have stressed the fundamental unity of the sacramental principle rather than its differentiation into the seven sacraments enumerated by the Council of Trent. Contemporary discussions of the sacramental principle, in line with patristic thought, have highlighted the analogy which exists between the Father's love of humanity, the pattern of Jesus' life, death and resurrection, the contours of the life of the Church, and the shape of a humane and just society. Jesus Christ is the symbolic-real expression and embodiment of God's covenant of love with all of humanity. He is "the sacrament of the encounter with God."[36] The Church, in turn, is the sacrament of Christ—the human community in which the saving grace of Christ is made visible and effective. Though the presence of grace is not restricted to those who are members of the Church, this grace comes to its most explicit symbolic expression in the Christian community. God's covenant of love, moreover, extends to the whole of humanity. It is the most radical basis of the unity and solidarity of the human race. Therefore, as a community which both proclaims and attempts to live in this covenant, the Church is, in the words of Vatican II, "the universal sacrament of salvation simultaneously manifesting and realizing the mystery of God's love for man," "a kind of sacrament or sign of intimate union with God, and of the unity of all mankind."[37] The sacramentalizing of divine presence and covenant, then, is not restricted to the traditional seven sacraments of the institutional Church defined by Trent but occurs in the entire Christian life and the whole cosmos regarded as the symbolic manifestation of God's love.

Louis Dupré has pointed out that this broader interpretation of sacramentality was common in the days before the polemics of the Reformation age caused its suppression:

> A clearer recognition of the intrinsic nature of religious symbolism could have constrained the bitter polemics among Christians over the number of sacraments. The positive, institutional element peculiar to each faith, is undoubtedly more important than modernism and liberal Protestantism allowed, yet it should not eclipse the primary truth that sacramentality is a universal form of symbolism. It must not be restricted, then, to those particular forms of which we know the historical institution. Christian tradition itself professed the all-pervasive nature of sacramental symbolism in its respect for "sacramentals," now all but abolished by the institutional legalism of the last centuries. Another instance of sacramental symbolization is the veneration of images, so important in the cult of the Eastern Christian Churches. Far from being idolatrous, as some Byzantine emperors thought, the sacramental character of the Christian cosmos is directly implied in the incarnation. If God communicates himself in Christ, the image of God, then he also communicates himself in the images of that image.[38]

The range of the Christian sacramental imagination, then, is not restricted to the seven traditional sacraments. It is capable of seeing in the whole cosmos and in all human relationships a kind of symbolic realization of God's covenant with humanity. This, of course, does not imply that the entire cosmos and all human relationships are in fact realizations of the covenant love of the Kingdom. To maintain this would be to maintain that the Kingdom has already fully arrived. It is to maintain, however, that all of human existence is open to interpretation and action which rises not simply from the theoretical perspective of theology and the principles of social ethics but also from the Christian sacramental imagination.

Within this context the differentiation of the sacramental life of the Christian community into the traditional seven sacraments can be viewed in a way which gives it secondary but important relevance to the prophetic role of the Church in society. Each of the seven sacraments places one of the key moments or events in human existence and the human life-cycle within the symbolic-real world of Christian imagination. This is a world in which God's creating and redeeming covenant of love is seen as acting not only *on* human life but *within* it. The central events which provide the texture of human existence—birth, maturity, communion in a shared meal, marriage, vocation, forgiveness and death—are all bearers of the grace of the new covenant. The seven sacraments are the concrete realization and enactment of the fundamental sacramental reality of the Church in those events which give human life its shape. In Rahner's words, "A fundamental act of the Church in an individual's regard, in situations that are decisive for him, an act which truly involves the nature of the Church as the historical, eschatological presence of redemptive grace, is *ipso facto* a sacrament."[39] This sevenfold differentiation of the sacramentality of the Church represents the historical differentiation of the Church's awareness of key ways in which redemption is realized in human form. Though this differentiation is subordinate to the sacramentality of the entire fabric of human existence, it is a differentiation which provides a rough outline of the shape of the Christian imagination as it has evolved through history.

The relevance of this view of the sacraments to the public and prophetic role of the Church is suggested by the fact that each of the sacraments is a specification of the fundamental sacramentality of the Church which is called to be a sign of "the unity of all humanity."[40] The symbol of each sacrament points to the world beyond the sanctuary. Each of the seven sacraments has an intrinsic dynamism which carries the Christian imagination toward the perception of the grace of God's covenant love in social existence as well as in the interpersonal and private domains of human struggle and fulfillment. Each of the sacraments has a social relevance which arises from the universality of the grace it bears. The sacramentalizing of God's grace which occurs in the Church is not solely for the benefit of the internal life of the Christian community but also for the whole world. Baptism expresses not only the call of a select few to the Kingdom but the invitation which God's grace holds out to all persons. The Eucharist expresses not only the participation in the death and resurrection of Christ which is the source of Christian unity, but the radical source of the unity of the human race. Thus the Christian imagination whose contours are outlined by the sacramental system is an imagination which can shape existence and stimulate action in the whole of life, not just in the personal religious life of individual believers.

This social relevance of the sacraments has been largely absent from both sacramental theology and Christian ethics until very recently. A rediscovery of this relevance was begun in Henri de Lubac's great work, *Catholicism: A Study of Dogma in Relation to the Corporate Destiny of Mankind*. A contemporary American Protestant theologian, Langdon Gilkey, has argued that the sacramental imagination of the Catholic tradition has the potential to make a major contribution to the struggle for justice and peace if it is allowed its full social range. In Gilkey's words:

> Strangely, in denying or abjuring—or being forced by the twentieth century to do so!—the great *temptation* of a sacramental form of religion to absolutize the relative and sanctify the ambiguous, Catholicism may discover the vast strength of a sacramental form of religion, namely, the divinely granted capacity to allow finite and relative instruments to be media of the divine and to endow all of secular and ordinary life with the possibility and the sanctity of divine creativity; and thus more than Protestantism, Catholicism may be able to bring Christianity alive and well through the turmoil of the modern world. However, if Catholicism or Protestantism is to achieve this task of mediating the divine grounding, judgment and possibility to our secular existence, it must widen the scope of both word and sacrament far beyond their present religious, ecclesiastical, dogmatic, and "merely redemptive" limits.[41]

This widening of scope for the sacramental imagination is called for by the pain and ambiguities of contemporary social life. It is more than a matter of attempting to insure the survival of Christianity in the future, however. This widening of scope for the sacramental imagination is called for by the nature of Christian faith itself.

The need for such a widening of the range of the sacramental imagination suggests that the influence of sacramental symbolism on secular life is not a one-way influence. The secular experience of Christians will influence their experience of worship and liturgical celebration. The way they understand and experience baptism, the Eucharist, marriage, ministry, forgiveness and death is not shaped solely by their experience within the worshiping community, but also by the contemporary social situation. Thus, once again, any effort logically to deduce a Christian approach to social and political action from the shape of the sacramental symbols is doomed to failure from the start. Worse than this, it would amount to an effort to impose a religious structure on secular life in an imperialistic and alienating way.

The imagination does not create by deduction. In arguing that the sacramental imagination is a central source of the Church's prophetic action in society, I am not proposing that sacramental symbols drawn from the tradition be used as the first principles for a theory of the Church's prophetic function in contemporary society. My suggestion is that the synthesis of the experience of the joys and struggles of life in all its dimensions with the experience of redemption and grace which occurs in communal sacramental worship is a synthesis which can and should provide insight into the concrete role which the Church should play in society. There is a dialectical relation between the shape of the sacramental symbols of the worshiping community and the realities of the social community. This dialectic may be much more helpful for clarifying the relation between Christian faith and specific social options than are general moral principles. This is so because the dialectic between sacred and secular in the Christian imagination is *already* concrete. It does not have to *become* concrete by a process of deductive reasoning as is the case with general moral principles. It is a dialectic *within* concrete experience. To the extent that sacramental worship of the community is both true to itself and in touch with realities of contemporary society and culture it can lead to concrete communal action. On the basis of historical evidence Hans Bernhard Meyer has pointed out the kind of influence which sacramental liturgy can have in public life when it is thus related and open to secular experience:

The more completely the expression of a culture is taken over for the liturgy, the more closely the language and symbols of the liturgy correspond with the social features of a period, the more likely it is that celebrations of the liturgy will have secondary effects which will be felt in the life of society outside worship. When this happens the liturgy can perform its function of providing meaning and motivation which will help to shape the lives, not only of individual believers, but also of the whole believing community, and go on to influence the wider society outside this.[42]

Though Meyer rightly calls this influence secondary, since sacramental worship is not social action, such an effect on society is a primary and essential dimension of a form of faith which lives through sacraments.

The appeal to the sacramental imagination as a source of communal prophetic action in society was one of the central themes of the 41st International Eucharistic Congress whose theme was "The Eucharist and the Hungers of the Human Family." A main theme in the Congress was the link between the symbolically shared meal of the Eucharist and the responsibility of the Christian community to take concrete action to alleviate world hunger. Some reflections on this theme will serve as an example of the function of the sacramental imagination envisioned in this essay.

The Eucharist is the representation and everlasting memorial of the new covenant which God established with all of humanity through the death and resurrection of Jesus. This covenant is the source of Christian unity, and the Eucharist is the pre-eminent sacrament of unity. It both signifies and realizes the unity of the followers of Christ in a shared meal. In the concreteness and materiality of shared bread and wine the covenant between God and human beings becomes the covenant which forms the human community of the Church.

The covenant sacramentalized in the Eucharist, however, is not an exclusive covenant with those who are members of the Church. The new covenant is a universal covenant with all humanity. If the Church is the "sacrament of the unity of mankind" and if the Eucharist is the primary enactment of the shape of that unity, then the shared meal is the pre-eminent symbol of God's will for the human race. Because of the presence of the universal grace of God's covenant in the sacramental sharing of food, the Christian imagination is drawn to both perceive and experience the relations between all persons as a covenant relationship, a relationship of partnership, communion and solidarity only adequately expressed in the sharing of bread. This synthesis between the Eucharistic faith and efforts to satisfy human hunger is essential if the symbolic reality of the Eucharist is to remain alive and authentic. Philip Rosato has made this point forcefully:

> The Eucharist would seem magical to many if it were understood as the only bright moment in an otherwise dark and godless world. . . . Christ's presence, then, in the hungry of the world (Mt. 25:35) and his presence in the Eucharist (1 Cor. 12:23-26) must be seen as complementary. The Eucharist is not only the place where Christ encounters man, but it the place where all of man's existential encounters with Christ—even in the suffering caused by human starvation—come together in one incandescent encounter with the crucified and glorified Lord.[43]

If an alienated and magical sacramentalism is to be avoided, the action of Christians in a hungry world must become eucharistic. And it will be eucharistic to the extent that it is action which brings food to the hungry.

This line of thinking does not exhaust the full significance of the Eucharist for the Christian imagination.[44] Nor does it spell out a policy for the solution of the tragic problem of world hunger. In the area of policy-making, however, this approach does provide the basis for corporate prophetic action by the Church as a whole. In the Eucharist Christians are not presented with a moral ideal or general principle of human action. They are graced with a concrete manifestation of the shape of God's covenant with all humanity as a covenant which *is realized* in the sharing of food. This covenant, Christians believe, is a *fact*, not simply an ideal or a general norm.

The covenant confronts Christians with a call or vocation, a call which has the weight of a moral imperative, but which also enters human experience as grace—as a gift which makes response to the imperative possible.

Consequently there is an intrinsic affinity between the Christian sacramental imagination and the assertion that all human persons have a "right to food." The affirmation of this right provides the intellectual foundation for quite specific policy proposals.

The existence of a "right to food" provides the basis for the proposals of the National Conference of Catholic Bishops' statement on "The World Food Crisis" and the "Statement of Policy" on the right to food issued by the ecumenical group Bread for the World.[45] These policy proposals include calls for specific action such as a national nutrition program in the United States, U.S. participation in a world food reserve program, increase in U.S. food assistance, the separation of food policy from military policy, the lowering of trade barriers for imports from poor countries and special preferences for their exports. These policy proposals are not deduced from the Eucharist. They do possess an imaginative affinity to the Eucharist, however. They "make sense" in a non-rationalistic way, in the context outlined here. Their very concreteness is one of the reasons why they make sense in this way, for the imagination is a concrete rather than abstractive faculty. The prophetic voice which the Church addresses to the world food crisis thus has deep roots in the shared experience and identity of the Christian community. It can be defended as a normative expression of Christian faith.

The appeal to sacramental imagination does not absolve the Church from the rigors of social, political and theological analysis. All of these are essential if the imagination is to be informed by the realities of both the actual social world and of the Christian faith. There are times and situations, however, where the imagination can outrun this analysis and lead the Church to corporate prophetic action which cannot strictly be "proven" to be the only Christian response. The sacramentalism of the Catholic tradition provides a framework within which it is possible to argue for the legitimacy of such prophecy in a way that will prevent the cultural tendencies toward the privatization and fragmentation of Christian

faith from destroying the Church's public influence. The link being
drawn between the Eucharist and world hunger is just such a case.
I believe that a similar impetus toward prophetic action can be discovered in the other sacraments. Examination of these other possible developments is not possible in an essay already too long. But
further investigation and developments along these lines seem imperative if the Church wants to act as a people and wants to do
this in a public way. The pressures toward privatization and fragmentation of Christian behavior will continue to be present in our
society. I have argued that the Church possesses both the practical
and theoretical resources that make common action for justice
possible in spite of these pressures. These resources are in part to
be found in the sacramental experience which has shaped the
Roman Catholic identity. If Catholicism can tap the prophetic potential of its own identity, the entire ecumenical Church stands to
gain new insight and strength in its attempt to serve a struggling
world.

NOTES

1. "Dogmatic Constitution on the Church" ("Lumen Gentium"), no.
9, in Walter M. Abbott, S.J., and Joseph Gallagher, *The Documents of
Vatican II* (New York: Guild Press/America Press/Association Press,
1966).
2. Max Weber, "Science as a Vocation," in H. H. Gerth and C.
Wright Mills, ed., *From Max Weber* (New York: 1967, Oxford University
Press), p. 155.
3. Karl Rahner, "Theological Reflections on the Problem of Secularization," in *Theological Investigations*, vol. X, trans. David Bourke
(New York: Herder and Herder, 1973), p. 318.
4. For a parallel discussion of the two approaches outlined here, see
James M. Gustafson, "Two Approaches to Theological Ethics," in his
Christian Ethics and the Community (Philadelphia: Pilgrim Press, 1971),
pp. 127-138.
5. For a synthetic discussion of the recent literature on the Church as
sacrament see Avery Dulles, S.J., *Models of the Church* (Garden City,
N.Y.: Doubleday, 1974), chap. IV.
6. Karl Barth, *Community, State and Church* (Garden City, N.Y.:
Doubleday Anchor, 1960), p. 169.
7 Paul Ramsey, *Who Speaks for the Church? A Critique of the 1966*

Geneva Conference on Church and Society (Nashville, Abingdon, 1967).

8. *Ibid.*, p. 34.

9. *Ibid.*, pp. 17 and 152.

10. *Ibid.*, pp. 16 and 149.

11. *Ibid.*, p. 169, n. 4.

12. James M. Gustafson, "Moral Authority of the Church," *The Chicago Theological Seminary Register* LXI (1971), no. 4, p. 6.

13. For a general account of these recent developments and the official documents which reflect them, see *The Gospel of Peace and Justice: Catholic Social Teaching Since Pope John*, presented by Joseph Gremillion (Maryknoll, N.Y.: Orbis Books, 1976), esp. pp. 7-10 and 531-567.

14. Wolfhart Pannenberg, *Theology and the Kingdom of God*, ed. Richard John Neuhaus (Philadelphia: Westminster Press, 1969), p. 79.

15. Jürgen Moltmann, *Theology of Hope: On the Ground and Implications of a Christian Eschatology*, trans. James W. Leitch (London, SCM Press, 1967), p. 324.

16. Pannenberg, *op. cit.*, p. 83.

17. Johannes B. Metz, *Theology of the World*, trans. William Glen-Doepel (New York: Herder and Herder, 1969), pp. 123-124.

18. Gustafson, "Moral Authority of the Church," p. 11.

19. Gustavo Gutierrez, *A Theology of Liberation: History, Politics and Salvation*, trans. Sister Caridad Inda and John Eagleson (Maryknoll, N.Y.: Orbis Books, 1973), pp. 224-225.

20. See Rahner, "On the Theological Problems Entailed in a 'Pastoral Constitution,' " in *Theological Investigations*, vol. X, pp. 293-317, and Edward Schillebeeckx, "Church, Magisterium and Politics," in *God the Future of Man*, trans. N. D. Smith (New York: Sheed and Ward, 1968), pp. 141-166.

21. Rahner, "Theological Reflections on the Problem of Secularization," p. 322. See also Rahner, "On the Theological Problems Entailed in a Pastoral Constitution," p. 303.

22. Schillebeeckx, "Church, Magisterium and Politics," p. 151.

23. See Schillebeeckx, *op. cit.*, p. 152, and Rahner, "Theological Reflections on the Problem of Secularization," p. 330.

24. Schillebeeckx, *op. cit.*, p. 156.

25. Rahner, "Theological Reflections on the Problems of Secularization," p. 331.

26. Rahner, "On the Theological Problems Entailed in a Pastoral Constitution," pp. 304-306.

27. Schillebeeckx, "Church, Magisterium and Politics," p. 154.

28. *Ibid.*, p. 159.

29. Gustafson, "Moral Authority of the Church," pp. 9-10.

30. The place of symbol and root-metaphor in Christian theology and ethos has been analyzed in a seminal way by H. Richard Niebuhr, *The Responsible Self: An Essay in Christian Moral Philosophy* (New York: Harper and Row, 1963), Appendix A, "Metaphors and Morals."

This topic has received extensive discussion among Christian ethicists in recent years.

31. Iris Murdoch, "Vision and Choice in Morality," in Ian T. Ramsey, ed., *Christian Ethics and Contemporary Philosophy* (London, SCM Press, 1966), p. 212, n. 37.

32. David Power, "The Song of the Lord in an Alien Land," in *Concilium*, new series, vol. 2, no. 2 (Feb. 1974), "Politics and Liturgy," p. 92.

33. Karl Rahner, "The Church and the Sacraments" in *Inquiries* (New York: Herder and Herder, 1964), p. 219.

34. *D.S.*, 1639 and 1606.

35. Joseph Gelineau has pointed out the complex relation of simultaneous continuity and discontinuity between the sacramental and eschatological realization of the kingdom in a way that is relevant here: "There is a dialectic of continuity-rupture-communion at the basis of liturgical dynamics. But the liturgy is practice rather than theory. It does not stop at the level of -logies (anthropo-logy, theo-logy); it is concerned with the order of -urgies (liturgy). It is symbolic action and an inductive force; it institutes a new existence. That is the way to look for its political power and liberating power"—Joseph Gelineau, "Celebrating the Paschal Liberation," *Concilium*, new series, vol. 2, no. 2, p. 112.

36. The phrase is taken from the title of Schillebeeckx' important and influential study, *Christ the Sacrament of the Encounter with God* (New York: Sheed and Ward, 1963).

37. "Gaudium et Spes," no. 45; "Lumen Gentium," no. 1. See also "Gaudium et Spes," no. 42: "Lumen Gentium," nos. 9 and 48, "Sacrosanctum Concilium," no. 26, "Ad Gentes," no. 5. For recent discussions of these texts, see Dulles, *Models of the Church*, ch. IV; Juan Luis Segundo, *The Community Called Church*, trans. John Drury (Maryknoll, N.Y.: Orbis Books, 1973), ch. 4; Edward Schillebeeckx, *God the Future of Man, op. cit.*, ch. IV; idem, *The Mission of the Church*, trans. N. D. Smith (New York: Seabury, 1973), ch. 3; Richard P. McBrien, *Church: The Continuing Quest* (New York: Newman Press, 1970), Louis Dupre, *The Other Dimension: A Search for the Meaning of Religious Attitudes* (Garden City, N.Y.: Doubleday, 1972), ch. 4.

38. Dupré, *The Other Dimension*, p. 185.

39. Rahner, "The Church and the Sacraments," p. 223.

40. "Lumen Gentium," no. 1.

41. Langdon Gilkey, *Catholicism Confronts Modernity: A Protestant View* (New York: Seabury, 1975), pp. 196-197.

42. Hans Bernhard Meyer, "The Social Significance of Liturgy" in *Concilium*, New Series, vol. 2, no. 10, p. 37.

43. Philip J. Rosato, "World Hunger and Eucharistic Theology," *America* 135 (Aug. 7, 1976), p. 48.

44. For a reflection on the relation between this emphasis and the more familiar Catholic stress on the themes of presence and sacrifice in

the context of shifting social and cultural structures, see William J. Byron, "Eucharist and Society," *America* 135 (Aug. 7, 1976), pp. 43-46.

45. National Conference of Catholic Bishops, "The World Food Crisis—A Pastoral Plan of Action," Nov. 21, 1974, and "The Right to Food," in Arthur Simon, *Bread for the World* (New York/Grand Rapids: Paulist/Eerdmans, 1975), pp. 165-172. For an analysis of these documents from a perspective similar to that adopted here, see Drew Christiansen, "Society and Ethics: The Church and World Hunger," The Catholic Theological Society of America, *Proceedings of the Thirtieth Annual Convention* (1975), pp. 129-139.

Jesus as the Justice of God

John C. Haughey, S.J.

In the past eighty years there has been a notable increase in the Church's understanding of its responsibility in the social order (as has been treated elsewhere in this volume).[1] At the same time there does not seem to have been a parallel increase in the concern of Christians for the social order. While major things are being said by the Church, minor things at best are being done by believers in their dealings with the world and its injustices. Justice remains pretty much as it has always been, namely one of the virtues in the galaxy of virtues that it is incumbent on Christians to practice. It has not moved onto center stage or become a passion with Christians as the Church's developing self-understanding would have it be.

I believe that Christians will stand pat in their attitude toward justice and the injustices that surround them until they see the ideal the Church is preaching incarnated in the person of Jesus. This essay will suggest some of the ways in which this might be done. It will begin to re-image Jesus in terms of justice. By re-imaging Jesus I am not recommending that we super-impose on the image we have of Jesus alien ideas or categories or perspectives, but only that the newly developing understanding of our responsibilities as Christians be traced to and, if possible, be integrated by the person of Jesus. The essay will indicate some of the lines of thought that, though somewhat hidden in the Scriptures, many concerned Christians are beginning to tease out either by study or by prayer and reflection. Although this essay will take its data largely from the Scriptures, it will be more interested in getting the reader to re-examine his ordinary justice hermeneutic than it will be exhaustive in its treatment of the suggested lines of thought that a new hermeneutic might take. In brief, the primary assumption behind this essay is that new things do not become part of the behavior of Christians unless they are seen in the behavior of Jesus after whom devoted Christians pattern themselves. In this case, aspiration for the ideal will be commensurate with their perception of Jesus' call and ministry as one of justice.

There is a second reason for this essay. A reader of this volume might find that the word justice, though many-splendored, is too much so to be intelligible. It touches every level of human existence. Like happiness, those who are most conscious of it and passionate about it are those who are the victims of its absence. Whether present or absent, justice touches every level of human existence from its most complex level which is political life to the simplest point of social order, the interpersonal. Even below all levels of social existence, the notion of justice refers in some of its usages to the individual touched at the deepest level of his or her being when they are made just by God, i.e., "justified." This study will contend that the many meanings of the word "just" can be illumined by the person of Jesus. It will likewise contend that the person of Jesus can be seen to integrate each of the meanings of this variegated and elusive notion of justice into himself.

The matter for this essay could also be put in the form of a question: How much should believing in and following Jesus entail concern for the social and political conditions of our contemporaries and modern society? How much is the oppression and poverty of much of our modern world the business of the community of believers in Jesus? I believe the answer is neither simple nor single. It is not simple because of the extraordinary complexity of the relationship of Church to world, not to mention grace to nature. Nor is it single since within the Christian community there are many different calls extended to individuals, the answering of which contributes in different ways to the Church's relation to the world.

One answer, of course, could be given which would be true for all Christians irrespective of their particular calls. This would be along the lines that each servant of the Lord is called to be the way the master was, neither greater nor lesser. But this leads to the crux of the matter. To what extent was Jesus of Nazareth con- cerned with social injustice? If the Kingdom he preached was "not of this world," then those who live in the Kingdom (insofar as they do) should not besmirch themselves by linking it with the ame- lioration of social ills. If, on the other hand, the Kingdom has re- sponsibility for the social order as a constitutive part of it, can Christians by and large be accused of following a Jesus who is too other-worldly and of their own making, so to speak?

How is the Church to answer this question? As the essays in this volume alone indicate, it has been about the task of answering it for a long time and in many different ways. Furthermore, the very fact of the volume indicates that it is not yet satisfied that it has fully discerned the degree of social realism to which the master is calling the believing community. This is as it should be since, in this matter as in all other questions that bedevil it, the believing community will not come to an end to what it can see and learn in the words, deeds and life of Jesus.

In the present era of the Church there is a fresh reflection on some relatively neglected facts about the Gospels, the recalling of which should serve to illuminate Jesus' stance toward the social order of his day. Jesus was neither a withdrawalist like the Es- senes, who were contemporary with him, nor an insurrectionist like the Zealots. His posture toward the justice and injustice of the social order of first-century Palestine developed between these two extremes which equivalently held that "God will take justice into his own hands in the end times" or "we must take it into ours now."

But these two facts alone suggest that a good place to begin our inquiry will be with some of the socio-political attitudes and judgments about social structures that were extant in Jesus' gener- ation, having been handed down to him by the devout Jews of previous generations. These attitudes and judgments which are contained in their Scriptures are always presented in connection with Judaism's understanding of salvation.[2]

Yahweh prepared Israel over the course of the centuries to ex- pect a salvation which was social in its form with justice as its con- tent. From the beginning of Israel's understanding of what was going on in her, she saw herself as a people, a nation among nations whose uniqueness was traceable to the promises made to Abraham. He was told that he was to be the father of many nations. Although this understanding developed through the many stages of the revelation she received, it never lost its initial socio-political, yet personal, stamp. Even the introduction late in the Old Testament of hitherto unsuspected notions which connect salvation to a life-after-this-one in a place other than this earth did not change Israel's basic understanding that it was the nations as nations that were to be saved. These after-life notions which came practically as an after-thought into the Old Testament serve to purify her ideas about salvation, but they do not rob them of their socio-political cast or the social reality of their form.

Just as the nations were a component part of Israel's conception of salvation, so also was justice. Israel was to be the means whereby the nations would be blessed. But before that would happen Israel would be vindicated by Yahweh before all of the nations. Justice would be done to them on Israel's behalf if Israel herself was transformed radically into a people after Yahweh's heart. If she remained true to "the way of the Lord by doing righteousness and justice" (Gen. 18:18) by her own internal comportment and behavior with one another, she would have justice done to her.

To this end Yahweh anointed special individuals with his own Spirit, some of whom were judges, some prophets, some kings, each in his own way bringing about justice in and for the people or exhorting Israel to it. In all instances justice was an essential part of the vocation of each of these individuals. As a result of Israel's experience of these especially endowed individuals, an idealized future figure was conceived by Israel, one who would have the courage of a judge, the royal ways of another David, and the piercing message of the prophets. Like Moses himself this Messiah would lead Israel out of her constant condition of victim of others' injustices.

Once she was vindicated through the Messiah she awaited, Israel would become the epicenter of international peace and justice and order, the nation to which all nations would come, where God would be Lord of all nations and acclaimed as such by them. All nations would then be under the conscious sovereignty of the one Lord; they would acknowledge his sovereignty by the universal worship of him. This universal order would be achieved when the justice of God was freely accepted by his creatures as the ultimate determinant of human order.

Notice how many different shades of meaning the aspiration for justice brings together and, in turn, how closely each of them is linked to salvation. Justice is something Israel is to do for herself, and, at the same time, something she cannot achieve of herself. It is gift and responsibility. It is eschatological and yet socio-political. It is religious and ethical. It is to be yielded to and done, an export after it is imported.

There is no reason to believe that Jesus thought other than in this frame of reference. He was thoroughly Jewish as every modern exegete is at pains to point out to us. He purified the notions of his hearers and his followers, of course, concerning their expectations, but he did not disabuse them of these expectations.

One of the caricatures or reductionisms Christian catechesis has been frequently guilty of has been with regard to Israel and Israel's expectations about the Messiah. The caricature runs like this: "The Messiah whom Israel awaited was expected to bring about a political and social transformation of the fortunes of Israel; what our Jesus did was to teach his hearers how wrong-headed those expectations were by teaching them about heaven." As a consequence the Christian Messiah is depicted in what is supposed to be a rectified version, one in which he is a depoliticized figure whose role is to bring about a spiritual kingdom. Gone is the realism of the Old Testament. While the Kingdom preached by Jesus is purified by him and transcends the socio-political realities of this world, it was never meant to leave these or disdain them or prescind from them. Even though some portion of the population of Jesus' contemporaries riveted their expectations to the intra-mundane, it was the confinement of their expectations to the intra-mundane that Jesus railed against, not the socio-political framework of those expectations. It would seem a cruel trick if the long-awaited Messiah had a wholly other-world, "the next life," in mind when every expectation entertained by Israel was social and national in character, since this was what their Scriptures had taught them to believe.

The first matter, then, for a Christian examination of conscience is to ask ourselves whether we have been giving ear to the scriptural word of God in a way that hears the social realism of that word. Although the issue is not an easily resolved black and white kind of thing, the Jewish background of the Christian Scriptures must be kept to the fore, unless one wishes to give quite a different hearing to the verses one contemplates and the reality the revelation would have us perceive. The Magnificat, for example, can be heard in two quite different ways. "He has put down the mighty from their thrones and exalted those of low degree," among whom was his handmaiden whose "low estate he regarded" (Lk. 1:52-53), can be heard in the typical way which prescinds from the empirical reality of social power. In this hearing a spiritual world of virtue and disembodied grace is being referred to. Or one can hear these verses in a way that expects the divine action to take place in and on the socio-political realities of human affairs.

The traditional hearing does not create expectations in one about degrees of social change, nor does it provoke one to see his or her Christian responsibility as having to deal with this world and the use of social power within it. Then one is happy to interpret one's faith in an interior way and content to stay with personal trust in God, leaving such macro-issues as the uses of power in his hands rather than bringing them into our own as part of our religious responsibility. In effect, then, the word of God has encouraged a world-escaping attitude, not a world-transforming one.

I
RE-IMAGING JESUS

The re-imaging of Jesus must begin with the Scriptures. These give the re-imaging its basic data and they bespeak the need for a re-imaging. The evangelists themselves, notice, had to deal with this question which the Church is presently asking itself and we are inquiring into here. Each evangelist had at hand more material than he used. He had to be selective with his material according to the theological motifs he wished to underscore and the problematic he wished to address. Since this was the case, we could ask, for example, why Luke chose the famous passage from Isaiah 61 to have Jesus introduce his public life and his understanding of himself to his fellow Nazarenes. Since there is no way of knowing whether the incident of Jesus' reading in the synagogue on the Sabbath day happened as Luke describes it (and in fact we have good reason to believe it did not), we can nonetheless be sure from Luke's decision to make use of this material in this place and way that he perceived the mission of Jesus in justice terms. Thus Luke attests that the Spirit was conferred upon Jesus in order to "proclaim release to the captives and recovery of sight to the blind, and to set at liberty those who are oppressed" (Lk. 4:18-20).

Both from its placement in this Gospel and from the content itself, one can be sure that at least Luke's Jesus who identifies himself with the figure predicted by Isaiah—"Today this Scripture has been fulfilled in your hearing" (Lk. 4:21)—sees himself with a mission and vocation of social responsibility. We do violence to the realism of Judaism if we choose to hear the terms which connote poverty, bondage, deprivation and oppression as metaphors referring to the "spiritual" life. If they do not mean what they say, if Luke's Jesus is suggesting that the political and economic order and the world of social systems are to be circumvented in order for his hearers to be religious, then he has certainly chosen a peculiar text for saying so.

Once again without wanting to sound as though the matter is clear and simple, what is being recommended here so far is that the Christian remain open to the possibility that the evangelists' Jesus, or so far at least Luke's Jesus, inherited the social realism of the Israel he had been born into. If this was the case, Jesus would have looked quite directly at the world of matter and power, and, having seen his people surrounded by bondage, oppression and poverty, he would also see its alleviation as an intrinsic part of their salvation and, consequently, his mission.

Since he went about that alleviation in quite a different way than most of us ordinarily think about the transformation of social systems, perhaps we have allowed his wholly different way for bringing about a radical change in the social order to obscure the intention he had to bring this about.

Once one is prepared to be open about this question he begins to see other possible interpretations of so many different things in the New Testament. Weigh, for example, what is being said by Jesus by his choice of disciples. He did not choose those who were socially influential. With intentional selectivity he went out and attracted to himself the powerless, and even in some cases, like Matthew, the despised. It seems that he chose to minister to those in need with those who were uncredentialed, and in some cases even disreputable, in the eyes of society. The broadest of overviews of his life reveals a predilection toward the least favored, the "outs" of society. In this connection there is the tantalizing contention made by the respected Oscar Cullmann and picked up by many since then that perhaps as many as five of the twelve that Jesus called into a close relationship with himself had been recruited from among the ranks of Zealots, the most radical of the political parties in the Israel of Jesus' day.[3] Even if it is off base by a few, it seems that at least some of Jesus' closest companions were former Zealots, a strange choice to say the least if the Kingdom he preached was beyond time and the systems of power within which human lives were lived.

Some of the theological motifs that Luke used to reinforce the Christology we have begun to sense in his Gospel are mentioned elsewhere in this volume.[4] We will touch on only one other of Luke's more revealing Christological statements. It is inserted into a situation of conflict between the apostles who are concerned with the power and position they will enjoy in the Kingdom that Jesus is preaching and establishing. Jesus' response to their conflict is illuminating both about his own self-understanding, at least according to Luke, as well as his understanding of social power itself and its purpose in his Kingdom. In a word, Jesus does not eschew it, but describes himself as employing it. He does so differently from those whose social power is greater than any his fellow Israelites would have known, namely the power of the kings of the Gentiles. In contrast to them, Jesus explains that his power places him "among you as one who serves" (Lk. 22:27). His Kingdom, in other words, is not going to be without power, but the purpose for which it is given, both to Jesus and his followers, is not to govern others or dominate them, but to serve them.

One serves people, of course, but one serves to some purpose;

one has power in function of something. Each of the New Testament authors dealt with this question as well as the questions of the degree of social change intended or envisioned by Jesus, but each of these authors handled it in a different way. Nonetheless it is clear that all three Synoptics had a predilection for the suffering servant of Isaiah as an apt vehicle for gaining some understanding of Jesus' social mission and Jesus' understanding of the power he was given to accomplish that mission. Since all three see Jesus in terms of the suffering servant of Isaiah, all three would see Jesus' mission as fulfilling the servant's mission foretold in Isaiah 42:1-4 which was the establishment of justice among the nations.

Mark, the evangelist, in the same scene of conflict between the apostles about position in the Kingdom, is even more explicit in his use of the suffering servant motif than Luke was. But like Luke's Jesus, the Marcan Christ does not upbraid his apostles for thinking about the power they are to receive nor does he deny that they will be given it, but he chastises them for seeing it in terms of themselves rather than those for whom it is bestowed: "Whoever would be the first among you must be the slave of all" (Mk. 10:44). Mark's Jesus then proceeds one step further in appropriating the mission of the suffering servant of Isaiah to himself by explaining not only the style of his use of power, but also the way in which he would employ this power. "The Son of Man came not only to serve, but to give his life as a ransom for the many" (Mk. 10:45).

Mark does not focus on the source of Jesus' power quite as much as Luke does. Luke's two volumes are held together by the theme of power which comes from above, overshadowing first Jesus, then the community of those who believe in him. This power is, of course, the Holy Spirit. But in all three Synoptics the power is given for purposes that are world-transforming, not world-escaping, purposes that are linked to the mission which Jesus takes upon himself. This mission is one of justice.

It is clear that these servant songs are one of the first sources of intelligibility, one of the earliest frames of reference used by the earliest communities to interpret the deeds and the life of Jesus. Since the community of those who believed in Jesus saw him as the servant of Deutero-Isaiah, the mystery of Jesus cannot be unrav-

eled unless both his mission and his unique manner of accom-
plishing it are traced back to these servant songs.

Matthew contributes something unique to the servant Christology when he connects the healings done by Jesus with the justice
mission explained in the first of the servant songs: "Many followed
him, and he healed them all, and ordered them not to make him
known . . . to fulfill what was spoken by the prophet Isaiah:

> 'Behold, my servant whom I have chosen,
> my beloved with whom my soul is well pleased.
> I will put my Spirit upon him,
> and he shall proclaim justice to the Gentiles.
> He will not wrangle or cry aloud,
> nor will any one hear his voice in the streets;
> he will not break a bruised reed
> or quench a smoldering wick,
> till he brings justice to victory' " (Mt. 12:15-20).

Jesus is depicted here as thinking he would not have been able
to fulfill his justice mission if he had been prematurely hailed as
the one destined for this, and the one with the power to do this.
The manner of the fulfillment of his role, in other words, did not
include acceptance or acclamation before his death since that was
the act which healed par excellence—not only healed but reorient-
ed society and brought "justice to victory." This is at least how the
community of believers and Matthew, Mark and Luke saw Jesus'
life and death. Inextricably interwoven, of course, with this is
Jesus' own self-understanding. Where the community's belief joins
with Jesus' understanding and where it reads back into his life and
mind something that could only be known after Pentecost is a
question we are not dealing with here, important though that
would be for a full treatment of the question being posed by us.

There is every indication too, both here and elsewhere, that
the messianic secret which Jesus insisted on trying to preserve was
not a refusal of power (otherwise why should he have exercised the
power he had?) but a refusal to have the power crowned by the
forms (religious and/or political) chosen by those who were enthusiastic about him because of the short-term, superficial effects his

power had on them. Is not the servant of Isaiah described in notably empowered terms, with the Spirit of God and God's own righteousness poured out on him? But he is also notably bereft of any of the usual forms of power as he executes his mission on earth. The only form of his power, it seems, was his person. The irony about the servant is that while he is without a political base, the effect of his call is pre-eminently social, even political. "He has established justice on the earth" (Is. 42:4) while shunning the acclaim that his power is greeted with and enduring the obloquy that comes with being rejected by the powers that be.

Although his death was not in itself a political act either by intention or ultimate import, nevertheless the cross spelled an end to the powers that put him to death, although it took some years before this was evident. In and through his death the believer can see the beginning of a new source of power and justice and vindication. "When power crucifies truth, it signals to all the world that it has come to its effective end."[5] The enormity of the effect of his death on the power structures which managed human interaction in Jesus' age was only gradually felt in Israel as it was also in the other centers of power beyond Israel. In words that still communicate their awe, the author of the letter to the Ephesians bears witness to the political consequences of Jesus' death and the mystery unfolding before his very eyes of the coming together of the nations with the Israel of God "in one body through the cross" (Eph. 2:16). "In Christ Jesus you [Gentiles] who were once far off have been brought near. . . . He is our peace who has made us both one and has broken down the dividing wall of hostility by abolishing in his flesh the law . . . that he might create in himself one humanity instead of two and reconcile us both to God in one body" (Eph. 2:13-15). In modern parlance one might say that Jesus in death was able to effect an intra-mundane systemic change at a depth not even dreamed of by his contemporaries.

The ironies of Jesus' relation to social power, and, through it, social change, should not be missed. He insisted on performing the actions which had him acclaimed, at times all the way to the point of coronation by acclamation. But the more he was acclaimed, the further he removed himself from the powers of his day. "Perceiving then that they were about to come and take him by force to make him king, Jesus withdrew again to the mountain by himself" (Jn. 6:15). The further he removed himself from contemporary configurations of power the more threatened they became. "So the chief priests and Pharisees gathered the council and said, "What are we to do? For this man performs many signs. If we let him go on thus, everyone will believe in him and the Romans will come and destroy both our holy place and our nation' " (Jn. 11:47-48).

At no time does he call for the overthrow of the religious or political authorities of his day. He seems even to concede the validity of their authority in itself: "Render to Caesar the things that are Caesar's" (Mt. 22:21). "The scribes and Pharisees sit on the chair of Moses; so practice and observe whatever they tell you" (Mt. 23:2). At the same time he confronted them, critiqued them, exposed their hypocrisy, and eventually brought them down through the power of the truth of his person exercised despite or over against them. As Paul Lehmann has put it: "The weakness of power is that when power is confronted by the authority of truth, it is no match for the power of weakness that bears the mark of truth."[6]

The truth of his person was the only political "form" he used. This form released its power primarily through his death and resurrection. The price then for the establishment of justice was his own life. The primary medium of Christian justice after Jesus, one could argue, is still the person who, like Jesus, stands in the truth the Spirit gives one to see. This truth unmasks untruth even when that untruth is systematized and ensconced in political, social and religious power configurations that appear impregnable.

II
JESUS' TEACHINGS ABOUT JUSTICE IN MATTHEW

The evangelists' Christology touches and illumines many levels of justice; what Jesus taught does the same thing. In the interests of brevity we will inquire into only one Gospel—Matthew's. In Matthew, Jesus informs his followers that their kind of justice must exceed that of the scribes and Pharisees (Mt. 5:20). What the scribes and Pharisees teach and practice about being upright before God and neighbor, his listeners are exhorted to go beyond. The key address given by Matthew's Jesus to teach the meaning of justice in the Kingdom coming into existence through him is the Sermon on the Mount. This sermon is the first formal address given by Matthew's Christ and the leitmotif of the sermon is justice. Righteousness or justice *(dikaiosynē)*[7] is the key word used by Matthew and the main quality characterizing the new order. It is used at every important juncture in the sermon to indicate the uniqueness of the Kingdom that Jesus preaches.

The Sermon on the Mount begins with the Beatitudes. These in general describe the right order which God will establish imminently when his reign has its full effect, even though the human condition at present, when the reign is only partial, involves the followers of Jesus in mourning, poverty, strife and persecution. The Beatitudes promise a blessedness now and hereafter for those who are poor in spirit, meek and merciful, peacemakers, etc.

The two Beatitudes that are of particular interest to us explicitly mention righteousness. The first is: "Blessed are those who hunger and thirst for righteousness, for they shall be satisfied" (Mt. 5:6). On the basis of this statement alone one would conclude that righteousness is not present in any great evidence or in the possession of those addressed, since they are described as hungering and thirsting for something beyond themselves and in the future. It appears, furthermore, that the primary meaning of righteousness cannot be ethical conduct since the hearers are described as being in quest of this quality rather than capable of bringing it about through their efforts in the present order of things. The second Beatitude referring to righteousness complicates the matter of present versus future: "Blessed are those who are persecuted for righteousness' sake, for theirs is the Kingdom of heaven" (Mt. 5:10). In contrast to the first, this Beatitude suggests that the righteousness Jesus is referring to cannot be a wholly future thing because some are now experiencing or will soon be experiencing persecution for righteousness' sake in the present order.

Although the reason for the persecution is not alluded to in this Beatitude, the one that immediately follows makes the motivation for the persecution quite concrete: "Blessed are you when men revile you and persecute you and utter all kinds of evil against you falsely *on my account*" (Mt. 5:11). The reason for the persecution is obviously the relationship that the followers in question have with Jesus. It follows, therefore, that the righteousness referred to in the prior Beatitude is enfleshed by this one. The abstract notion of righteousness is in the process of becoming concrete. There is a remarkable implication here, for if to be persecuted for the sake of righteousness and to be persecuted for the sake of Jesus are synonymous, then Matthew's understanding of Jesus must be that in some way he is God's righteousness or justice incarnated. Paul will be even more explicit about this.

One should be able to see from this why the otherwise abstract notion of justice becomes a christological one for Christians. Matthew implicitly and Paul explicitly situate the subject of justice ultimately in these terms. One can see also how the conflict between the present versus the future in the Beatitudes already cited is also reducible to the mystery of Jesus himself. By his presence he was the reign of God he preached and yet he preached the reign of God as coming albeit imminently.

The next appearance of *dikaiosynē* in the Sermon on the Mount serves to confirm these points. After Jesus tells his disciples that their righteousness must exceed that of the scribes and the Pharisees or "you will never enter the Kingdom of heaven" (Mt. 5:20), the next twenty-seven verses spell out in detail how the scribes' and Pharisees' righteousness was impoverished. The actions which expressed the quality of the relationship they had with God and one another, although in material conformity frequently enough with the Law, were not undertaken from within the spirit of the relationship either to God or to man that the Law called for. In all six antitheses which follow verse 20, the insufficiency of the righteousness of the scribes and Pharisees is described by contrasting the norms which supposedly guide their behavior with the kind of righteousness and justice Jesus expected of his followers In each instance Jesus teaches either an abrogation or an interiorization of the law governing believers' behavior.

In the first contrast he cites the commandment about not killing. He heightens the quality of the network of relationships that his followers are to knit together with one another by indicating that the slightest anger between brothers must be resolved before one brings one's gift to the altar to express one's union with God. In the second contrast between the conduct of the Pharisees and that of his followers he speaks of the sin of adultery. Here again he goes much deeper than the action forbidden by the commandment by calling for a disposition of heart toward others which would keep them from using one another for their own exploitative purposes. In the third contrast Jesus shows his sensitivity to the interdependence of relationships between people by tracing the guilt of a person's adultery back to the partner responsible for the breakup of the marriage relationship in the first place. In the final contrast between the respective behaviors, Jesus abrogates the *lex talionis*, that is, that norm of conduct in human relationships that sought parity in retribution, or an eye for an eye and a tooth for a tooth resolution of conflict. In its stead, Jesus does not give a norm but he exhorts his listeners to an attitude which would not return evil for evil but which would have one remain non-retaliatory if dealt with unjustly or harshly. By turning the other cheek one defangs a situation of stress.

The attitude Jesus is calling for here is to go beyond abstract norms in one's conduct to a way of relating because of the experience of God's own goodness. Jesus experiences his heavenly Father as acting in the same manner that he is exhorting his followers to act. His Father "makes the sun to rise on the evil and on the good, and sends rain on the just and the unjust" (Mt. 5:45). Just as his Father acts from a center of benevolence toward his children rather than on the basis of a pre-judgment about their relative merits, so Jesus' listeners are urged to act toward one another. In other words, his Father's own goodness was to become normative for the conduct of Jesus' followers just as it was for him. Jesus is here abrogating the ordinary mode of human behavior that, on the basis of pre-determined judgments about another, considers hatred appropriate in some cases and caring appropriate in others. This final antithesis raises inter-personal Christian conduct to the axiological level of an *imitatio Dei*. With this the Sinai stage of divine guidance of human affairs has been superseded. God is no longer giving norms of conduct to his people. Rather Jesus is making his Father's own conduct their norm: "You must be perfect as your heavenly Father is perfect" (Mt. 5:48).

But the imitation of the Father's perfection is not left to the speculation of the would-be followers of Jesus in Matthew. There is a final dimension to Jesus' teaching with regard to God's justice and the imitation of his Father. This dimension is found in the only other place in Matthew where Jesus speaks of being perfect. Unlike the other Synoptics, Matthew explains to the rich young man who came to him, "If you would be perfect [this is the unique Matthean phrase], go, sell what you possess . . . and come, follow me" (Mt. 12:21). In other words, Matthew's Jesus is saying that conducting oneself after the manner of his Father and following Jesus are virtually the same thing. Both are characterized in terms of perfection. Rather than leaving the imitation of God to the speculations of believers, Jesus becomes the flesh and blood embodiment of the perfections of God, according to Matthew.

In brief, Matthew's Jesus is saying something wholly new about justice. He is saying: "If you take justice to mean conformity to abstract norms, then you must transcend it." The Kingdom of heaven to which he is inviting his followers radically transforms justice into a familial pattern of behavior. In this Kingdom, one is to act the way one experiences God, the Father of Jesus, acting toward them. But this becomes even more tangible as the Matthean commands of Jesus indicate: Follow me, learn from me, hear me. The followers of Jesus can exceed the justice behavior of the scribes and Pharisees by their union with Jesus who is the embodiment of the justice of God. Paul says this more explicitly than Matthew.

Matthew's Jesus has one further lesson to teach about justice in the Sermon on the Mount. The last line of the sermon recapitulates the whole sermon and brings the teaching one step further: "But seek first his Kingdom and his righteousness and all these things will be added unto you" (Mt. 6:33). "Things" here refers specifically to food, drink and clothing. The hearers are exhorted to have confidence both in God's knowledge of their needs and in the fact that he will care for them. If they expend their energies seeking his Kingdom and his righteousness, they will find themselves cared for by him. But over and above the immediate material things about which they need to shed their anxiety, one could argue that something is also being suggested in this final exhortation about the way of doing justice and being just in the everyday world of people and things. If his followers are exhorted to seek it first and foremost, then God's righteousness must have been conceived of not only as a quality peculiar to God but also as something of his that he chooses to make "giftable." Since it can be bestowed, seek it, for he would bestow it, Jesus is saying. The action which reorders the space one occupies more profoundly than any other is the action of seeking God's Kingdom and being imbued with his own righteousness.

Jesus himself is the best lesson about his exhortation. He was peacefully but totally concerned to be under God's reign, confident that the righteousness received from God would begin to reorder human chaos. He was also confident that it would do so soon. Since everything else was secondary to Matthew's Jesus, he taught that it should be to his followers. If he had spoken in a more philosophical mode of statement, he would have said: "The righteousness of God which operates in me as a principle of life and action is the source of the new order of existence I proclaim." Righteousness as gift and the advent of the new order which is to be characterized by *dikaiosyne* are in continuity one with the other. The latter flows from the former.

Jesus' life has an uncanny ability to enflesh and simplify the complex and multiple levels of justice without collapsing them. His teaching about justice is best seen when he himself is taken to be the exemplar of the lessons he taught. When these lessons are abstracted from him, theorized about and systematized, the personal love of Christ which is meant to reactivate and empower the believer is lost.

There is still another level to the meaning of justice in Matthew. Justice as God's gift is complemented by the equally essential soteriological dimension of Christian justice. This, in turn, is closely linked to the moral action meaning of justice. It is something done or left undone. Persons are just or unjust depending on what they do or fail to do, and their salvation is determined accordingly. The scene is the famous end-times scenario in Matthew 25:31ff, where all the nations are appearing for the Final Judgment. The new lesson here has to do with how Matthew's Jesus sees himself and with whom he identifies himself. He identifies himself with the suffering members of humanity, so that those who have concerned themselves with these same sufferers even without knowing the full meaning of what they have done, by trying to meet the needs of those who were hungry or thirsty or who were in isolation or naked, are touched by the righteousness of God because they have served his Son who incarnates that righteousness. (Later theology will develop the doctrine of the whole Christ which sees the risen Lord with his members as intimately one with him as a body is to its head.)

The criterion used by Jesus here in his role as eschatological judge for separating the sheep from the goats in the end-times is what the individuals in the nations have done or failed to do to the least of his brethren with whom Jesus most fully identifies himself. The choice to be uninvolved with them merits damnation. On the other hand Jesus welcomes into the Kingdom those who have chosen to involve themselves with him in the person of the needy. They inherit the Kingdom prepared for them from the creation of the world because they have taken upon themselves responsibility for him in his brethren. The transition from the Old to the New Testament, from Old Testament righteousness to New Testament righteousness, is now complete since Matthew's Jesus insists that concrete individuals with whom he identifies himself are so many means to and ways of access to the justice of God. Obviously, following Jesus does not take one away from the world of injustices; rather it takes one further into it and into those battered portions of humanity that are most needy. The needy, the victims, those unjustly treated, the marginal are like so many sacraments, so to speak, whereby the person is touched by the righteousness of God if one chooses to be affected by the needs of "the least of these, my brethren." Jesus makes the doing of justice a serving of him because of his identification with the needy, and he makes the serving of him a salvific event for the server.

Admittedly, this puts things together that can't be found in the text itself, but any text can be illumined by the rest of one's beliefs. The Matthean 25 scenario provokes many questions which this text alone doesn't answer. How could the Son of Man describe some as sheep and some as goats and proceed to assign them to their respective fates on the basis of activity and inactivity, the import of which was unknown to them? The only Christology that makes such judgment plausible is one which sees Jesus as the righteousness or justice of God even in his members. Then his suffering members would be so many sources of the saving righteousness of Jesus. The scene, therefore, would be a description of the Son of Man perceiving the righteousness already in some because they had ministered to him in his bedraggled members and therefore were ministered to by him. Their salvation had already begun irrespective of their knowledge of it. One would have to conclude that there is more than an ontological marvel in describing Jesus as the justice of God, since such a fact also has enormous soteriological significance.

But there is more. If one takes this scene seriously and fills it out with its theological dimensions, one should also be able to see the degree of social change and "this world" significance of Jesus. If he is God's justice and identifies himself with the oppressed, poor, homeless, and hungry, then where they are he is; or one's salvation is where they are.

One can see why John McKenzie sees in this passage the core of the moral teaching of the New Testament.[8] I would go much further and say it is a point at which the moral, ecclesiological, soteriological and Christological dimensions of the New Testament converge most profoundly. In other terms, one can begin to see in this passage in particular how the following of Jesus, concerning oneself with the injustice of society, receiving God's own righteousness, imitating the benevolence of Jesus' Father and attaining to salvation are only different perspectives or modes of one and the same reality.

III
JUSTICE IN THE PAULINE CORPUS

We will take just one other New Testament author who attempts to deal with the question addressed in this essay. To be more exact, we will take the *corpus* attributed to Paul and, inasmuch as that is possible, selectively treat those aspects which give promise of illumining the subject of justice through the Christology he developed. Paul furnishes us with a unique understanding of justice by seeing Jesus as God's justice (1 Cor. 1:30; Rom. 1:17). Paul is much less interested in the historical actions and sayings of Jesus than any other New Testament author, so he presents us with quite a different picture of Jesus than the Synoptic one we have already seen.

Even though Paul was steeped in Old Testament thought, he reworked all the facets of his previous understanding of justice into his Christology. Paul saw that the death and resurrection of Christ created a radical upheaval that affected all humankind and moved the world out of a "dispensation of condemnation" and into a "dispensation of righteousness" (2 Cor. 3:9). Jesus' self-gift in obedience to his Father for the sake of his brethren is described by Paul as "an act of righteousness" that leads "to acquittal and life for all men" (Rom. 5:18). Jesus' resurrection is taken as proof that God's entrustment of his righteousness to Jesus was not ill-conceived.

I believe that Paul never ceased to taste the irony of it all nor did he cease to marvel at the chasm between God's ways of achieving justice and our own. We should not fail to contemplate the same irony. To begin with, the only one who deserves no punishment at all, God allows to be punished all the way to the point of death so that all other human beings who surely deserve punishment because of their loss of innocence are acquitted because of the death of Jesus. Through an injustice, as it were, to his own Son, we who were not even distant relatives at the time were justified. This brings up the second peculiarity of God's way of doing justice in Paul's mind. Not only does God declare persons who deserve the sentence of "guilty" to be declared innocent, but he makes them innocent. Their acquittal does not remain something extrinsic to them as if only their records were tampered with. The acquittal given by God transforms persons at the deepest level of their being. They become "justified." Nothing they could do for themselves or for one another could merit such a degree of transformation. The kind of justice we can win for ourselves or for another at best changes the conditions we and others live in; it remains at the level of the circumstances of human life. But the kind of justice God does in Christ transforms persons at the level of being.

The image now changes into one which contrasts the old creation with the new creation. The justice of God did not stand over against the world he had created, condemning it. Rather, in and through the person of Jesus it entered the world to become a principle in the new creation God was to bring about in Christ. The favorite image used by Paul to describe the new order of justice God was to establish in Christ was the new creation. Paul speaks of it as if it were a place one enters even though the old creation is not thereby annihilated. Thus the two creations exist simultaneously and co-terminously with justice and injustice interwoven into the fabric of human existence. The author of each of these creations is, of course, God himself, but death is the finality of the old creation drawing everything in it like a vortex, while the finality of the new creation . . . is glory. The risen Lord draws all things into his eternity and destiny. The old creation, which is neither glorious nor eternal, will eventually succumb of its own weight since the principalities and powers attempting to govern it are not synchronous with divine righteousness. The new creation, on the other hand, is glorious both in its destiny and its present reality although it takes the power of faith to see that. One comes into the new creation by believing in Christ Jesus. And by believing one comes within range of and has access to the justice of God. Being in Christ and being in the new creation and being just or among the justified are virtually one and the same thing. Entering into the new creation is a process, a process of being drawn beyond the pull of the dynamisms governing the old creation, the chief of which is sin and the end of which is death, into the dynamism governing life in the new creation, God's righteousness. Jesus entered into the center of the old creation characterized by sin and death and proved its undoing. "For our sake God made Jesus to be sin who knew no sin, so that in him we might become the justice of God" (2 Cor. 5:21). The power governing the new creation is the justice of God exercised by Christ. In this justice we have a share.

Justice in Paul's mind is first and foremost theological, rather than ethical or juridical. It comes from God, is received by believers, manifests God's presence in the world and leads to God. It flows into the world of persons and things, not through law but through Christ who alone can justify all and in whom all will eventually be justified. Not that those who are justified arrive at some state of perfection in this world whereby the reality of God's justice subsists in them. Rather they are through God's goodness brought into union with the person of Christ who becomes their justice. God's righteousness remains peculiarly his, but in Christ Jesus we can stand within God's own righteousness. "In him we become the justice [or righteousness] of God" (2 Cor. 5:21). Without the divine and the human being fused or confused one with the other, Jesus is the place at which the divine and the human come together. He is what makes the new creation new.

Admission into the new creation is contingent upon belief in Christ Jesus. For Paul one stands within the righteousness of God only if one is incorporated into Christ through faith. All believers would have to echo Paul when he asserted that he did not have "righteousness of my own . . . but that which is through faith in Christ, the righteousness from God that depends on faith" (Phil. 3, 8-9).

If the teaching of Paul were to be left at this point, the social dimensions of the Christianity he believed in and preached would not be adverted to. The person is brought into the new creation and into the dynamism of the justice of God in order that justice might also be done through him and through the body of Christ of which he has been made a member. One of the powers the justified "enjoy" is the power to "do" justice in such wise that their actions are intrinsically linked to God's actions in redeeming and reordering the world. Just as Jesus' death and resurrection have brought us to an acquittal we did not deserve, so that acquittal has won for us the power which we have not merited. That power is nothing less than God's own justice enabling us to perform actions which no human capacities would be competent to perform. Not only are the justified brought into a new order of justice, but they become instrumental in the co-creation of that new order. Those who have received the righteousness of God are capable of reflecting and making tangible the new order which that righteousness generates. Insofar as human beings are rooted in the justice of God, so the justice of God can be enfleshed in human actions and human structures and human institutions. Just as the justice of God has transformed the innermost being of those who are saved in his Son, so those who are saved in his Son are capable of transforming the social realities they touch upon and are touched by.

In Paul, as in the whole New Testament, the gift of union with Christ becomes the radical basis of the Christian's social responsibility. "Yield yourselves to God as men who have been brought from death to life and your members to God as instruments of righteousness" (Rom. 6:13). Doing justice in Paul includes but is not confined by what modern generations call social action. Paul himself showed himself capable of no small degree of social action, but it is Paul's social consciousness tirelessly acted upon that is worthy of note here. Maybe one could say that the primary social action of his Christian life was the continual indication to others by his words and deeds of the consciousness he had come to about the social action that God was doing in Christ. As he saw it, Jesus' life, death and resurrection revolutionized the entire meaning of justice at every level of meaning. Paul's primary social action, consequently, was proclamation of the awareness that was continually nurtured in his spirit about what was going on in the social order—one that only the most fervent faith could perceive. This awareness did not keep him from undertaking nitty-gritty actions on behalf of the poor, of course, but all his actions were undertaken with a buoyancy born of hope and a single-mindedness born of certainty that the victory was already won not only for the new Israel but for all the nations in Christ.

It is superficial, consequently, to wonder whether Paul's life manifests a concern for social justice. His life gives a number of indications as to how a Christian, knowing what he knows, might go about being instrumental in bringing more clearly into the social existence of mankind the reordering effects of Jesus' victory over unrighteousness. Indefatigably driven by the power of God's righteousness, Paul was preoccupied with adding to and building up the social entity of the body of Christ within which the first-fruits of the victory of justice were to be manifested. It was his Lord whom he saw in the body's members, and whom he clothed, fed, and visited in all the material and spiritual ways in which they showed themselves in need and he saw himself capable. Paul re-imaged the whole meaning of religion and relationship with God because of his faith in Christ Jesus, but nothing that he saw or did was beyond the pale of that personal relationship, yet all of it was social in effect. Every action he undertook in society and for its reordering was reconfigured by his faith-drenched imagination with the features of the person of Christ Jesus.

Two final observations need to be made to fill out the picture of Pauline justice. While for Paul one of the ways of being an "instrument of righteousness" was to express the consciousness that one came to through proclamation, this consciousness just as certainly led to other actions which Paul calls "good works." Although in Matthew it appears that one can come into the new creation and be synchronous with the justice of God because of certain good works done for the suffering members of the whole Christ, it seems in Paul that good works come about only because one has been justified and brought into Christ. The gift one has received in Christ Jesus makes good works possible; the good works do not win for one the gift of union with him. What is more, one is judged, in Paul's mind, in the Final Judgment by the faith one has in Christ, not by the good works one has done. Paul contends that each person's works will be tested as to their vintage and origins on the day of the Lord Jesus. At that time, "the fire will test what sort of work each has done. If the work which any man has built on the foundation survives, he will receive a reward. If that man's work is burned up, he will suffer loss, though he himself will be saved, but only as through fire" (1 Cor. 3:13-15). This appears to be at variance with the Matthean scenario analyzed in the previous section of this paper.

Paul, finally, is helpful about what we might call the stature of the gift the Christian receives in Christ. Like the Spirit-gift itself, so the gift of divine righteousness (two different symbols for the same reality) is of a first-fruits or down-payment nature. What is to be ours is already here; the Kingdom which is coming has already arrived but in the same manner as a harvest is anticipated by the first-fruits or a purchase is represented by a down-payment. This is why righteousness for Paul can be both a gift received now and "a crown" still to be awarded on the day of the Lord Jesus (2 Tim. 4:8). This is why Paul can both exercise the gift of righteousness and still live "in the hope of righteousness" (Gal. 5:5).

By extension this imagery also gives some indication of the

social impact that graced Christians should expect from their efforts in the social order. Their social impact will be commensurate with the stature of the gift they have already been given. Just as that gift represents the beginnings of blessedness, so its outworking through them should represent the beginnings of the new order of justice that Christ's death and resurrection has won for humankind. To expect more will lead to despair; to expect less will lead to inaction in the social order and irresponsibility in actualizing the gift of justice won for us in Christ.

IV
POSTSCRIPT

The above reflections are presented with full awareness that the Christian task of re-imaging Jesus in terms suggested by this essay is just in its beginning stages, here as elsewhere. The fact that it is still in an initial stage of conception calls for several observations about what is needed to successfully accomplish such a task. First of all, such an undertaking will certainly be done ineptly and in fact should not even begin at all, if it is attempted without the continual input which scientific exegesis can provide. On the other hand, however, this task is not only an exegetical one. Exegesis is only one step in a complex process of discernment which the Church must be about in this matter of justice. Scripture is to Christology, as an individual's genetic structure is to his growth. A justice Christology will require both an uncovering of what can be found out about Jesus of Nazareth from the sacred texts as well as a discovery of that which is true about the risen Lord as he reveals himself to the contemporary community of believers united to him in the Spirit. What is being re-imaged, in other words, is not only the Christ who was but who is now—about whom our knowledge will never be complete even though he remains the same yesterday, today, and forever.

Several other observations seem appropriate at the same time. The practice of justice or the lack of it on the part of would-be discerners will be a major factor in determining the quality of the product. The truth to be perceived in this instance will be in part determined by the truth that has been and is being done by the perceiver. Where one is standing and has stood vis-à-vis injustice, poverty, and need (one's own and others') creates a climate which allows insight to deepen or encircles one in a virtually impenetrable haze. Finally, it goes without saying that there is a history of perception, a sacred tradition, regarding the person of Christ that contemporary Christians have inherited from erstwhile generations of believers. Any new understandings will be true only if they build on and are in continuity with this christological tradition.

Christians are gifted with a special power to see into the depths of things, including the depths of Jesus. That gift, of course, is the Holy Spirit. "The Spirit searches everything, even the depths of God" (1 Cor. 2:10). To decipher the justice hermeneutic which so many of us modern Christians feel impelled to do in order to be faithful to the following of our risen Lord, the action of the Holy Spirit in us and our communities is an absolute necessity. Maybe there is an analogy between one of the specific gifts of the Spirit and what we need to accomplish our search today. Paul mentions in 1 Corinthians 12:10 that some have the gift to "interpret tongues." There are tongues all around us: some shrill, some barely audible, some foreign in language, some merely foreign to our sympathies. They appear to be speaking mostly of justice and injustice. The need to decipher them, the gift to interpret them, seems increasingly critical. To be faithful to the Lord, Christians must increase their capacity to interpret these tongues. They could be the Lord speaking to us about himself and the ministry he would have us perform. Or they could be something quite other, coaxing us into concocting an anti-Gospel that would deprive humankind of the Good News.

NOTES

1. Cf. especially the Hollenbach essay in this volume "Modern Catholic Teachings Concerning Justice." Also see Joseph Gremillion, *The Gospel of Peace and Justice* (Orbis Books, N.Y., 1976), pp. 5-133.

2. Cf. Walther Eichrodt, *Theology of the Old Testament* (The Westminster Press, Philadelphia, 1961), Vol. I, esp. pp. 472-501; A. de Groot,

The Bible on the Salvation of Nations (St. Norbert Abbey Press, De Pere, Wisconsin, 1966), esp. pp. 11-63, 109-118; Joachim Jeremias, *Jesus' Promise to the Nations* (S.C.M. Press, London, 1950), *passim*.

3. Oscar Cullmann, *The State in the New Testament* (Scribner, N.Y., 1956), p. 17.

4. Cf. especially Donahue's essay in this volume, "Biblical Perspectives on Justice."

5. Paul Lehmann, *The Transfiguration of Politics* (Harper & Row, N.Y., 1974), p. 66.

6. *Op. cit.*, p. 59.

7. Justice and righteousness are both legitimate translations of the Greek *dikaiosynē*. As the Donahue essay shows, this New Testament term translates both *mishpat* and *sedāqāh*. Miranda lists thirty-four instances in the Old Testament where they appear together as synonymous parallelisms and thirty-two other times where their roots are paired together. Cf. José Miranda, *Marx and the Bible* (Orbis Books, N.Y., 1974), pp. 93-94, 107, nn. 35-38.

8. John L. McKenzie, "The Gospel According to Matthew," *Jerome Biblical Commentary*, eds. R. E. Brown, J. A. Fitzmyer, R. E. Murphy (Prentice Hall, Englewood Cliffs, N.J., 1968), II, p. 107.

Biographical Data

JOHN R. DONAHUE, S.J. (Ph.D. University of Chicago), associate professor of New Testament of Vanderbilt University, sabbatical year 1976-77 at Woodstock Theological Center; author of several books and an editor of the upcoming series in biblical theology *Overtures* (Fortress Press).

AVERY DULLES, S.J. (S.T.D. Gregorian University) is a research associate of the Woodstock Theological Center, a professor of systematic theology at Catholic University and the author of innumerable books and articles

WILLIAM V. DYCH, S.J. (Ph.D. Münster) is a research associate of the Woodstock Theological Center. In the academic year 1976-1977 he has been visiting professor at both the Gregorian University in Rome and Princeton University. He was formerly a professor of systematic theology at Woodstock College 1970-1975.

JOHN C. HAUGHEY, S.J. (S.T. D. Catholic University) research associate of the Woodstock Theological Center; formerly a member of theology faculties at Fordham and Georgetown Universities; author of several books and innumerable articles on theological subjects.

DAVID G. HOLLENBACH, S.J. (Ph.D. Yale) is an assistant professor of moral theology at the Weston School of Theology, Cambridge, Mass. He is a specialist in social ethics and author of many articles in his field.

JOHN P. LANGAN, S.J. (Ph.D. Candidate in Philosophy, University of Michigan) is a research associate, Woodstock Theological Center; author of articles on philosophy of religion, religious ethics and politics.

RICHARD R. ROACH, S.J. (Ph.D. Yale), an ethicist, is a member of the theology department at Marquette University and author of innumerable articles in the area of religious ethics.

WILLIAM J. WALSH, S.J. (S.T.D. Catholic University) is a member of the faculty of Lancaster Theological Seminary where he teaches historical theology; he is also a spiritual director of Jesuit Novices and Tertians.

Index